THE HOPELESS BIKER

THE HOPELESS BIKER

Who Went Twice Round the World

MILES MORLAND

MUSWELL
PRESS

First published by Muswell Press in 2025
Copyright © Miles Morland 2025

Maps copyright © Emma Charleston
Typeset in Bembo MT by e-Digital Design

Printed by CPI Group (UK) Ltd, Croydon CR0 4YY

A CIP record for this book
is available from the British Library

ISBN: 978-1-06838-932-0
eISBN: 978-1-06838-933-7

Miles Morland has asserted his right to be identified as the author of this work in accordance with the Copyright, Designs and Patents Act 1988.

Apart from any use permitted under UK copyright law, this publication may not be reproduced, stored or transmitted, in any form, or by any means without prior permission in writing from the publisher.

Our authorised representative in the EU for product safety is
Easy Access System Europe, Mustamäe tee 50, 10621 Tallinn, Estonia
gpsr.requests@easproject.com

Muswell Press, London N6 5HQ
www.muswell-press.co.uk

CONTENTS

An Apology	9
Across Europe: Orient Express	11
Life Before Bikes	31
South America: In the Tyre Tracks of Che	35
India by Bullet	55
Japan with Beemer-San	79
Australia: Roo Dodging with Brenda	105
Southwest USA: Daisy in the Desert	137
Iceland with Björk	159
New Zealand: Kiwiland with Cooky	175
Australia: Priscilla, Queen of the Desert	197
Mexico: Baa Haa Boy	225

With love to Tasha, my often-imaginary pillion-rider, although I know how grateful she was not to be.

AN APOLOGY

You may have bought this book thinking it is about motorbikes. Let me apologise if you did. I know as much about how a motorbike works as I do about ukuleles. I have no idea where to find a spark plug and am incapable of changing a punctured tyre. Finding the right hole to put the petrol in is a challenge.

No, this is not a book about motorbikes but a book about going off into the back of beyond, somewhere over the mountain, and finding out what is on the other side. Despite my utter incompetence as a mechanic, I did sort of learn on the job how to ride a motorbike and it was motorbikes that took me off beyond the horizon. I usually did it by myself because going solo gives you complete freedom and freedom is what biking is all about. This is a book about finding freedom.

When I gave this book to a few friends to read, several said that it was moronically stupid, not to say irresponsible, of me to head off on a motorbike into places like Patagonia on tyre-shredding back roads with no passing traffic, out of reach of a phone signal, and with nothing but circling vultures for company because, if the bike had broken down, I would have been incapable of fixing it and the vultures would have had an excellent lunch.

However, I am an optimist and believe that things will always work out for the best in the end. They did, moronically stupid maybe, but what adventures I had. I hope you like them as much as I did although, as you will see, there were some scary moments on the way.

Enjoy the ride but please don't think it'll teach you anything about spark plugs.

ANOTHER APOLOGY

You may have bought this book thinking, thanks to the subtitle, that I had ridden a bike twice round the world.

Yes, but no.

When I added up the distance I had travelled on my bike trips outside England, they came to a bit over 50,000 miles. The circumference of the world is just under 25,000 miles so, yes, the distance travelled was more than twice round the world, but the trips themselves were on five different continents and took me wherever that month's wind happened to be blowing. Circumnavigating the globe like Magellan, no. But shooting off on random trips to the back of beyond, yes.

ACROSS EUROPE: ORIENT EXPRESS

In 1989 I had chucked in my job in the financial world, I was in my forties and in good health, I had an understanding wife and two lovely daughters, and just enough money in the bank that I didn't need to get another job right away.

So, I took motorbike lessons.

The first part of the test required you to drive round a course of cones laid out in the empty parking lot of Wimbledon Greyhound Stadium. After a bit of coaching, I passed that with some ease. A month later I took the second part of the test, on a tiny 125cc bike rented from the driving school (some lawnmowers have bigger engines). This test was on public roads in Croydon with the examiner on a motorbike behind me. I had earphones connected to him by radio. I crept along, careful not to make a mistake, as he barked, "Next available left", or "Emergency stop" into my headphones. Everything was going swimmingly until, right at the end as we were returning to base, I carved up a Ford Mondeo at a mini-roundabout and was summarily failed. To this day I don't know who has right of way at a mini-roundabout. Ignominy. Two months later I took the test again, met no Mondeos on mini-roundabouts, and passed.

Once I had passed the test, I didn't buy a bike. Guislaine, my half-French wife, pointed out quite forcefully that I had no need for a motorbike and as we were counting our pennies at the time it would be an unnecessary extravagance. The French have never really got motorbikes. Sadly, I couldn't disagree.

However, ever since I was a child I had looked with longing at motorbikes as being a short cut to freedom and the best way to find out what lay on the other side of the hill. I am no petrolhead and mechanics are a mystery to me but having passed my test I began reading biking magazines. I did this in private as I didn't want to have to explain why I was doing it, but a man can dream.

I knew little about bikes, but I knew roughly what I wanted. I didn't see myself crouched like a jockey over the tank of a Japanese sports bike or an Italian racing machine. I certainly didn't want a Harley. I wasn't sure who Harleys were for, but they weren't for me. I wanted a powerful, long-legged, touring machine that would allow me to sit up straight and that would keep on going for ever.

A friend of mine from university, an American called Jim Rogers who had been wildly successful in the financial world as the original partner of George Soros, had given up his job years before me and ridden a motorbike around the world. Later he wrote a best-seller about it called *Investment Biker*. Jim had ridden a thing called a BMW R100RT. I had little idea what this was, but I remember Jim writing that he didn't want a bike that was going to break down and he was confident that the BMW wouldn't. Nor did it. If it got Jim across Africa, Russia, Australia, and China, it was the right bike for me.

I was too broke to splash out on such a big purchase at the time I passed my test. but over a year later I made some unexpected money on a rash speculation. I suddenly found myself with what felt like enough found money to go out and do something silly but not enough to do anything serious. I consulted Guislaine, who could have found many uses for the money but who knew about my secret longing and suggested I buy a bike before we spent it on anything sensible. Thank you, Guislaine.

The next day I found myself standing in the BMW showroom on Park Lane, stroking a steel grey BMW R100RT: a massive creature with fairings, slanting windscreen and the legendary "boxer" engine that looked as if it belonged in an industrial museum. This was not surprising as it had been originally designed in the 1920s, five years before the first Zeppelin crossed the Atlantic. BMW had had seventy years to iron the bugs out with its boxers. I liked that. Fixing bike engines was not part of my biking dream, and this was the bike that had got Jim round the world without breaking down.

In 1991 you had to have held a licence for over a year before you could purchase a bike bigger than 250cc, the idea being that you would have a full year to gain experience on a smaller bike first. In my case I hadn't owned a bike since passing the test, so I had gained no experience whatsoever and had practically forgotten how to ride one, yet here I was stroking a beast weighing almost half a ton with an engine of 1000cc, bigger than many small cars. As I had held a licence for over a year, I was now technically able to buy a bike of any size. The salesman was no fool. He smiled but said nothing. He recognised the moon-struck look of a man who has just fallen in love. I bought the 1000cc bike.

"I'll come back tomorrow to pick it up," I said to the salesman in my gruffest voice, hoping to sound like an experienced biker. "Oh yes, and can you get me a crash helmet for tomorrow too, please?" I had never owned a crash helmet. For my test I had rented one from the bike school.

"Of course, sir, what kind of helmet?"

"Um, yes." Helmets came in different types? I looked wildly round the showroom. "Just like that one there," pointing in what I hoped was a decisive manner at a nifty-looking thing with a chin-piece you could raise.

Next afternoon I was back in the showroom. The salesman took me round to the garage in the mews behind where a giant BMW R100RT stood, gleaming grey, and looking slightly threatening. The salesman presented the bike to me, gave me a run-down of what the switches and buttons did, and waited for me to ride off. Was that a smirk on his face? I didn't want to admit to him that I had never ridden anything bigger than the near-moped on which

I had taken my test. The BMW, at 1000cc, had an engine eight times bigger.

"Um, remind me exactly what this does," I said in as nonchalant a voice as I could muster. He gave me another detailed explanation which passed straight through my brain without making a permanent home in any part of it.

I mounted the bike with what was meant to look like swashbuckling confidence. This evaporated as I struggled to move the thing off its centre stand.

"Sir, you'll need to push harder than that," said the salesman as I threw my weight into the handlebars. "Are you sure you're OK on this?"

"Am I OK on this? Ha-ha, yes, no problem," I put on my gruff voice again. "Oh yes, more than OK, been riding bikes for years."

He smirked again and I wobbled off out of the garage into the London rush hour. I was terrified. I was about to ride something eight times more powerful than the biggest bike I had ever been on out into the maelstrom of Park Lane rush-hour traffic.

I inched the bike out of the mews and on to Park Lane where I began to creep down the bus lane. Traffic screamed past. The terror was mounting but I gradually became aware that this giant bike was on my side. It was going to look after me. It was like a faithful horse as it steered me round the six-lane vortex of Hyde Park Corner. I felt it respond as I banked gently into the corner, and I only had to give a gentle tweak on the throttle to find us accelerating away from the taxis which were coming at us like Focke-Wulfs.

Later that afternoon I set off to drive the bike up to Norfolk where we were living in a little house on the marshes, and where Guislaine was waiting for me. It would be a three-hour drive. Other than the Wimbledon bike lessons, I had never ridden on the open road before. I discovered that when riding a bike you become a different driver. You start to use senses that are asleep in a car. What excitement when I got off the main road passing Newmarket and onto an empty side road and felt the huge creature bank and swoop into bends with the grace of a butterfly. That gave me a feeling I had never had in a car. Open-cockpit flying must have been like this.

The bike, my new companion of the road, had already acquired a name. Motorbikes, like cars and boats, are feminine. My BMW might have been feminine and even curvaceous but underneath those curves she was also big and muscular. Being a BMW I felt her name should begin with a B, but she was no delicate Barbara or Bella: this was Bertha the pride of Bavaria. As we cruised through the Norfolk countryside, I felt that Bertha and I had become a team. We were a We. I sensed that she would look after me.

Like many people who have spent much of their lives working in offices, I have always had an active fantasy life. One dream had been a journey across Europe, not for the sight-seeing, but for the journey and the feeling of being free of anything to tie you down. Anyone who had to ask, "What's the point of that?" wouldn't understand any more than I can understand why people run marathons. The weekend after buying Bertha, she and I set off for Istanbul. I had never ridden a bike in the rain, at night, or on a busy motorway. I had made no plans. My total bike mileage had been the trip to Norfolk and back. Now, I was proposing to set off on a round trip of 4,000 miles. I would have to learn on the job.

Guislaine understood. She worried but she understood. We talked about her flying out to join me in Istanbul, but we didn't want to tempt providence by making firm plans till I got there.

This was October, a time of volatile weather. I had intended to leave on a Monday morning but the forecast, "France very stormy on Monday: heavy rain likely to be accompanied by winds as high as 100 kph", meant that I fled down the M2 to Dover at dawn on Sunday hoping to stay ahead of the storm. I had yet to ride in the rain and wasn't looking forward to it.

We lived then in Norfolk, but we also had a houseboat on the Chelsea Embankment as our London pied-à-terre, or rather pied-à-l'eau. I spent the last night before leaving aboard the boat with Bertha parked on the Embankment. Having decided on the trip I had spent much of the week in motorbike shops buying kit. Bike shops are storehouses of wonder. Who knew how much kit bikers can buy? Leather; Gore-Tex; PVC; exotic fabrics; gloves; goggles; helmets; boots; chaps; one-piece suits; back, knee, and kidney guards; all with a multiplicity of pockets and zips. There would be rain: this was October in Europe. I would need to be rain-proof. It would be cold: we would be crossing Alpine passes. I would need gloves. Goggles? No. But special glare-defying glasses? Yes. Leather was a problem. Real bikers wore leather, but I didn't feel I was yet ready for leather. That was for real bikers, not amateurs like me. I settled for Gore-Tex.

On Sunday, in the pre-dawn light, I carried the pannier bags out from the boat to Bertha.

Soon Bertha was packed and ready for the road. I fastened my helmet, zipped up the new biking jacket, slipped the map into the transparent pocket on top of the tank-bag, opened the petrol tap, pushed Bertha off her stand, fired up the engine, and glided out into a chilly grey dawn.

I had no exact route as I wasn't sure how far I'd be able to go each day. I had imagined that about four hours in the saddle would be enough, but a bike-riding neighbour told me that he had once covered 500 miles in a day. Allowing for stops that could be twelve hours. Istanbul was almost 2,000 miles away. I had calculated on two weeks to get there and back and I wanted a couple of days' rest in Istanbul, but I had no idea whether this was do-able or not. I would have to average around 400 miles, further than London to Edinburgh, every day. Was that possible? I didn't know.

I had spent hours with my newly bought maps spread out on the floor working out possible routes. When, and always if, I reached Istanbul I didn't want to take the same route coming back. And this was 1991, with communism in Europe having only ended a year earlier, so eastern European roads were likely to prove a challenge.

I decided on a northern route out, dropping down through France, Germany, Switzerland, Austria, Hungary, Romania (rioting miners trying to overthrow the new post-Ceaușescu government permitting), and Bulgaria to Turkey, while taking a southern route back, across Greece and through Italy and France, using the overnight ferry from Greece to Italy to bypass the terrible civil war in Yugoslavia, a country caught in the ferment that accompanied the end of communism.

The storm and I hit France at the same time. I arrived in Nancy that night, after four hundred terrifying miles from Calais, exhausted from a day fighting gale-force winds and stinging rain. Despite singing to keep my spirits up I had been scared and miserable most of the day. Fighting the gale, adjusting for the bow-wave of cork-screw air pushed out by huge trucks, and trying to gauge the slipperiness of the surface occupied every ounce of my brain. These were new sensations I was having to learn on the job at 70 mph on traffic-heavy wet roads.

For a moment in the afternoon, the rain had stopped and a pale sun had come out long enough to dry the road as Bertha and I came down the Meuse Valley. The road curved gently along the valley and, as the surface dried, Bertha began to find firm footing round the corners. For a surreal hour we found ourselves biking along with participants, so the stickers on the cars proclaimed, of a Liege–Rome vintage car rally; Bertha and I glided along avenues of poplars escorted by gleaming Delahayes and Frazer-Nashes.

Then the rain returned, spitting bullets, and the wind rose once more to give me a final buffeting before docking for the night at the Hotel Mercure in Nancy, a grim and charmless place. I called Guislaine to tell her I had crossed France. I told her about my day.

"Darling, why exactly are you doing this? It doesn't sound much fun. No-one apart from me knows what you're up to. Why don't you just turn round and come home?"

"Well, no," I stuttered while asking myself why not do exactly that. The day had not been fun. "Tell you what, I'll do one more day and if it doesn't get any better, then I'll come home."

Next morning I was woken by the noise of cars splashing through water in the street. The dawn sky was thick with rain clouds and the wind still whistled. I contemplated giving up, but continued, with dread. I'd give it one more day. My biking dream was crumbling around me. With a sinking heart, I put on my rain gear, stowed the luggage and pointed Bertha to the road.

Dodging through the mist-shrouded mountains of the Vosges, the view was dramatic and the driving a nightmare. On a bike the front brake is the one that has the power, the back being an auxiliary like the parking brake on a car. This works well in the dry. In the wet, if you use the front brake too hard when you are going anything other than straight you skid out of control. I had to learn that while edging my way through the leaf-sodden bends in the Vosges mountains.

Things got worse when we crossed the border into Germany and found ourselves sucked into the autobahn system to get past Freiburg. It was an old autobahn, and the road was a narrow two lanes each way with a slippery concrete surface and traffic on the slow lane going at 75 mph. Welcome to Germany. Overtaking in these conditions was hard. I discovered that a big truck, just like a big boat, leaves behind it a quarter-mile bow-wave of turbulence which builds to a climax as you pull out to pass it, but, as you go past, sucks you back violently the other way.

Then everything changed. We had reached the Black Forest, and the road was dry. The traffic was left behind on the autobahn and the road curved sinuously through the pines. Bikers from all over Europe came to ride there just for the fun of it. The Black Forest had long swooping bends through undulating glades, and little traffic apart from bikers, there for the sheer enjoyment of biking these swooping roads. It was a strange but gratifying feeling to find myself part of a new fellowship. As bikers pass on the open road they salute each other. At first I found myself returning their salutes with a majestic wave, until I realised this made me look like the Queen Mother and learned the appropriate acknowledgement of a two-inch lift of the outside hand and an upward flick of the little finger.

I stopped for lunch: a sandwich and a glass of fine German beer, sitting outdoors by Lake Konstanz. The ride through the Black Forest and sitting in the sun by the lake had restored my spirits. I was on a high. So this is what biking was all about. I set off with my visor up and my Ray-Bans on. And then the rain came down. This set the pattern for the next few days. Just as I would be wondering how much more punishment I could take, everything would come right and there would be an hour or two of sun-filled ecstasy.

I avoided motorways where I could. They make for boring riding and, even when they pass through scenery as beautiful as that between Innsbruck and Vienna, you don't have the spare concentration to admire the views. My rule became that when it was wet I stayed on the motorway and ate up the miles and when the sun came out I sought out the small roads and the mountain passes.

The high point came when the rain paused and I left the autobahn for the Alpine road up through Lech and Zürs over the Arlberg Pass and down to St. Anton. The Arlberg Pass is the watershed of Europe. Everything to the North and West drains into the Atlantic, most of it through the Rhine, while everything to the South and the East joins the Rhone, the Po, or the mighty Danube on their journeys to the Mediterranean or the Black Sea.

The bike rose and fell like a lapwing on the long mountain bends. Brake, change down, bank to the right, lean in, knee out, change down again, let the bike fall sideways as the bend tightens, just a touch of throttle to pick her up before she goes over, and now some more throttle to bring her upright and then, throw the weight the other way, and bank to the left for the next bend. The sparse traffic was left behind like sweet wrappings. The best moments were those instants on a long S-bend when I flowed out of one curve and brought the bike up and into the opposite bank for the next. The sensation and the high was the same as slaloming down a field of fresh powder on skis.

If those were the high points, things didn't get much worse than the four stomach-clenching hours from the Hungarian border at Nădlac to Sibiu in Romania, where I spent the night. In 1991 there were few private cars on the road in Romania. The traffic consisted of Romanian-made diesel lorries which sputtered and coughed and left bits behind them in the road, agricultural machinery, horse-drawn wagons, and weary peasants plodding from one village to the next. The main road was just wide enough for a tractor to overtake a hay wagon. In the rain the already slippery road surface was made worse by a top dressing of diesel oil and horse dung from the hay wagons. This gave a surface on which riding something with two wheels required skills which I wasn't sure I had yet learned. When night fell it became worse. The tractors and horse carts had no lights and my powerful headlight wasn't much use through a smear of mud.

But that night I felt like a star. There was a hotel in Sibiu, the Imperator Romaniul, which Nicu Ceaușescu, son of the recently assassinated dictator, had had restored to a point where every surface was either marble or mahogany. Bertha, a rarity at that time in Romania, was parked in the place of honour under the main canopy and soon attracted a crowd. The old-fashioned architecture of her great finned engine was something they could appreciate.

Next morning, when I left, again a crowd gathered and I felt like a medieval knight preparing for battle as I slipped on my helmet, waterproof over-trousers, and gloves, stowed the luggage in the panniers and inserted the folded map in the transparent cover of the tank bag. The more knowledgeable spectators pointed at the bike and kept up a commentary: "Now he's turning on the petrol. Look at those carburettors." I felt like a fraud as they knew so much more about engines than I did.

Bertha's star quality in Romania was a blessing. There was a petrol shortage at the time with queues of a hundred cars or more at the infrequent petrol stations. I drove hesitantly up to the front each time and, instead of the other drivers objecting as they had every right to, they got out of their cars to wish me well and admire Bertha. My GB plates identified me as coming from overseas and everyone seemed genuinely happy that despite its troubles Romania could still attract foreign visitors.

By the time I reached Bucharest, the rioting miners, who had sworn to bring down the post-Ceaușescu government, had gone home. I was able to photograph the bike in front of the recently burned Parliament building until President Iliescu's motorcade came out and the guards, who had been quarrelling about who was next going to sit on Bertha and have their picture taken, hurriedly shooed me away.

That night, after five days on the road, I reached the Black Sea near Varna in Bulgaria.

I had crossed Europe.

After five days of battling with gales, rain, German autobahns and Romanian roads, the Bulgarian coast was a paradise. There were neat white hotels set in lush gardens and a shoreline of rocky coves and sandy beaches. After checking in, I biked to dinner in the next village, just in T-shirt and jeans – no helmet, no gloves, no jacket. I had an illicit feeling of freedom with the wind through my hair and on my bare arms for the first time.

It was here that the great Roman poet Ovid had been exiled in 8 AD for eight years of moaning after he wrote *Ars Amatoria*, one of the great love poems of that era. What was he complaining about? What a charming place. Next morning I saw his point. A great storm had rolled in from the Black Sea. I looked out with a mixture of excitement and terror and was thankful that I only had 300 miles to cover that day to reach Istanbul.

Bikers develop a blind person's sensitivity to road surfaces – the slipperiness of the white line in the middle, the join left by a road mender, the qualities of grip of different types of tarmac and concrete. This new skill was tested to the limit when I took a short cut, an inland route, to the border through the mountains. The road ran through forest and over heath, the surface varying from leaf pulp to sheep droppings. In places the road had collapsed over a cliff edge and Bertha and I had to pick our way over the debris. The cold was intense. I had stopped in a bus shelter in Varna to put on a sweater. I hid from the rain under a cliff to put on a second. By the time I reached the Turkish border at the pass beyond Malko Tarnovo I had on almost all the clothes I possessed and the noise of chattering teeth echoed round my helmet. I tried singing to keep my spirits up, but that fogged the visor.

There was a two-hour delay at the border while Turkish officials sipped tea and bullied Bulgarian traders on their way to Istanbul. I was sent to a special room to get a visa; a moustachioed officer flicked through my passport and then left the room with it. After fifteen minutes I asked where he had taken it. "Toilet." I was relieved when he eventually brought it back with its pages intact and a visa stamped in it.

Every day I kept reassuring myself that I'd broken the back of the journey and things couldn't get worse. Each time, I was soon proved wrong.

I still don't like to remember the four hours from the Bulgarian border to Istanbul. The fiendish Edirne–Istanbul road was narrow but it was the main artery connecting Turkey with the rest of Europe, making it a thundering road-train of speeding trucks.

The rain never let up while the cold and wind increased. Water had penetrated my rainproof suit and I felt as if I was sitting in cold rice pudding. Each time a truck swept past in the opposite direction it was like standing on the edge of a station platform when an express screamed through. We were hit by a wall of solid air and tossed about like a canoe in the rapids.

At last, the Edirne road was behind me. I was in the suburbs of Istanbul and almost glad to see rush-hour traffic, even if it was Turkish rush-hour traffic. At least it moved at a slower speed. The only problem was that I had no idea where to go. I vaguely remembered Istanbul from my one previous visit, but I had no map of the city. God and Bertha would guide me. We took a random turning through a gate in the medieval city walls and nosed our way gingerly into Istanbul proper.

Suddenly a sparkle of light on water popped up on the right – the Bosporus. The twinkling lights the other side were in Asia. Now I truly had crossed a continent. I had been to Istanbul once before and locating the Bosporus allowed me to get my bearings. We puttered past the six minarets of the Blue Mosque, over the Galata Bridge, and up the hill to my hotel. There are many luxury hotels in Istanbul but only one that was right to stay in after crossing Europe: the Pera Palas. The Pera Palas is a wonderfully old-fashioned place, built in 1892, an Ottoman palace to accommodate the first passengers from the Orient Express. I had arrived on Bertha, a one-passenger Orient Express. The Pera Palace was the only place for us to stay.

I was received with grave courtesy by Hakan at the hotel desk as I stumbled in dripping and steaming in bike clothes and helmet, trailed by a smartly uniformed porter carrying the pannier bags. I had no booking, but when I told him I had biked from London he bowed and said, "Sir Morland, you are welcome. I will give you the suite where Agatha Christie liked to stay." Agatha Christie had written much of *Murder on the Orient Express* in the

Pera Palace. When I was shown into the room it looked as if Agatha might be popping back to write another chapter at any moment. It was room 411 and has been preserved unchanged. Bertha was parked in a place of honour by the main entrance. When I next saw her, poor, bedraggled, road-stained Bertha was shining and spotless. The hotel staff had cleaned and polished her.

Next morning, I met Guislaine off the plane from London. She had told me to telephone when I arrived and she would then get on the first plane out. Superstition about tempting providence stopped us from making plans sooner. We had a weekend of bazaars and mosques and little fish restaurants. It rained most of the time but we didn't care. Bertha stayed in the Pera Palace garage, apart from a trip to the Blue Mosque to pose for photographs. Guislaine was worried when I told her how bad conditions had been on the journey out.

"How awful. You must have been miserable. You look changed."

That made me think. I probably was changed, but first I was filled with gratitude at surviving.

"You know, I was tired, cold, uncomfortable, and often scared, but I was never unhappy. I wouldn't say I enjoyed it all, but it was a great thing to do and the bits that were good were fantastic."

I would have liked to say more because the trip had been so much more, but I could not find the words. The experience I had been through was not one I could share.

On Monday, I said goodbye to Guislaine, who was staying on for some sight-seeing before flying home, and headed off at dawn into the obligatory thunderstorm. Another thunderstorm? Hadn't I been punished enough on the way out? We'd even survived a dust storm in Bulgaria. Surely I had seen it all.

Not quite. The thunderstorm washed a mudslide onto the motorway so that it had to be closed and traffic diverted to the old, clogged coast road. This was flooded, the water a foot deep. Would Bertha be able to handle it? I hesitated but then put my head down, engaged second gear, and prayed. Clouds of steam rose as brown water washed over Bertha's hot flanks, mud splashed on my visor, and bow waves from passing trucks slopped over us. I

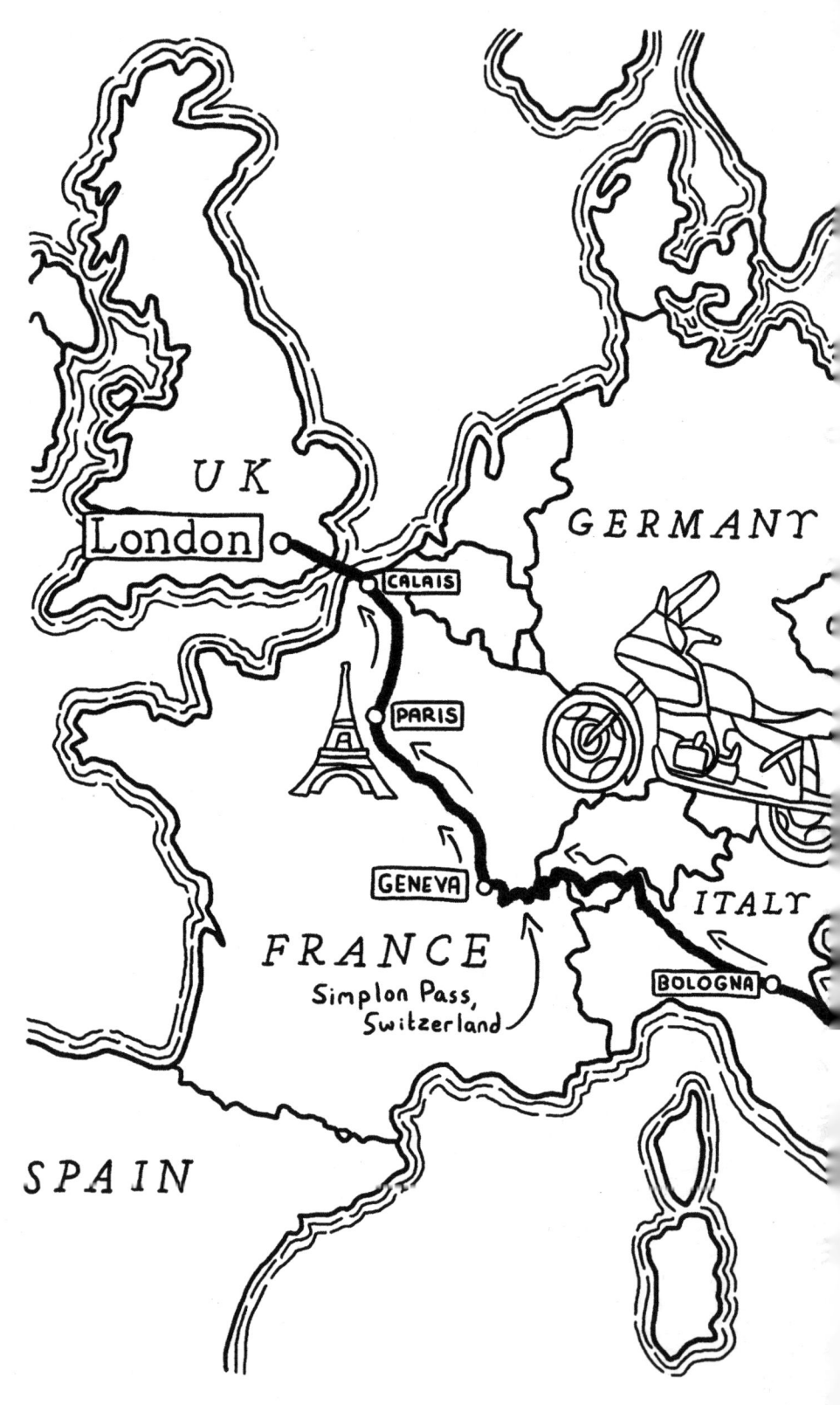

held my breath, waiting for the engine to sputter and fail as water got into it but Bertha chugged through without a hiccup. When we reached dry land I tested the brakes and revved the engine. Everything was good, the only casualty being Bertha's horn whose imperious Teutonic klaxon had been reduced to a mere burp.

That was the last trial. It was as if I were being tested, and the rest of the way home was a reward for surviving. The sun came out and the wind dropped. Bertha and I coasted along the Aegean, swept across the glorious Pindus Mountains on a road that flirted with the Olympian Gods, and came down to the Ionian Sea on the other side of Greece. I took breakfast in an olive grove and a ferry up a tranquil Adriatic. I stood at the stern rail after dinner with a glass of brandy in my hand looking to the East at Yugoslavia in the depths of its civil war. While the boat sliced quietly through the calm water, 50 miles away thunder and lightning flashed and rumbled over the war-torn land.

There followed a night in Stresa on Lake Maggiore and a pink dawn. At 6 am Bertha and I set off to cross the Simplon Pass. There is an excellent modern tunnel through the Simplon. Only idiots take the old, long, bendy way over, rather than through, the mountain. How glad I was to be an idiot. Crossing the old Simplon was the high point of the trip, like surfing the perfect wave in Hawaii – two hours of long bends that floated round the flanks of the mountain. At the summit was the old monastery that had looked after travellers and from time to time sent out St Bernard dogs to find them.

The plan was to spend the night in Paris and then drive on to Calais the next day, but I was on such a high when I came down from the Simplon that I didn't want to stop. We arrived in Paris as night fell. I nosed Bertha onto the *périphérique*, but instead of heading for the centre of the city, I thought, "What the hell, let's go for it." We cruised round the *périphérique* and an hour later popped out the other side of Paris, "*Direction Calais*".

Seventeen hours after leaving Lake Maggiore, Bertha and I skidded onto the midnight ferry from Calais. Three hours later at 2.30 am we banked gently into a deserted Parliament Square after twenty hours in the saddle and

800 miles on the road, the longest drive I had ever done in one day. Just three more miles to go to the houseboat.

Along the Embankment I was slaloming Bertha from side to side, Europe twice crossed and 4,000 miles behind us. When I had set off two weeks earlier I hadn't known how to ride a motorbike. Now I did. I had my visor up and was singing with joy while tears rolled down my face. I hoped a policeman would stop me.

"Now, now, sir. Going somewhere are we?"

"No, officer, I've been."

2

LIFE BEFORE BIKES

The motorbike trip to Istanbul and back came at a dividing point in my life. Before that I had spent twenty-two years working in London and Wall Street for investment banks. It was a different era to that of today. Banking was a more civilised pursuit then and a less well paid one. All the same, it had been hard, and at times gruelling, work. After ten years on Wall Street I had returned to London during the 1980s to run the branch office of First Boston, a big US investment bank.

The work could be exciting, particularly when we were working on a big deal, but the satisfaction was visceral more than intellectual. I did not want to spend the rest of my working life shouting down a phone. At the time First Boston was one of the most successful firms on Wall Street thanks to its dominance of the late 1980s mergers and acquisition business. We became overconfident and began taking big bets with our own capital in what later came to be called private equity. Too many of the big bets were going wrong and in 1989 we had to be rescued. One of the giant Swiss banks, Credit Suisse, which had been trying to become a major player on Wall Street for many years, took us over.

Although it had often been tough, I had enjoyed working for First Boston, but the acquisition had come at a time when I was already thinking it was time for a change. I had no wish to work for a Swiss bank, so, shortly after the acquisition was announced, I resigned. I was then in my mid-forties. I had saved up enough that we, that is Guislaine, my wife, and Tasha and Georgia, our two daughters, could get by for a couple of years if we sold our house in London, but before the end of that period I would have to have found a way of earning a living or I would be forced back to Wall Street. And so, in April 1989, I packed up my desk and left. After twenty-two years working for other people, having nothing to do and no-one to report to felt strange, but also strangely exhilarating.

I began taking motorbike lessons … Twenty-two years chained to a desk breeds a desire for freedom and nothing gives greater freedom than an open road and a motorbike.

Now that I was jobless, we had to downsize. We sold our house in London and moved to a holiday cottage in Norfolk. The cottage was in Blakeney, a little village on the north Norfolk coast, a place of tides and salt marshes, looking out over the angry North Sea, with geese wheeling in the sky and seals lolloping on the sandbanks. If the south coast of England is cosy and twee, the north Norfolk coast is wild and elemental, a place of big skies and shimmering horizons.

I needed to earn enough to save me from having to return to Wall Street. I have always been fascinated by markets, particularly stock markets, governed as they are not by numbers but by psychology, fear, and greed. I have also always liked doing the opposite of what other people think is a good idea. If you follow the herd there are too many people smarter than you who are there already, ahead of you. If you go off by yourself and root around in an undiscovered corner of the forest you might find something worthwhile no-one else has noticed.

This led me to Africa. I had never been to Africa, but its attraction to me was that, in investment terms, neither had anyone else. It was shunned by the investment world. Africa was the last virgin corner of the investment universe. For investment people it was as empty and unmarked as Mars. That intrigued me.

I did mention to a few knowledgeable friends that I was thinking of looking for investments in Africa. Their reaction varied from scorn to hilarity. The lack of interest appealed to me. One thing was certain. No-one else was stupid enough to do what I was setting out to do.

I began travelling to places like Ghana, Nigeria, and Egypt, all places with fledgling stock markets. I did some homework first and set up meetings with local companies, government privatisation ministers, journalists, and academics so I could get a rounded picture of these new, to me, countries. What they must have made of me I don't know. To them, I was a strange old white man who was showing an unaccountable interest in their companies, something no other foreigners were doing at the time.

I formed Blakeney Management Ltd which I registered at Companies House. It had £100 in paid-in capital. I was the chairman and chief executive, as well as being its sole employee. I now had a job and two titles. I told anyone in Africa who asked that we were a leading African markets investment firm. That was true enough as we were the only one. And the garden shed of our little Blakeney cottage turned into Blakeney Management's Global HQ.

I now needed some clients. I began doing the rounds of my more adventurous investment friends from my previous life. I told them I was doing research into the next investment frontier, Africa, demographically the world's fastest growing continent. I doubt if any of the people I went to see had the remotest interest in investing in Africa but, like smart people everywhere, they were curious about the new. I told potential clients that if they paid me a consulting fee I would do my best to find them attractive investments in Africa.

Gradually I signed up a few clients. For most of them the motive was probably friendship or pity rather than the belief Blakeney Management might bring them anything useful. For instance, I went to see the legendary Barton Biggs, the man who had set up Morgan Stanley Asset Management, whom I knew as I had worked with him at Morgan Stanley in the 1970s. I told Barton what I was doing. At the time his firm was managing hundreds of billions of dollars invested round the world, much of it in emerging markets. He laughed.

"Miles, I've never heard of anyone investing in African markets. The only functioning place is South Africa and we can't touch that because of apartheid. However, I can promise you that Morgan Stanley is not going to dick around in places like Ghana and Nigeria itself so if you want to dick around for us, go ahead. I'll tell my people to sign up to your service."

So, it was the dick-around factor that got Blakeney Management its first client.

Barton, who sadly died a few years ago, was the first and I will always love him for that. My second was Soros Management. George Soros in those days employed a mercurial American, Gerry Manolovici, to look at newly emerging markets. He was known universally on Wall Street as the Prince of Darkness, although I never found out why as he seemed to me a charming man. I went to see him. He was delighted by my stupidity. He rocked with laughter.

"Man, you have as much chance of making me money as I do of being the next Pope, but I like your chutzpah. Sign me up."

I did.

Quite soon, I had ten clients signed up, each paying me what to them was loose change but to me made the difference between having to head back to Wall Street with my tail between my legs to find a job, and making an independent living. I loved it. Finding things out first hand for yourself is the best thing in the world and possibly the thing that sent me off on motorbikes to undiscovered corners of the earth.

Once more I found myself working very hard but this time I was working for myself, not a big Wall Street firm. I was lucky. Africa, while remaining a complicated place, began doing better and big investors like pension funds began coming to me and asking me to invest money there on their behalf. Tiny Blakeney Management went from being a consultancy to managing over $2 billion of institutional money. Later, Development Partners International (DPI), an African private equity firm I set up after I handed Blakeney Management over to my partners in 2006, managed another $2 billion.

I was back in business and I was my own boss.

3

SOUTH AMERICA: IN THE TYRE-TRACKS OF CHE

Apart from the trip to Istanbul which happened in 1990 before my new African venture got going, biking had to take a back seat to business for a long time. The better the business did, the less time off I had. After all the years working for big firms, I found, like so many people, that building your own business was exhilarating but left little time for holidays, let alone bike trips to far-off places.

Bertha, the faithful BMW R100RT on which I had made the trip to Istanbul, was starting to look old-fashioned as BMW brought out new, more stream-lined bikes, but still with the legendary "boxer" engines. I said an affectionate goodbye to her and traded her in for a more modern and streamlined BMW R1150RT, which had an even bigger engine.

Sadly it was spending most of its life locked up in a garage. Occasionally, I would get away for a long weekend and head for a cross-channel ferry. I made two trips to Italy, one crossing the Alps via the Mont Cenis pass, the one which Hannibal had taken with his elephants on the way to Rome, and one over the same Simplon pass that I had last crossed on the way back from Istanbul.

Once I had to go to Madrid for a business meeting but instead of flying, I popped the bike on the overnight ferry from Portsmouth to St Malo, crossed the Pyrenees over the Roncesvalles pass, where, 1,200 years earlier, Charlemagne's army had been slaughtered by the Basques, down to Pamplona and on across the high plains to Madrid. I remember coming down from the Pyrenees into the flat lands below, fighting my way through a black thunderstorm, and then, as I biked along a drying road by the side of a beautiful lake, I went through an endless cloud of yellow butterflies. I stopped to clear my visor and found my biking gear covered in yellow butterfly smudge. Biking had not lost its magic. You don't get that kind of experience in a car.

As Blakeney Management grew, I found myself with little time for play or indeed motorbiking. We had, with sadness, sold our cottage on the Norfolk coast and moved closer to London as I needed to be there for my job pretty much full-time. Blakeney's office moved from the garden shed in Norfolk to a converted loft building on the river in Chelsea close to the houseboat I had bought when I gave up my job, now our London base.

The bike trip to Istanbul became a distant memory. Had I really done that?

Then, one day in 2007, fifteen years after the Istanbul trip, by which time Blakeney was big enough that I could get away for a two-week holiday leaving the firm in the hands of the excellent people who had joined me, I went to see a film. It was in the Chelsea Cinema opposite the Old Town Hall in the Kings Road. The film was called *The Motorcycle Diaries*. It told the story of how in 1952, Che Guevara, later to be Fidel Castro's *consigliere* as ruler of Cuba but then a medical student in Buenos Aires, took a trip with his fellow student, Alberto Granado, across Patagonia, over the Andes, down into Chile and on to Bolivia to work in a leper colony. The trip was made on *Il Poderoso*, The Powerful One, an ancient 500cc Norton. The bike broke down constantly, struggled to get over the Andes, and eventually expired in Chile forcing them to do the rest of the trip by bus. Che drove the bike with Alberto on the pillion.

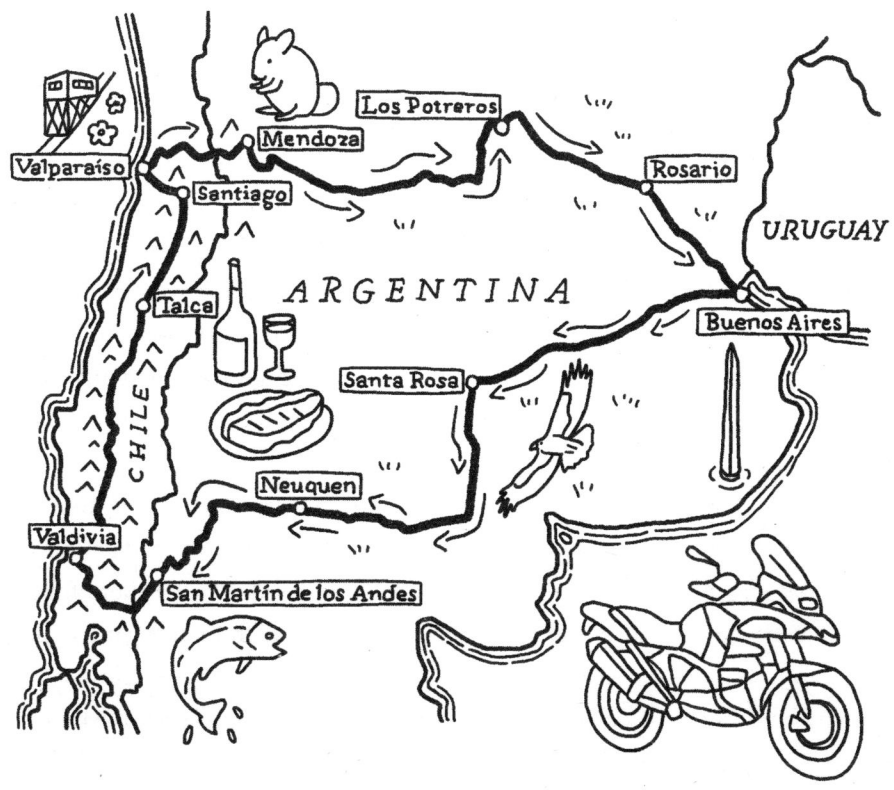

I watched the film, enthralled. As *Il Poderoso* struggled out of Patagonia into the Andes, memories of my crossing the Alps on a bike some fifteen years earlier overwhelmed me. I was banking with Che and Alberto into the bends. I could feel my pulse quicken. As they descended into Chile, a thought began to worm its way into the back of my brain. If them, why not me? If then, why not now?

There were many excellent why not reasons. I had never been to South America. I didn't speak Spanish. I couldn't reasonably take my bike to Argentina. I was a hopeless mechanic. I had hardly any off-road biking experience. These were just the first reasons not to do it that popped into my mind. Above all, it would be lunacy for a 64-year-old man with no real experience and no local knowledge to undertake such a trip.

Wouldn't it?

By this time, Guislaine and I had parted. We both came to the conclusion that we were not partnership material. We divorced but have gone on loving each other. We had given it a good go, thirty-one years from start to finish. And we had had two much-loved daughters, Tasha and Georgia, although we had lost Georgia a few years earlier, something for which nothing prepares you.

Tasha, now a grown-up woman in her thirties, was my closest family. I did talk to her about my following in the tyre-treads of *Il Poderoso*. She was not enthusiastic about her aged Dad heading off into the God-knows-where on a bike, but she didn't try to stop me or blackmail me into not going. Thank you, Tasha.

I don't think I seriously thought I was going to make the trip but, "just for fun", I began buying maps of Patagonia, and reading up about people braver and more qualified than I who had made bike trips in South America. Of course, one of the things that made my trip an impossibility was that I would not have the time to ship my bike all the way to South America and no one in Argentina would be foolish enough to rent a big BMW to a 64-year-old Englishman who had never been to South America.

However, a little time on the Internet produced the impossible, a firm in Buenos Aires who were happy to do just that: Rentamoto. Their website proclaimed: "We are the first Argentine company that rents BMW motorcycles. Our motorcycle rental has an actual fleet of 30 BMW GS motorcycles. We choose to rent BMW motorbikes because they add quality, comfort and safety to your way of riding, adapting, due to their versatility, to the diversity of Argentine roads. We offer premium services for those who share the adventure spirit, passion for motorcycles and searching for new and inspiring tours." Today, Rentamoto no longer exists but, if you are tempted to head off to Patagonia on a big Beemer, I believe you will find that R40Moto is their successor company.

Suddenly, my autumn after-work evenings began filling up with calls and emails to my new friends, Pablo and Nicolas at Rentamoto. Would I have to join a group tour? I didn't want to do that. No, señor, just pick up your bike, ride it a couple of times round the block to show us you are competent, and off you go. What about insurance, breakdowns, and crossing the border into Chile? No problem, señor, we will take care of all those things. Um, you do know I'll be 64 when I come to pick up the bike? Don't worry, señor, it is true that most of our renters are in their 30s and 40s but last year we had a man of 75 and he loved it.

I found myself going to work in the morning singing Peter, Paul and Mary's "Leaving On a Jet Plane".

And on my 64th birthday, 18th December 2007, I did. I boarded a big silver bird bound for Buenos Aires. Nicolas had told me that my Beemer would have two big steel panniers and a steel top-box behind the pillion. I would also be able to attach a tank bag to the top of the petrol tank inside which I could keep a passport, bike papers, a bottle of water, Ray-Bans, and the other essentials that I would need to access on the road. It had a useful transparent panel on top of it into which to slip a map with the route traced out on it. Satnav was not going to help in Patagonia or the Andes as most of the time I would not have a phone signal. I had already been along to BMW in London and bought bags to go inside the panniers and a tank bag.

On landing in Buenos Aires, I caught a taxi straight to Rentamoto whose depot was close to the airport. I must have looked like a Christmas tree festooned with bags, all hanging off different parts of me. Nicolas greeted me with a clap on the back.

"Señor Miles, we have been waiting for you. Your flight was good, I hope?"

He showed me the bike. It was a gleaming silver almost new R1200 GS Adventure. The engine was similar to my bike in London, but the GS series were taller and more rugged, built to go off-road as well as on. They are the bikes on which nearly all the great round the world bike trips have been taken. The Adventure series had a bigger petrol tank and was even further off the ground than the normal GS bikes. I am over six feet but found my feet were only just touching the ground when I sat astride it. To my relief the controls, brakes, and gear lever were all but identical to those on my London bike so, despite its height, the bike felt comfortingly familiar.

"Take it for a little ride while we do the paperwork," said Nicolas.

He wanted to be sure I could ride the bike before he let me have it. I fired her up, gently eased her into gear and tootled off down the road for a minute or so, did a gentle U-turn and returned with a bit of show-off slaloming on the way back.

"Ah, señor Miles, I can see that you and the bike are already friends."

We were, and half an hour later, bags and papers safely stowed, the bike and I were on our way to Buenos Aires.

At least I was booked into a hotel in Buenos Aires. For most of the trip I didn't know where I would be staying. Booking.com did not exist in Argentina in 2007 and I wasn't sure where my stopping places would be. I had no proper idea of the route as I wanted to get a feel for the road before deciding where to stop. Apart from my first night, the only place I was certain of was that I would be spending Christmas in San Martín de los Andes, a little hill town in the mountains near Bariloche on the way to the same border crossing to Chile that Che had taken in 1952. I had become friends with Heather, an Anglo-Argentinian woman, in London in the 1960s. She had returned to her family ranch in Argentina which she now ran with her husband and children. Their summer house was in San Martín and she had very kindly invited me to spend Christmas there with her and her family; Christmas in Argentina is of course in mid-summer.

Some earlier research in *Lonely Planet* and other books indicated that I might have to stay in some basic places along the way, but this was Patagonia and I travelled in the wake of Che. However, to make up for possible privations ahead I had booked myself into Buenos Aires' most elegant hotel, the legendary Alvear Palace for my first night. At least I would start off in style.

I knew no-one in Argentina apart from Heather but, having parked the bike in front of the Alvear Palace, I was taking out the pannier bags, when I heard behind me, "Miles, what on earth are you doing here?"

It was Ioana Beju Miller, someone I knew in London, married to Martin Miller, who started the famous Miller Antique Guides.

"Heavens, Ioana, what a surprise."

She looked at my bike and then at me.

"I thought you were delivering pizzas."

We both burst out laughing. I did look as if I was delivering pizzas.

After I had checked into the hotel, I met Ioana and Martin at the bar, a bar so 1950s elegant that you expected Katharine Hepburn and Humphrey Bogart to be sipping dry martinis on the bar stools next to you, and we later went out for my first Argentinian steak dinner. I went to bed the happiest of men, wonderfully full of delicious grass-fed ribeye washed down with powerful malbec. I was ready for whatever the road could throw at me.

The next day, a brilliant sun shone, porters from the Alvear Palace escorted me to the bike and helped me load the panniers, and at 8.00 am, Spike and I were on the road, heading west. The adventure had begun.

Ah. Yes. Spike…

My 1200 BMW GS Adventure was similar to the ones Ewan McGregor and Charley Boorman rode on the trip they wrote about in *Long Way Round*. Bikes, like cars and boats, and indeed dear Bertha who had taken me so faithfully to Istanbul, are feminine. The GS Adventure with its big, boxy steel panniers did lack obvious feminine characteristics. I had however been staying with a friend a couple of months earlier in Key West in Florida. My friend had a wonderfully muscled female personal trainer whom I met and whom everyone called Spike, the perfect name for the GS Adventure. I soon found that whenever I stopped, Spike attracted attention. Big bikes were a rarity in Argentina. Everywhere she went crowds gathered to admire her shiny metal panniers, twin bulging cylinder heads, and muscular lines.

Our first day on the road was easy but long. We were crossing the Pampa, the great Argentinian plain, the perfect place for rearing horses, cattle, and wheat. Ranching country. I had feared the Pampa might be as boring as the American Midwest, but it turned out to be a place of ethereal beauty. The road undulated under a sky the light-blue of the Argentinian flag, not the azure of the Mediterranean, as it wound its way through salt pans flecked with egrets, ducks, and black-necked swans, and past county-sized fields of open pampas grass flickering in the brilliant sun. Hawks, harriers, and eagles hovered along the edge of the road. Three hours out from Buenos Aires I saw an eagle snatch a dove in full flight.

It was 600 kilometres from Buenos Aires to Santa Rosa de la Pampa. The streets were lit and decorated while people danced in the plaza for their Christmas fiesta. My hotel had seen better days. The window was cracked, the shower had no hot water, and the noise from the fiesta went on till 3.00 am. I didn't care. Spike and I travelled in the footsteps of Che. Who needed hot water?

Patagonia and Timbuctoo are the two most famous bywords for the back of beyond, so I had a thrill the next day as we left la Pampa behind and took a bridge across the Rio Negro. On the far side was a big sign saying, "PATAGONIA".

So far, the biking had been easy. Halfway through the second day I was cruising along thinking that I had now travelled over 1,000 kilometres and the roads had been smooth and metalled, easy riding but not much of a challenge, so I decided to leave the main road and take a clever short cut. I had gone about 10 kilometres into the short cut when I saw a sign saying '*Camino Deformato* 75 kilometres'. Never were truer words put on a sign. This was a once-surfaced road that had decayed into 75 kilometres of pothole. Four out of five potholes Spike could bounce through, but the fifth had the depth and a hard enough edge to shred a tyre and crack a wheel-rim. The fifth needed to be avoided or I would be alone with a shattered and unrideable bike in the middle of the wilderness with no phone signal, no passing traffic, and none but circling vultures for company.

In places I had to stand on the foot-pegs for a mile or two to spot tyre-shredders so I could skid round them. I tried driving along the dirt by the side of the road. That worked on the gravel but then suddenly gravel became eight-inch-deep sand and poor Spike was fish-tailing wildly as she tried to throw me broadside into the thorns. It was back to the potholes. Welcome to Patagonia.

Somehow we made it through the deformed camino without shredding a tyre, rejoined the main road, and found ourselves at a much nicer hotel than the previous night. We were in Neuquen: according to *Lonely Planet*, "the diving board into Patagonia". How exotic was the diving board into Patagonia? Well, about as exotic as Norwich. It was a town of high-rises and pedestrian precincts but, unlike Norwich, when I strolled through the streets of Neuquen at midnight, it was thrumming with life. The town centre, deserted earlier in the evening, was crowded with laughing people, the motor-scooters were revving, the girls were giggling (in between eating plate-sized helpings of *bife de chorizo*, sirloin to you), the boys were strutting around in leather jackets, and everyone was happy and smiling.

Biking across la Pampa had been an easy introduction to the trip, but with the exception of the horror of the 75 kilometres of *deformato*, it had so far lacked things that make the heart beat faster. At least by now Spike and I had got to know each other. As we began to climb out of the Pampa and into the Andes, we felt like a comfortable old couple, ready to face the mountains together.

Christmas with Heather in San Martín de los Andes turned out to be a unique experience. We were a big group thanks to much of Heather's extended family of fourth generation Anglo-Argies showing up. Her family had lived in Argentina for four generations, having originally emigrated there from Scotland, but not one of her relations had ever married someone with Latin blood. For four generations they had always married into the surprisingly large Anglo-Argentine community. They all spoke Spanish perfectly, had been to local schools, had many non-Anglo friends and indeed they thought of themselves as Argies, not Brits.

We were thirteen for dinner on Christmas Eve. To avoid bad luck, the dog reluctantly agreed to join us to make us up to fourteen. Heather's mountain house was a graceful old wooden structure with shutters and balconies. It would not have looked out of place in Chamonix. A trout stream bounced through the bottom of the garden, but the thing I remember most is that it was surrounded by acres of wild blue and yellow lupins. I'd only seen lupins in small clumps in tidy English gardens before. Here were fields of them, interspersed in places with lilies.

Despite the fact it was mid-summer, we had a traditional British Christmas dinner on Christmas Eve: turkey, Christmas pudding, badly remembered carols, lots of presents, and then after dinner we found ourselves at around 1.00 am outside in the surreally starry Andean night. "Damn, we don't have any fireworks," said a cousin. "I can fix that," said Jesse, Heather's Che-lookalike son who made a living teaching Argentinian ski instructors to hurl themselves off cliffs with skis on. A minute later he was back waving a water pistol around. I didn't want to get soaked by the water-pistol, so I ducked under a trestle table. Then I realised the pistol was doing loud banging, not squirting.

"Hang on," I found my Malbec-fuddled brain saying, "That is no water-pistol. We are in the pitch darkness with an inebriated ski-suicide instructor discharging live bullets from a Smith & Wesson."

Everyone sensibly got on all fours while the bullets brought down passing boughs and sleeping sparrows until Jesse's magazine was empty.

"There. Fireworks over," said Jesse.

On Boxing Day, I set off from San Martín. The more I saw of Argentina, the more I liked it. How lucky I was to have met Heather forty years earlier in London.

The Argies think Chile a pathetic runt of a country, so they make sure the roads leading to the high Andes border passes are kept in maximum disrepair, nowhere more so than the 80 kilometres of "rip-rap": iron-hard corrugated mud studded with sharp, grapefruit-sized flint, road-grenades, leading to the Puyehue Pass into Chile. The Argies, having exterminated most of the indigenous people like to name their passes and lakes after them to remind themselves in a sentimental way that they too had native peoples once upon a time. What happened to them is a question best not asked while in Argentina.

The only bad thing about Patagonia for a biker was the wind, which varied between gale, storm, and hurricane force. Patagonia is in the heart of the Roaring Forties, that band of the world 40 degrees south of the equator where only Tasmania, New Zealand, and the sharp point of South America interrupt the southern oceans, hardly any land to break the wind that screams around the Southern Ocean. This made biking tricky when a full-force gale was coming in from the west and trying to flatten you.

Half the time I felt like I was sailing a dinghy as I skimmed along at 120 kph with Spike 45 degrees off vertical as I leant into the wind on what would have been a broad reach if we had been sailing with a Patagonian howler screeching in across the beam. Tricky, particularly when the wind dropped suddenly as you passed a bit of shelter and scrabbled to get the bike upright again.

Rentamoto said the only bike they had ever lost was a result of a young American failing to hike into the wind when the Roaring Forties hit him on the famed and feared Ruta Cuarenta. Ruta Cuarenta, or Route Forty, is one of the world's legendary biking roads and one of its longest, a kind of bikers' Everest. It runs down the spine of Argentina along the east side of the Andes, from the tropical Bolivian border in the North, 5,000 kilometres south to Tierra del Fuego and frozen Ushuaia, the southernmost city on Earth. I have long dreamed of biking the Ruta Cuarenta. The southern bit is still almost all gravel, gravel with 100 kph winds barrelling in from the West. Worse, the gravel has ruts from the trucks who thunder up and down the road. The sheer concentration required to keep a bike going in those conditions is possibly more than I could handle.

Despite the rip-rap and much of the road to the border resembling a water-course, Spike and I finally arrived at the Argentinian customs house. It was in the middle of the day. The Argie border guards waved us through, more interested in their lunch than passing gringos on bikes. Things were very different in Chile. Smartly suited officials in grey uniforms scrutinised me, Spike, and our papers for half an hour, occasionally disappearing into the immigration hut to confer amongst themselves.

I remembered the old saying that Argentina is a Spanish speaking country inhabited by Italians, there being more Argies of Italian descent than Spanish, while Chile is a Spanish speaking country inhabited by Germans. That may be an exaggeration, but it is certainly true that things are efficient and bureaucratic in Chile, where you better have your papers in order and be ready for inspection, while they are inefficient and bureaucratic in Argentina, where no one will inspect your papers during siesta time. I had not been biking long in Chile before I was waved down by a man in a uniform who had caught me exceeding the speed limit by 10 kph with his laser gun. He did not fine me, but I got a stern lecture. Argentina has speed limits, but the police have better things to do than enforce them.

I couldn't decide about Chile. In Argentina you think you are in Europe's forgotten but loveliest country. In Chile you are definitely in South America. Just as I was starting to like it, a cold and clammy sea-fog rolled in making the place as appealing as Dundee on a Sunday afternoon in Lent and then, suddenly, the mist disappeared and all around were heaped baskets of cherries and apricots by the road and the scent of wild oregano.

The people too were different to the other side of the Andes. In Argentina every second woman had looked like a young Sophia Loren. Not many Sophia Lorens in Chile. In Argentina I had seen very few indigenous people whereas in Chile they were as numerous as the European immigrants. And goodbye to the dignified colours of Argentina. Here every building was painted retina-bruising shades: sherbet yellow bungalows, lipstick purple cathedrals, and Paisley orange schools.

A couple of hours after crossing the border high up in the mountains we had descended to Valdivia on the Pacific. Spike had now taken me Ocean to Ocean, Atlantic to Pacific. I was by the harbour drinking pisco sours and eating grilled albacore caught by one of the hundred battered old Humboldt current trawlers in the harbour while the sea lions roared. Chilean sea lions are like seals on steroids. The Valdivia ones wallowed and slobbed around on the wooden bathing platform in the harbour and roared when the tourists stopped throwing them bits of fish. They reminded me of Chelsea soccer supporters.

One of the best things about Chile is the food and, of course, the wine. Not only are the fruit and vegetables some of the best in the world but Chile is in the vanguard of the new South American cooking revolution. I had been getting bored of the steaks and sausage in Argentina, good though they were.

In Chile, it rained. I am no meteorologist, but I suppose the wind blows in to Chile over the cold Pacific and hits the mighty Andes, which makes it offload all its moisture, whereas the other side in Argentina you sit in the rain shadow of the mountains and seldom see rain.

Spike and I did eight hours from Valdivia to the wine country in weather you might find in Aberdeen. I arrived cold and drenched at Casa Donoso, a winery cum château-hotel in mid-Chile which I had found through Google. It was a posh hotel set in its own vineyards. En route it had been so wet that I had to change into my black leather jeans and discovered that they too let the water in. Casa Donoso, I learned that evening from the only other guests, a German couple living in Brazil, was owned by a French Tahitian, married to a Chinese woman, who had become a billionaire by cornering the black pearl market. He lived in Tahiti. His representative on earth, or at least at the Casa Donoso in Chile, was Maria, its manager, who looked like a film noir star after a long night with the absinthe.

It soon became apparent that she liked men in leather. Far from recoiling from my road-stained, sodden figure, she greeted me by stroking my dripping leather jeans and murmuring, "Mmm, *mojado*". When we discovered that we had schoolboy French for a common language, I learned that *mojado* meant wet. I was shown to a room the size of a tennis court and, as I peeled off wet things, Maria kept tripping into my room with bottles of wine and plates of fruit to enquire in French whether I'd like *un vin special*. "*Oui, oui, certainement,*" I said, and it was only when she began describing the post-*vin* massage opportunities and how *le vin* was *plein du sel* (salt? in wine?) that I realised it was *un bain special,* a special bath, that I was being offered. I thought it best to say no.

After dinner, she, the German couple, and I sat sloshing red dessert wine, "*C'est spécial pour toi, Señor Che,*" murmured Maria, who said that my bike trip had fired her up. We were sitting in a tiny private cinema built of mud and horse-dung in the middle of a field of ripening cabernet sauvignon.

Later, as I was cleaning my teeth there was a scratch on the door and Maria slipped in wearing something floaty to ask if I needed *quelque chose pour la nuit*. "No, no, hrrrmph, *merci beaucoup*, quite OK thanks," said I, feeling like the Major in Fawlty Towers. After all that I had an undisturbed night. I had no idea what a pair of wet leather jeans could do.

I now had a decision to make. Unlike Che, who had continued on to Bolivia, I had to return Spike to Rentamoto in Buenos Aires so I would have to cross the Andes once more. There are only three practicable border crossings for a biker. I suspect this is because the Argies can't imagine why anyone would want to go to Chile if they are already in God's own country of Argentina. I didn't want to retrace my steps so I would aim for the middle one, which ran between Santiago, the Chilean capital, and Mendoza, where the finest Argentinian wine is made. I had been studying the route on the map. This is the highest border crossing in the Americas, peaking at 11,000 feet. That is almost twice as high as Zermatt at 6,000 feet. It sounded like good biking. I would take that route.

I also had to decide where I wanted to be on New Year's Eve. On leaving Casa Donoso I was going to head to Valparaiso. This was further, but sounded more funky and fun than Santiago. Santiago has 6 million people, no place for a biker, thank you. Valparaiso was the port of Santiago, 100 kilometres west. It was meant to be a hilly, student city with crazy art. Apparently on New Year's Eve, the students got drunk and threw anyone they could catch into the freezing Pacific. That too sounded interesting, but sadly I had worked out that I would need to be back in Argentina by New Year's Eve.

Valparaiso lived up to its billing, the hilliest city I had ever seen with cable cars and cog railways running up from the port area to the funky hilly bits, a wild mish-mash of clashing colours, San Francisco on acid. The New Year's three-day party was just kicking off. Winter Carnival, Valpo style. I had checked into a tiny wooden hotel on a street at what seemed like a 45-degree angle and had to spend ten minutes trying to get Spike on her stand so she wouldn't topple over. Dinner was drowned out by the crashing throb of street-samba echoing round the hills which were seething with drunken students preparing for the traditional Valpo New Year's Eve massacre. It was a fun place to be for my last night in Chile.

I had been wondering what to do for New Year. Ignore it completely? I had a plan. I had been in email contact with my new favourite unmet person, Astrid. Astrid was the sister of my 22-year-old London friend Richard 'Haz' Harrisson, a man who once rode a 1937 Velocette motorbike from London to Cairo, a feat beside which my trips are like a stroll round the Serpentine. His sister Astrid was doing things with horses at Los Potreros, an upmarket Anglo-Argie estancia near Córdoba. The estancia took in paying guests from England. It was fully booked over the Christmas holidays, but Astrid had persuaded the owners to liberate a tiny room by the stables for me on 30th and 31st December. She told them I was riding round Argentina. I suspect she omitted to mention that I was on two wheels, not four legs. That was in two days' time. First I had to cross the highest road pass in the Americas.

Spike and I were now attuned to the mountain roads, but nothing I had seen so far compared with the climb up to the 11,000 feet Cristo Redentor Pass, so called because on the top of the mountain was a statue of Christ the Redeemer while the traffic went through a tunnel below. The road was an endless series of hairpins, with just enough space between bends for Spike to accelerate past the huge trucks labouring up the mountain. It was a bare-cliffed place of heart-stopping wildness and grandeur where the screaming wind all but lifted Spike into the void, and vegetation was a stranger, mountains a million years older than the Alps. How the conquistadores had the courage to cross these mountains ignorant of what lay on the other side is a humbling thought.

Once over the pass there was an equally winding descent into Mendoza, the Argentinian wine capital and a city as elegant as a 1950s Alfa-Romeo. The plains around it and the city itself are all but rainless, but the Argentinians had learned from the Spaniards who had learned from the Arabs who had learned from the Persians the art of irrigation. Every street had a guttered brook of snow-melt which fed the roots of the majestic trees which lined the graceful avenues. The temperature in January was over a hundred degrees Fahrenheit, but the near-rainless city was as green as Seattle.

Then I travelled on to Los Potreros, a place of pilgrimage for horse-mad English people, where the Begg family, like Heather, Anglo-Argies of four generations standing, inhabited a wild and apparently endless estancia, 50 kilometres north of Córdoba.

During the day the Beggs put their guests on horses, took them riding, set up polo games, and taught them to lasso calves, but, in the evening, everyone sat sipping excellent Argentinian Domaine Chandon champagne on a cool verandah, looking out at a view of wildness and harmony, while gauchos set up huge grills where they barbecued everything from steak to sausage with a bit of grilled thymus and thyroid in between.

I am no rider of horses, which I regard as scary and dangerous animals, so while the guests had been galloping around, I had gone for a two-hour wog (half walk, half jog) into the rolling hills. Owls were perched on fences. I learned that these owls hunted in daytime. They slept at night in deep burrows dug by the local chinchillas. The chinchillas left the burrows to hunt at night. Perfect harmony.

Then I found myself in the middle of a field that felt as big as half a county and, looking around, I realised there were at least a hundred shiny black bulls and cows, many protecting their calves, stationed at twenty yard intervals throughout the field, each one half a ton of muscled, marbled, beef, motionless, and every one looking directly at me as if I had just bounced a cheque on it.

I looked for a hiding place in case one of these giant beasts chose to get sirloin's revenge and charge. Hiding behind a clump of grass, the only vegetation in the field, did not seem like a bull-fooling option so I walked purposefully on taking care to avoid the accusatory eyes and resisting the urge to break into a run. Two minutes of heads-down striding and I was able to clamber over a stone wall to safety. I looked round. A bull the size of the Minotaur was standing thirty yards away pawing the ground in a preparatory manner.

Before dinner, and I do not use the word dinner lightly, on New Year's Eve, at 7.00 pm as the shadows lengthened we walked half a mile from the house to stand on a hillside while a lone gaucho, all in black but for a crimson faja (pronounced fucker) cummerbund, stampeded a forty-strong group of wild horses past us. These were genuinely wild horses, descended from those brought over by the first conquistadores. It was a breathtaking sight as the herd galloped past into the sunset led by a white stallion.

Astrid had to help entertain the paying guests till after midnight but then the two of us managed to summon up a cab by phone, and at 1.00 am on 1st January we bumped our way to Rio Ceballos, the local town half an hour away down a corrugated mud track.

I don't remember much after that. Astrid's charm got us into Betaque, the hottest club in Rio Ceballos, and we found ourselves two amongst a thousand heaving, seething, Argie New Year party people. A nicer group of good-looking revellers I had never seen. Astrid, at 22, was probably three years older than the next oldest person there. I'm not quite sure what happened after our first couple of cocktails, as navigation became a problem. I remember more drinks, more talk, and dancing with Argentinian girls, all of whom had perfect manners and had decided that it was their turn to look after the aged gringo, but before you could say pisco sour it was 6.00 am and Astrid and I were in a taxi bouncing our way back to Los Potreros and a rising Argentinian sun.

Poor Astrid had to go to work as soon as we got back while I spent most of New Year's Day snoozing in the shade. I had an early start the next day and a 700 kilometre ride to Buenos Aires.

I left Los Potreros at dawn and at five that evening Spike and I nudged our way into Rentamoto's yard near the airport. Nicolas greeted me as if I had just been to the corner store for a packet of fags rather than 5,000 kilometres across the Andes and back. "Ah, señor Morland, welcome. Did you have a nice ride?"

"Thank you, Nicolas, I certainly did."

The drive that day had been straight and level, but just to show that

THE HOPELESS BIKER

Argentina had not gone soft on us, we had been hit by a huge thunderstorm at mid-day, and squalling winds which tried to blow us off the road, but by now it would have taken more than that to slow us down. I handed Spike's keys back to Nicolas and loaded my bags into a taxi he had summoned. I gave Spike a pat on her massive petrol tank. "She's a great bike, Nicolas. Never put a foot wrong. Thank you." I shook his hand and climbed into the cab.

In the taxi I was hit by a feeling of flooding exhilaration at the enormousness of where the ever-reliable Spike had taken me. There was also a growing sadness that my journey with Che was history now, and the heavy feeling that it was time to get back to being a grown-up.

Non-bikers don't realise how physical biking is, quite unlike driving a car. There had been a hundred kilometre stretch of long curves through the Sierra Chica to Córdoba, which local bikers, or so Nicolas had told me, used to train for the Isle of Man TT bike race.

Steering a bike of course is done with the weight, as in skiing, not by turning the wheel as in driving a car. You slow for a corner, pick the best line, being careful not to trespass over the mid-line for a left-hand bend as you do not want to be decapitated as you round the bend by an oncoming bus, and bank the bike. The sharper the turn, the steeper the bank, and then as you go into the turn and just as the weight of the slowing bike is coming close to making it fall, you wind the throttle to pour on power and the bike starts to move back to the vertical as the centrifugal force of the added power pushes it upright and back towards the outside of the bend. As soon as you come out of the bend you are picking your line for the next corner, the bike rising and falling like a slalom skier throwing her weight from left leg to right as she flips through the poles. After a few minutes of a long swooping run through the Andes or the Sierra Chica your heart is pumping so hard you are gasping.

Part of the intoxication comes from the knowledge that if you pick the wrong line going into a bend because you have underestimated its sharpness you do not have the option of braking halfway round, as you could in a car. Hitting the brakes on the bike would throw it upright and force you straight ahead and off the cliff. All you can do if a corner unexpectedly tightens into itself is to force the bike even further over on its ear and pray it too will tighten into the turn.

Then there had been the times floating along at a cruising speed of 5,000 revs, about 90 mph, across the limitless Pampa, Chuck Berry on the iPod, just making himself heard over the thrum of the engine, a blue sky bigger than any you had ever seen empty but for hawks and eagles with the Andes but a smudge on the horizon.

What a country.

Where else has such generosity, grandeur, and largeness of spirit? Despite no more Spanish than *hola, chau,* and *gracias,* it was impossible to be there and not have endless friendly encounters with people, whether they were buying you a rum in a bar or stroking Spike's thigh and saying *quel moto*. When I had somehow explained that Spike and I travelled in the tyre-treads of Che I got a squeeze on the arm, a clap on the back, a snort of appreciation, and a *viaje con dios*.

4

INDIA BY BULLET

My trip with Spike over the Andes came fifteen years after the Istanbul trip. When I went to Istanbul I had viewed it as a one-off experience. But after the trip with Spike, I realised I was acquiring a new addiction. I'm easy prey to addictions and the bike dream was feeding it. However much I loved my new work in Africa, biking had become my window to freedom.

Now that I was a single man, I only had myself to worry about. This meant that if I was able to take a holiday, I didn't have to consult anyone else. And as a single man the possibilities were endless. I even toyed with the idea of sailing around the world single handed. As my sailing competence went little further than a day skipper's course and some messing around in dinghies, it is lucky for the marine rescue services that this fantasy died quickly.

However the biking fantasy didn't. I had done the trip to Istanbul, quite a challenge for a trainee biker, and I'd done the Che Guevara trip, an equal challenge. Both of these I had done alone. Biking alone has many attractions. If the sun is shining and it's a beautiful morning, you can jump out of bed at 6.00 am and hit the road without worrying about what your companion wants to do. Or if the wind is howling and the rain drumming down, you can stay in bed till 11.00 am and hope it goes away, again not worrying about the fact you had agreed the night before to leave at 8.00 am.

In 2007 I had handed over Blakeney Management to my partners there and begun building a new African investment firm, Development Partners International (DPI), with a wider focus beyond just stock market investing. To start with I was working too hard to get away but as DPI got bigger, it became easier to take a couple of weeks off.

So it was that in February 2011, four years after the trip with Spike, I found myself on a plane to India. I love India. My father was stationed there with the Navy during the war, which is why I was born there in 1943. However, India was not a place for long distance solo biking unless you were a far better mechanic than I. This was going to be different. In India, I was going on my first group trip.

I was on a trip organised by Extreme Bike Tours. I don't know if the Istanbul and South American trips would be considered extreme. Certainly extreme for me but possibly not so for an experienced biker. I had come across Extreme Bike Tours while googling trips in faraway places. They promised to take you biking "on the edge of the world". They appeared to be run by a pirate with a ponytail called Zander Combe. Their most fearsome trip took you to the highest navigable pass in the Himalayas where, so the website informed me, Zander was hoping to get in the Guinness Book of World Records for cooking the world's highest prawn curry. I did not stop to think how fresh the prawns would be by the time they got to the top of the Himalayas in a motorbike pannier. If eating a prawn curry made from week old prawns on a Himalayan pass did not appeal, they also offered a wild ride through the mountains of southwest India. This kind of trip needed support. I would never be able to arrange it by myself.

India is above all a place of villages and I liked the idea of biking through ancient Indian villages more than bare Himalayan passes, so I had signed up for the southern India ride. We were going to start in Kochi, climb up into the mountains of the Western Ghats, and bike on to Goa by a circuitous route via Madurai; Ooty, the Queen of the hill stations; and Mysore.

I like to stay in hotels that have things like flushing loos, showering

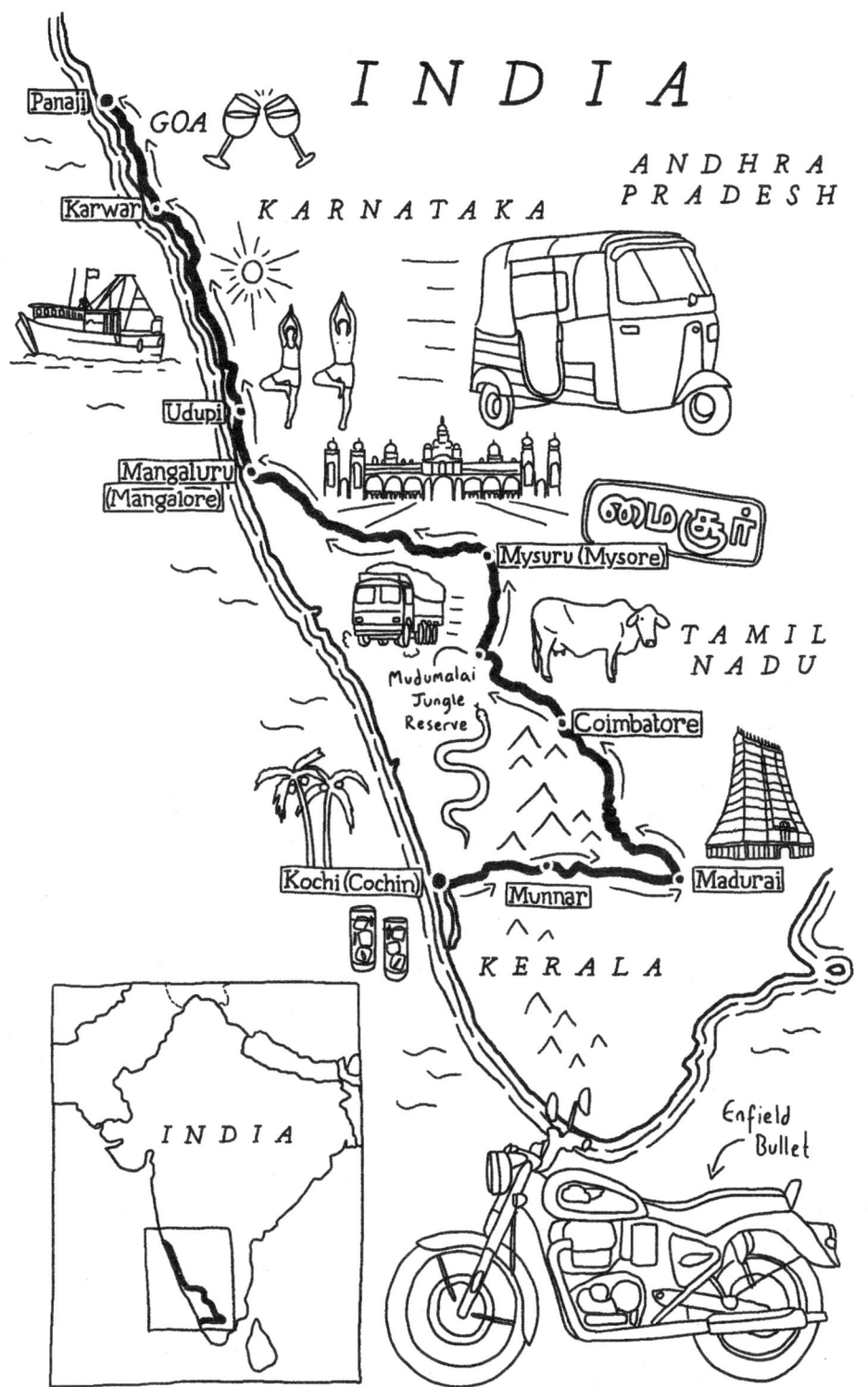

showers, unstained sheets, and curtains on the windows. On this trip we were going to be staying in two-star Indian hotels. Two-star Indian accommodation is not like Travelodge. I had looked some of the hotels up on TripAdvisor. The features they had in common were an abundance of sewage, little of it going down the right hole, and cockroaches the size of dachshunds.

Here's what TripAdvisor reviewers had to say about the "Royal Retreat" hotel in Munnar, a tea town up in the Western Ghats where we would spend our first night on the road.

Reviewer Mr Ankur Tewari reported:

"The biggest problem which I faced in the hotel was of fooding. The food quality is very poor. Most of the time the service is not available. Even the menu items are also not available. So if you want to stay make sure you eat out."

Meanwhile TripAdvisor reviewer "Coimbatore Sam" had this to say of his visit:

"It was an awful trip in my life ever ... Which was run by totally unprofessional people ... I started facing problem since I checked in. It's absolutely an worst trip and I never suggest this hotel and absolutely not for honeymoon couples. Please stay away."

Thank God I wasn't a honeymoon couple. And who cared about fooding? It was the bedding and the loo-ing which mattered more to me.

As for the bike it was an Enfield Bullet, a 1956 English bike still made in India as we had sold the factory to India when they stopped making them in England in 1956. Its slogan was "Built like a Gun, Goes like a Bullet", presumably because it exploded frequently. I was told we had "full Indian insurance".

"What does that cover me for?" I asked.

"Oh, $150 of damage to the bike."

"And what about if I run someone over?"

"Ah, that's a cash transaction," said Zander.

He did add that if you ran someone over in a village, for heaven's sake don't stop, because if you did, the village people would beat you to death.

And that it was important to settle matters in cash before the police turned up, as bribing them was far more expensive than buying off the person you had just run over.

We had arrived at 3.30 am on a February Saturday, St Valentine's Day, and spent Sunday in Kochi. What a lovely place it was, all fishing nets, crumbling churches, and Dutch forts. We met up with the other "Extreme Bikers" and learned how to drive our Enfield Bullets.

We were seven punters. My companion was Robert Maclean, who had been a close friend since Oxford. Robert had been a biker far longer than I, something I found reassuring. He also looked like Marlon Brando and never lost his cool, the perfect companion for the Indian road.

I had no idea what the other five Extreme Bikers would be like. Ravers? Biker babes? Karma-seekers? Dope-heads? None of those things. We had Bill, Ian and Charles, three hard men from Newcastle, who had, I suspected, spent many a Friday night head-butting Yorkshiremen; and two lads from Derby, Terry and Dave, both ex-enlisted army men. Terry was now a fruit and veg man while Dave drove the high-speed train to Newcastle from London. They were almost as old as Robert and me.

Our leader and the founder of Extreme Bike Tours was Zander. I discovered that he had been expelled from the same Victorian boarding school I had been sent to, something to do with girls or drugs, it never became quite clear which, like most things to do with Zander. He had been based for the last sixteen years in Anjuna beach, Goa's Hippy Valley, the place that made the world safe for ganja in the 1960s and our final destination. The team mechanic was Vijay, a gentle, smiling Goan and the only person who understood our ancient bikes.

On Sunday we were taught how to ride them. Unlike a normal bike the Bullet's gear pedal was on the right where the brake should have been, and to change gear you clicked down, not up. And there was a false neutral between each gear. Swapping the accelerator pedal with the clutch in a car would have had a similar effect.

The result was that when you wanted to do an emergency stop, you stamped on the gear lever, where years of instinct had told you the brake was, which promptly changed you up from third to a false neutral between third and fourth while the bike sailed on at 50 kph.

Starting was an act of mysticism known only to Vijay.

"The bikes are like women," Zander had told us, "treat them gently but with firmness and they'll do anything you want."

Zander was unmarried.

Starting required pushing the kick-start gently down while pressing the "decompression lever" at which the ammeter dial (don't ask) went to the left a bit and then you pushed the kick-start down further and the dial centred, at which brief but critical moment you let the kick-start come up and then quickly, gently but firmly, kicked the kick-start down.

After doing this ten times the bike was silent and the heat inside your helmet and your reinforced biker jacket had built to sauna proportions. Vijay then shimmied up, gave the starter a nonchalant prod with his left foot and the bike roared into action. And what a noise. The Bullet had none of the vulgar gargle of a Harley or the scream of a Ducati, it was a deep-throated "pocketa pocketa" of a 1950s English bike after a life in the tropic sun.

We went on a 15 kilometre trip through Kochi traffic to get used to the bikes.

"Only one thing is vital," said Zander, "the horn."

We were to sound it at all times. And if it broke, stop immediately and wait for Vijay as we would be invisible without a horn on an Indian road.

The trip was a qualified success. We stalled frequently and found ourselves stationary in the middle of maelstrom traffic, all using their horns at us, while we gently but firmly depressed the kick start while trying to watch the ammeter dial as the sweat cascaded in rivulets down the inside of our helmet visors.

Ian, one of the Geordies, meanwhile had overtaken a bus to follow a speeding police van which he had mistaken for Vijay's support van, so we had to wait in a sun hot enough to melt tar while Zander went off on a search and recover mission.

But after a bit our bikes did begin to exhibit their elegant 1950s Katherine Hepburn qualities as they glided along throatily pocketa-pocketing while we clumsily changed from third to fourth with no neutral in between and the coconut palms flashed by and the fragrance of Kochi's sewer-canals fell behind.

I was glad to get back to our hotel, a teetotal establishment, have a long shower, put on my new Kochi linen pants, and saunter off with Zander, Vijay, and Robert to the Brunton Boatyard, a five-star hotel, where we sat on the terrace by the sea, watched the fishing boats set out on the evening tide, and rehydrated with a number of the most delicious mojitos I had ever tasted.

The next day we would hit the road proper and head for Munnar, and the no-fooding Royal Retreat. It was at 4,000 feet and a five-hour drive away. I was both excited and apprehensive.

After a few hours on the road I was beginning to learn Indian hand signals. Well, hand signal. There was only one. A hand would come out of the driver's window and flap lazily in a Wildean manner. This meant one of seven things:

- Please overtake, the road is clear.
- A cement truck is hurtling towards us; you will be killed if you pull out.
- I am about to turn right.
- I am about to turn left.
- I'm hot and bored and feel like flapping a lazy arm out of the window.
- Look, children, there's Auntie's house.
- I have just picked my nose.

Once I knew this driving became much safer. The ride up to misty Munnar with its lakes and tea plantations and forests with tree canopies two hundred feet high and distant blue mountain peaks had been dramatic. Our hotel, the Royal Retreat, had not lived down to our worst Tripadvisor-inspired fears. It even had functioning western-style loos. To be on the safe side we had not counted on them for fooding but found a roadside stall which cooked us delicious dosas and veggie stuff served up on a banana leaf.

The next day, now feeling like veterans of the Indian road, we were swooping down to Madurai far below in the hot and dusty plain. The road down was a biker's dream, curve after tightening curve gliding through the forest. The trouble was that the road was narrow and an Indian bus could take up most of the road when it went round a tight bend.

Dodging an Indian bus could be tricky. Bill, an ex-British Airways 747 pilot, was about two hundred metres ahead of me, riding in a conservative style near the edge of the road so as to be clear of approaching traffic. The approaching traffic turned out to be a bus with people perched on its roof. The bus was not being driven in a conservative style. It barrelled round the corner, horn blaring, more on the wrong side than the right of the road. Bill had the option of being rammed or sliding into the shallow ditch. He took the latter course. The bike whip-tailed as it left the road and poor B.A. Bill was flat on his face in the ditch. The bus careered on, almost knocking me into the ditch as it passed.

Luckily, Bill had been going slowly and was quickly back on his feet. As if by magic, Vijay shimmied up out of the heat-haze, Bill and bike were repaired and we sailed on till Charles, one of the Geordies, caught a patch of sand on a hairpin and he too was off but again without hurting himself as he had landed in a pile of leaves. Vijay appeared to only have one tool, a large black hammer. This was produced, damage was repaired, and on we went.

We hit the plains and accelerated, now doing 80 kph (Indian kph are like dog years, except you multiply by two for normal equivalent), an unheard of speed. My buddy, Robert, was Easy-Riding along just ahead of me, Marlon Brando-style, the gum trees were whistling by, buffaloes saluted, tuk-tuks stood clear as the procession of mighty Enfields bulleted past, when Robert hit a reverse-camber sandy patch on a high-speed bend, his bike fishtailed violently, and I watched in slow-motion horror as the bike skidded on to its side and went down on top of Robert with both coming to rest in the ditch.

I skidded to a halt and rushed back. Robert was motionless under the bike. I sat him up gently while he croaked unconvincingly, "I'm OK." Before he could say anything else platoons of Tamils appeared from apparently nowhere and started fighting over which bit of Robert they would administer first aid to.

His legs and arms were seized and worked up and down; his head was rotated and wobbled. I did my best to fend them off before they did Robert a serious injury. When they reluctantly stood back we found that Robert was bruised but OK apart from possible cracked ribs. Zander, who had materialised out of nowhere with the support van, gave him powerful "muscle relaxants" from the First Aid bag and promised Goan ganja if that didn't work.

Robert's bike was hammered back into rideable shape by the wizardous Vijay. Vijay grinned in triumph and handed the bike back with a jolly, "Mr Robert, now good." Robert winced in pain as he took the handlebars. A swap took place. Vijay in his flappy sandals and no helmet rode the bike while Robert nursed his ribs in the support van.

Not for long. We stopped for lunch in a tiny village. Zander called Vijay who was riding as tail-end sweeper and discovered that we were another man down. B.A. Bill had had a blowout and ended up in a field. This was most unfair. What about the rule of three? We had thought that after three accidents in one day we were inviolable. Anyhow, it turned out that Bill was fine but the bike was not. Zander reported that Vijay had his hammer out and was busy reshaping the bike 10 kilometres back while we sat in a chai shop and ate honey balls.

We had now left the state of Kerala and were in the proud state of Tamil Nadu, the heart of South India, home to people who make the French look humble. Here the signs are written in ornate squirly script and the locals not only refuse to speak English but also Hindi so that they do not have to lower themselves by communicating with outsiders. Consequently, communication with lesser races (English, other Indians, Martians) is done by means of the Tamil Head Nod. So, having mastered Indian traffic indications, the Hand Flap, I was now studying Indian speech substitutes, the Head Nod.

Indians are of course famous for nodding their heads but in Tamil Nadu it is often the sole means of communication. Ask them a question and the head starts to oscillate sideways from left to right, picking up speed until it is almost a blur. The Tamil Nod, often accompanied by a patronising smile as if to say "what a stupid question", means "No, but it's more fun if you think I'm saying Yes." Such as…

- Thank you for ordering a sweet lime soda. It will be here immediately despite the fact we have no soda, and the last lime was used in the veg curry.
- Of course there are no knives and forks, what are your fingers for?
- All our ice is made from purified water.
- The hot water comes on at 6.00 pm.

Because from time to time we did need to communicate with local people, Zander had quietly recruited one, Shirath, and hired him to drive the support van in which Robert had been riding. Being a Tamil, he refused to admit to speaking English, but luckily Vijay had discovered a common tongue with him although most of their conversation was done by head-nodding vigorous enough to power a windfarm. Shirath's main purpose was, in the event of an accident, to leap out of the car, and negotiate a cash pay-off with the flattened Tamil. According to Zander, it was not uncommon for people to provoke accidents so they could get a pay-off. The important thing was to settle the matter to everyone's satisfaction before the police arrived. Being a policeman was a coveted job because you could make so much money by shaking down motorists.

Strange though it may seem, when we were not having accidents, I could not have been happier, perhaps because staying alive on the Indian road made me appreciate how good being alive was. We had fought our way through murderous traffic into the temple city of Madurai where we were spending the night. A prize lay ahead. I had looked on Tripadvisor and seen that, in this generally dry part of India, our hotel had a bar, the UFO Bar. Having not had a drink since Kochi we had in anticipation been eagerly discussing over lunch what we were going to drink that evening. Between us we had invented a special Extreme Biker cocktail: the Rumpy, fresh pineapple juice and dark rum. We were looking forward to having a few Rumpies before dinner.

Arriving in Madurai had been a challenge; fighting to follow Zander and the six bikes ahead, trying to stay upright while trying not stall in the maelstrom of Madurai traffic as tuk-tuks closed in like Messerschmitts. At one point I attempted to overtake a bus thundering towards me, proclaiming itself to be under the command of Lord Ram; it really was a monumental task. Heart in my mouth, I said thank you as the Bullet somehow found a hole between me and fatal contact with the bus. I popped out in time to see Zander attempting a U-turn because he had been foolish enough to ask directions.

Better to travel in hope than to arrive ... After we had checked in we met at the UFO Bar. We had noticed at check-in how promising the bar looked with flashing neon signs and renditions of sari-clad ladies perched on pulsating UFOs. I asked the barman what kind of rum they had.

"No, sir, not having rum."

"Oh, well, vodka?"

"No, sir, not having vodka."

"Well what alcohol do you have? I'd love a cocktail."

"Not having alcohol, sir."

Welcome to the UFO Bar. The lime soda was delicious.

I had hoped that a couple of rumpies would have eased poor Robert's pain, something a lime soda was not going to do. By the time we reached the hotel Robert, after what must have been a painful and bumpy ride in the van, was gasping whenever he raised his right arm and almost passed out when he sneezed. We needed to get him to a doctor. Madurai may have been the best place in India to find a doctor. Madurai had hospitals where normal places had coffee shops. Its stupendous temple made it a place of pilgrimage where people flocked in their thousands for the gods to heal. What more natural than after a healing trip to the temple but that you should have your spine fixed at Dr Ram's Spinal Intervention Clinic, or your boobs boobed at the Sunny Days Cosmetic Surgery Centre? Robert decided that cosmetic surgery could wait but his ribs could not. Escorted by Shirath, with whom we had no language in common, we headed off at 7.00 pm to find a hospital.

Vijay had made enquiries and had had recommended to him the Apollo, one of a chain of private Apollo hospitals throughout India. We were apprehensive about visiting an Indian hospital from which, we assumed, most people came out much sicker than when they went in. After being mis-directed six or seven times by people telling Shirath it was straight ahead we found a gleaming white building on the ring road, parked easily, and slipped into the 24-hour emergency centre. I knew from experience what emergency centres, or A&Es as they are called in England, were like. Many had been the long post-midnight hours I had sat when my daughters were teenagers in London A&Es waiting five or six hours to be seen while semi-decapitated people or those with painful things jammed in the wrong parts of their body jumped the queue. If it was like that in London, what horror awaited us in India?

The Apollo was as new, gleaming and clean as an Apple Store. You could have eaten your breakfast off the shining floor. A central casting doctor in spotless whites glided up, sat Robert on a bed, pushed and pulled his arms, listened gravely to the stethoscope, asked four or five questions, said, "Probably a rib fracture," and sent us off to X-Ray. We were asked to pay in advance for the X-Ray, 250 rupees or £3.50. Back in the ward our doctor conferred with an even smarter one. They slid the X-Ray onto a screen and pointed to where the third rib on the right-hand side was fractured but not broken in two.

"It will heal in eight to ten weeks by itself but meanwhile you should rest it. No treatment is necessary."

"Can I ride a motorbike?" croaked Robert.

"Mr Maclean, you are a very funny man. Of course. But you will take twice as long to heal."

We said thank you and trotted off to pay a further £8 for Robert's consultation and to pick up some prescription painkillers.

The entire treatment in this sparkling clean hospital had taken twenty minutes, less time than it would have taken to fill in an admission form in the Chelsea and Westminster. Everyone was polite, efficient, and treated you like a grown-up. Since taking the prescription painkillers Robert was walking around glassy-eyed with an odd grin on his face like a male Stepford Wife and I had been pondering the British National Health Service.

After Madurai we were heading to Kodaikanal, a hill station, where we would spend the night. The next day we would be going on to the Mudamalai Tiger Reserve for a much-anticipated rest day. However, between Kodaikanal and Mudamalai, Zander was going to spice things up. Instead of taking a relatively easy route through the forests we were going to drive all the way up to Ooty, stop there for lunch, and then head down and on to Mudamalai.

Ooty, or Ootacamund as it's now called, was important to Zander.

"Gotta go to Ooty," he said.

"Why?" we asked.

"There's nothing like it in southern India. The climb up and the descent down are hairpin after hairpin, blind bend after blind bend for mile after mile. Zoweee … Gets the blood pumping, I can promise you. You'll need to keep alert. Possibly the most dangerous road in south India."

Thanks, Zander.

Ooty meant little to the rest of our group, but it meant a lot to me and it wasn't because of the hairpin bends. In British days, it had been the Queen of the hill stations where the British in south India, like my parents when I was born, went to retreat from the heat of Madras for the summer months.

India is a special place for me. I don't have Indian blood, but India is in my blood. I was born, during the war in 1943, in India, at a port called Vizag, or Vishakapatnam as it now is, on the east coast, halfway between Madras and Calcutta. In 1943 it was a naval base and my Dad, commanding a Royal Indian Navy frigate, was stationed there. My Dad, and his father and grandfather before him, had all joined the Royal Navy and then transferred to the Royal Indian Navy during the days of the British Raj. On my mother's side too, most of her family had gone out to do things in India for four generations.

Today, this sounds outlandish. But for so many people of my colonial background, India played a huge part in our families' history. This is no place to argue about the rights or wrongs of the British Raj. I was four years old when India gained its independence in 1947.

My family left India in 1949, two years after independence, by which time my parents' marriage had ended. I have a powerful memory of the trip back to England on the *Circassia* of the Anchor Line, the P&O Line being too grand and expensive for us. I remember so vividly my shock at meeting 1949 England, grey, drizzly, food on ration, London a mess of bomb sites with the buildings black from a century of soot, everything and everyone subdued and without colour. After the heat, smell, noise, riotous colour, and sheer extravagant abundance of India, England was a shrivelled vision of purgatory for a five-year-old boy who knew only India.

This is a book about biking, not about memories of the British Raj. However, Ooty, to which we were about to bike, was somewhere I had been before, some seventy years earlier, in 1944. I was six months old then and my mother had taken Michael, my older brother, and me up there from Vizag for the summer before moving down to Madras. I had no actual memories of it, but I had heard many tales from my mother, a teller of extravagant stories, of the glamour of wartime Ooty life, where the Club was the trysting place for dashing off-duty officers with women whose men were far away fighting the Japanese in Burma. In going to Ooty I felt I was, in a funny way, coming home.

And there I was, seventy years on, following mad Zander from Kodaikanal up round the hairpins to the Queen of the hill stations.

I will never forget the drive up, a terrifying, heart-stopping climb of six thousand feet of hairpins from the plains to Ooty. It seemed that every bus and petrol tanker in the sub-continent had chosen to make the climb at the same time. We had the choice of going up at walking speed, choking in the fumes behind a struggling petrol tanker or overtaking the bus that was overtaking the tanker as we came into a blind bend (there were few sighted bends on the road to Ooty) with a mountain on one side, a cliff on the other, and a keen awareness that if another lorry was coming downhill at that point, then even Lord Vishnu could not save you.

It was fine for Zander, as lead bike, who normally waited till just before a blind bend before pulling out, throwing his bike on to the wrong side of the road and accelerating fearlessly. He had time to get past before the bend and could see if the road was clear. If you were riding third or fourth you followed heart a-thump as by the time you pulled out the visible space ahead had shrunk to nothing. I could feel every chamber of my heart fibrillating every time we overtook. Never had I been happier than when I finally saw a sign welcoming us to Ootacamund.

Even then, I got off on the wrong foot when I almost killed a cow on arrival. The streets, like everywhere in India, were a whirlpool of animals, humanity, and traffic. A cow turned suddenly from grazing at a vegetable stall and decided to graze on my front tyre. As anyone who has been to India knows, cows, sacred beasts that they are, wander everywhere in India without restraint. They walk through markets munching the cabbages, they sit in the middle of motorways, acting as traffic calming devices, and if God forbid you should hit one on a motorbike, you better hope that your bike can carry you away faster then an enraged crowd can run. I avoided hitting the Ooty cow, God knows my fate if I had struck the sacred beast, by diverting into a group of Tamil pedestrians, but somehow they too dodged the blundering red-face on his magic Bullet. Vishnu, God of the Indian road, must have had me in his care.

We were not spending the night in Ooty, just stopping for lunch. I decided to mark my return to Ooty by leaving the others to watch my bike and going for a walk by myself rather than have lunch. We had stopped on the edge of town with a view over wooded hills and valleys that seemingly stretched to infinity. I elbowed my way through the teeming streets into quiet old English cemeteries and deserted churches which looked as if they belonged in Gloucestershire. I had no memories of my own of Ooty, but I had my mother's stories. I was happy to go there but despite the English churches and cemeteries, Ooty is nowadays a very Indian city. I was glad to revisit it, but I won't go back. That chapter was closed.

Not only were Indian distances and speeds like dog years, equivalent to at least double, possibly triple their value in the normal world, Zander had started fibbing about them. Our trip from the hill station of Kodaikanal to the Mudumalai Tiger Reserve was, said Zander, "only 200 clicks" as Zander called kilometres, probably to make them seem shorter.

When we finally reached the end of the two-kilometre boulder-strewn watercourse that passed for the Jungle Reserve drive, after eleven draining Indian-road hours, we had covered almost 400 clicks of mountain hairpins, the drive down a near precipice beyond Ooty having thirty-six successive hairpins, not to mention roads closed by landslides, and random attacks by homicidal buses.

"Oh, was it that far?" said Zander innocently, and I could swear he was adopting the Indian head nod, "I had no idea it was so much…"

Arriving at the Jungle Reserve Hotel was like entering paradise. For the previous five days we had been staying in hotels where the fooding had been veg curry, the loo-ing a hole in the floor, and the drinking a disaster. It was wonderful to be in a place equipped with unimaginable luxuries like the first roll of loo-paper I had seen since Kochi. And, better yet, before dinner a smiling man shimmied out of the jungle and positioned himself behind the bar with a cocktail shaker in his hand, the first man for five days who did not say "Bless you" if you said "Mojito".

The Geordies, hard men that they were, spent the rest day going for a jungle hike. Robert and I spent ours, mojitos in hand, chilling by the Jungle Reserve pool which was alive with the giggles of fifteen teenage girls from the Ooty International School, who had come for a Saturday day out.

Before lunch I did however go for a walk round the hotel grounds with Max, the half-German, half-Parsee, camp botanist. When we reached my bungalow, he began laughing.

"Ach, Miles, zis is your bungalow?"

"Yes, why?"

He told me about the group of German guests that had just left. On their arrival, Max and the receptionist had been showing the group to their bungalows starting with mine. There was something sticking out and wiggling between the rocks used to build the bungalows.

Max had sent the receptionist off to get one of the staff. Then, eight newly arrived Germans stood around aghast, luggage in hand, watching while Max and his mate took hold of the wiggling thing and tried to pull it, a cobra, which had followed a frog into a hole in the wall and got stuck, out.

Eventually they tugged hard and Max's mate was left holding it by its tail, on outstretched arm. The enraged two-metre cobra was doing its best to climb up its own body to give it a platform for a strike. Every few seconds the holder gave it a flick to straighten it out, an action which enraged the snake even more. Max meanwhile was holding open a sack which his mate had brought, but was worried that the cobra would strike him as it was dropped in. The new arrivals stood watching, catatonic with horror.

"What then?" I asked Robin.

"Ach, ve got it in ze bag and took it off for first aid to make sure it wasn't damaged."

"First aid?"

"*Naturlich*. And the next day we released it into a distant part of the garden."

I knew exactly how the German tourists had felt and asked Max whether they had carefully checked the holes in the masonry of my bungalow for any more wiggling tails.

"Please, not worry," said Max. "Cobra gone."

"Phew. Thank heavens. Any other livestock in my room?"

"Nein, nein. Ach, ja, but not in the wall, in the roof."

"Roof?"

"Is only flying snake. It lives there. They flatten ze body and can glide 100 metres on ze wind. Don't worry, Miles, only mildly venomous."

I survived the flying snake, which must have been snoozing while I was in its room. We set off from the Jungle Reserve after our rest day refreshed and happy. Robert was back in the saddle, albeit with frequent winces. He had foolishly refused Zander's offer of Mysore Maddener, the local weed guaranteed to conquer all pain.

The drive to Mysore was uneventful, no hairpins or suicidal cows. Mysore turned out to be a tourist's not a biker's dream. It was big and flat and grand. During the British Raj, the rulers of Mysore had been among the most favoured of the princely rulers, allowed to rule their states independently as long as they didn't start invading their neighbours or burning their widows (the British had made themselves unpopular with the Hindu upper class by banning the practice of suttee whereby a widow was expected to throw herself on her dead husband's funeral pyre).

One of the features of a long bike trips is that well-meaning people give you advice before you set off about the wonderful things to sight-see on the way, some of which are en route and the others requiring a few miles of detour. What they don't realise is that when you are on a journey, you are on a journey, and that is the point of it. You're not a tourist on a sight-seeing trip. That may sound philistine and unimaginative but if you take real journeys you will understand. It is true that at times, such as in the evening before setting off from Kochi we had checked out the Dutch fort and the old town, and in Madurai in the evening we had gone to the temple. However, once you are on the road you do not stop or deviate to sight-see. You are living in the moment. The journey is everything.

However, when the day's journey was finished a wander was possible. Accordingly, Robert and I went to check out the Mysore Palace, one of the great marvels of India. Like the Umaid Bhawan Palace in Jodhpur, which is the biggest private residence in India if not the world, the Mysore Palace was built at the beginning of the 20th century. The architect was Henry Irwin, who had designed Raj buildings all over India. It is a grand three-storey Indo-Saracenic building with echoing mirrored halls and roofed with red cupolas. It reminded me of the slightly earlier Bombay Railway Station in Mumbai, one of the great Victorian buildings of India.

More important for us was that we had now left the very dry state of

Tamil Nadu and entered the not-so-dry state of Karnataka. As we had biked along I had noted in the towns establishments with dusty signs proclaiming they were "wine shops".

"Ooh, what wouldn't I give for a chilled Sancerre," said I to Zander.

"Sorry, mate, not available here."

"No, no," said I, "I've seen wine shops. I'll get some for dinner."

Zander explained in tones you might use to a six-year-old, "Wine shops sell beer. And spirits, mainly hooch and locally brewed whisky. But the one thing they can't sell is wine."

A day later, wineless, and after more than a week of sweat, terror, excitement, exhilaration, and pain (like most of us, I have a "Bullet tattoo" of red weals on the back of both calves from being branded by backing into a smoking exhaust pipe) and sheer hard work (eleven continuous hours from Mysore to Udipi), we saw the sea. We had arrived at Turtle Beach.

Getting here had not been easy. Zander had turned into a cross between Baron Munchausen and John Belushi.

"Don't worry, guys, only 280 clicks from Mysore to Turtle Beach. We'll be in Goa at last," he trilled.

We had set off at 7.30 am and arrived, near dead with fatigue after fighting our way through the suburbs of Mangalore, a singularly unattractive place, at 6.30 pm, having travelled almost 400 kilometres. To be fair, Zander had warned us we would encounter "lively lorries" on the road to Mangalore, one of the few accurate pieces of information he ever gave us.

After ten days, we had become fond of our quirky old bikes, their funny false neutrals, and decompression levers that you had to tickle if you wanted to start the bike. The riders had by now split into two groups. A suicide squad of four, including me, had been doing their utmost to keep up with mad Zander, the king of the blind bend. The other three, "I don't want to die on an Indian road", were the sensible squad, happy to drop behind. The sensible squad were the three who had come off their bikes: Robert with his fractured rib, B.A. Bill, and Charles, a civil engineer. The suicide team were Terry, the fruit and veg man; Dave, who drove the high-speed train from Leeds to London; Ian, an NHS manager; and me.

Indian roads were different. On the way to Mysore we had found ourselves on a divided highway with two lanes in either direction, like an English motorway. Unlike an English motorway, the outside lane featured tuk-tuks and buses speeding along in the wrong direction. Worse, they felt they had right of way. Indian roads had two traffic calming devices. One was the conventional road bump, except here they were unmarked, and so big that taken at thirty mph you would be airborne for the next five seconds and you might well bite your tongue off. The other form of calming device was a mobile one, also unmarked. It was a cow. Few things are calmer than an Indian cow, placidly ruminating in the middle of four lanes of crazed, beeping, braking, roaring traffic.

At last, exhausted from the drive, we puttered up behind Zander to the White Sands Hotel, ten palm-thatched huts with thick, soft mattresses and lilies on the bed, insane luxury after ten nights of hard boards and concrete platforms. It even had a stylish bar openly displaying hitherto-forbidden substances: rum, whisky, vodka, and even a case of Indian wine, which Zander had called ahead to order. In the restaurant building was a kitchen turning out spice-marinated grilled fish, crab masala, and fragrant coconut curries. And it was set on a mile of powdery white sand dotted with slender out-rigger fishing boats. The White Sands was £20 a day and another £6 for the best seafood dinner you had ever eaten.

We had made it to Goa. We had survived everything Zander had thrown at us. Blessed relief, and maybe one more mojito before a molten sun faded into an Indian Ocean whose surf broke on a mile of white sand.

For anyone like me who came of age in the 1960s, all journeys end in Goa. The first night in Goa I sat under a beach palm at midnight giggling like a nine-year-old, having had a mojito too many and a puff too far of the Mysore Maddener we had scored off a rickshaw driver, and I felt I had come home.

Juliebee was a friend who had taken time off from a job in London to work as a volunteer in an orphanage near Madras for two months. I had got to know her because she had been best friends in Los Angeles with Jane, an ex-girlfriend of mine. They were both English, but Jane was then writing for *South Park* and Juliebee was a Hollywood make-up artist.

I was delighted she was joining us because she was always cheerful and was one of the funniest people I knew. She had been given five days off and had taken buses and trains halfway across India to join us for the rest of the trip. A lesser woman might have been swamped by our very male group. She even chuckled politely as Terry, the Derby greengrocer, unleashed a torrent of his foulest jokes from the lads in Derby market, in the hope of embarrassing her. Having another friend in addition to Robert and having a feminine presence was a treat after many long evenings of chaps' talk.

Juliebee and I strolled down the pristine white sand beach in the evening, dodging our way through people in improbable positions doing the downward dog and the plank as they saluted the sinking sun. Yoga was compulsory in Goa. At the far end of the beach we had sat and sipped "Jungle Juice", lime, pineapple and cashew feni, the local hooch, and a painless passport to oblivion, at a little beach bar.

We had a rest day of beach, mojitos and coconut crab curry at the White Sands. The temptation to give it all up and become a permanent resident there was creeping up on me but the following day we were off to our final destination, Anjuna, where Zander and the bikes lived, and the hippies were older and more wrinkly than Keith Richards. We would be staying in the Joly Julie.

I learned at dinner that Zander had more metal than bone in his body. I was glad not to have known that earlier in the trip as I'd been comforting myself that if he had been risking his life on Indian roads for sixteen years and he was fine, then we should be too. If I'd known earlier that his forearm was titanium (a cow, which strolled away with hardly a moo after Zander had demolished his Enfield colliding with it), his right foot was steel (a fast-moving palm tree), and most of his joints were secured by pins and bolts after miscellaneous encounters with the flotsam of the Indian road, I would been even more scared than I was.

THE HOPELESS BIKER

Despite that, the trip to the Joly Julie, a group of startling red and white bungalows in the forest a mile or so from Anjuna Beach, the hippy Mecca, was uneventful and short. We arrived at lunchtime.

I had expected to feel elated but in fact I felt flat. I had had the same feeling when I had returned the mighty Spike after twice crossing the Andes. The trip was over. No more reason for heart-in-mouth and the pulse to quicken. Once more, there was gratitude that, apart from the Goa burn tattoos and a cricked back from one concrete mattress too many, we were unharmed. Even Robert, who had never once complained about his ribs, was looking perky.

Zander had proposed a bike trip the day after arrival to a deserted beach "only 30 clicks away". I remembered *Das Boot*, the wonderful German film about a U-Boat that survived everything from depth-charges to ruptured pressure hull on an Atlantic hunting trip. As the boat chugged serenely into Brest, its home port, sun shining, mission accomplished, with the crew on deck celebrating, they were suddenly wiped out by an RAF bomb. No-one voiced it but we all felt that one more outing, even if it was only 30 Zander-clicks away, on our brave Bullets could be throwing Providence one offering too many in the way of temptation.

Instead Juliebee and I were spending our last morning drinking lime and coconut cocktails at the Rock On!!! Cafe on Ozran Beach between Little Vagator and Anjuna. We found that almost every rock and empty bit of sand was peopled with near-naked pairs of Russian girls being photographed, bodies entwined, by the pot-bellied Russian men with extending lenses who had brought them to Goa.

Goa loved the Russians. Thanks to the financial crisis in the West, Goa had no Americans, a few French and Germans, some English tourists complaining about the price of everything, a handful of Israelis, some wonderfully flashy Indians, all gold, silver, and brilliantine, and platoons of Russians.

The Russian men were not Mr Putin's hard men; these Russians were flesh, gut, and wobble, but they were attended by blondes of such blonditude that a man could only admire and be grateful. The Indians loved the Russians as, unlike the English, who bargained over the price of a chapati, the Russians thought it beneath them to haggle and thrust fistfuls of rupees into every outstretched hand. Goa would have been Gone without them.

India and mad Zander's Magical Mystery Tour had been grand. I, who led a spoiled life in England, had spent two weeks in conditions that would have made an 18-year-old backpacker blanch. Most of our meals had been veg curry on a banana leaf, or dosas cooked on a hot stone in a tiny roadside shack with a tin cup of chai: hot, syrupy, milky tea. Yet I had survived a trip to India without Delhi belly in contrast to previous trips when I had stayed in five-star hotels.

India remained the fascinating, ensnaring, infuriating enigma it would always be. Time and again you caught yourself thinking, "It would be so much easier if only they…" but then you remembered that the Indian way is not our way. And their way did seem to be working. I'd seen fewer beggars on this trip than I'd meet on a Saturday morning on the King's Road.

Eight years earlier I had been on a trip round India with a charity I supported, and we had stopped off in Bangalore to meet Mr Nandan Nilekani, chief executive of Infosys, one of India's iconic new companies.

I asked him, "Mr Nilekani, China is doing very well and India is also doing very well, but you are two such different countries. How do you see that?"

"Simple, Mr Morland. In China they thrive on order. In India we thrive in chaos."

Just before leaving on our last day, I sat with Juliebee over a coffee, a newly bought wooden-chunk bracelet with mystic Om-signs on my wrist, watched a cow chewing contentedly at the edge of the surf, and thought back over the longest 3,000 kilometres in the world. I reflected that this trip was the nearest I was ever likely to come to assisted suicide, but I would not have changed a thing about it.

Thank you, Zander, and thank you, India.

5

JAPAN WITH BEEMER-SAN

India had sated the biking urge for a time but a year later I found myself, like Mr Toad, dreaming of the open road once more. But where? Europe? Popping my bike on a ferry and heading up to Scandinavia and along the fierce Norwegian Atlantic coast to the Arctic Circle was certainly a possibility but the weather? South America was intriguing, but surely nothing could match the trip with Spike over the Andes. Australia and New Zealand? Yup, both firmly on the bucket list. Then one evening I was in a Japanese restaurant in London. The waitress slipped a plate of sashimi in front of me with a graceful dip and it hit me. Japan.

Japan was to me a truly foreign place, unlike, say, Argentina or India both of which had many familiar points of cultural reference. I had been to Japan a couple of times but only on business, always just to the centre of Tokyo, and never for more than three or four days at a time.

Through the internet I had found Japan Bike Rentals. They turned out to be run by Jonathan, an Australian who lived in Tokyo. He could rent me a BMW 1200RT. Better yet, he knew Japan very well and would be happy to propose an itinerary. I had told him I wanted to spend nights in tiny fishing villages and on wild mountainsides.

"Perfect," Jonathan had said. "So many people just want to do Tokyo,

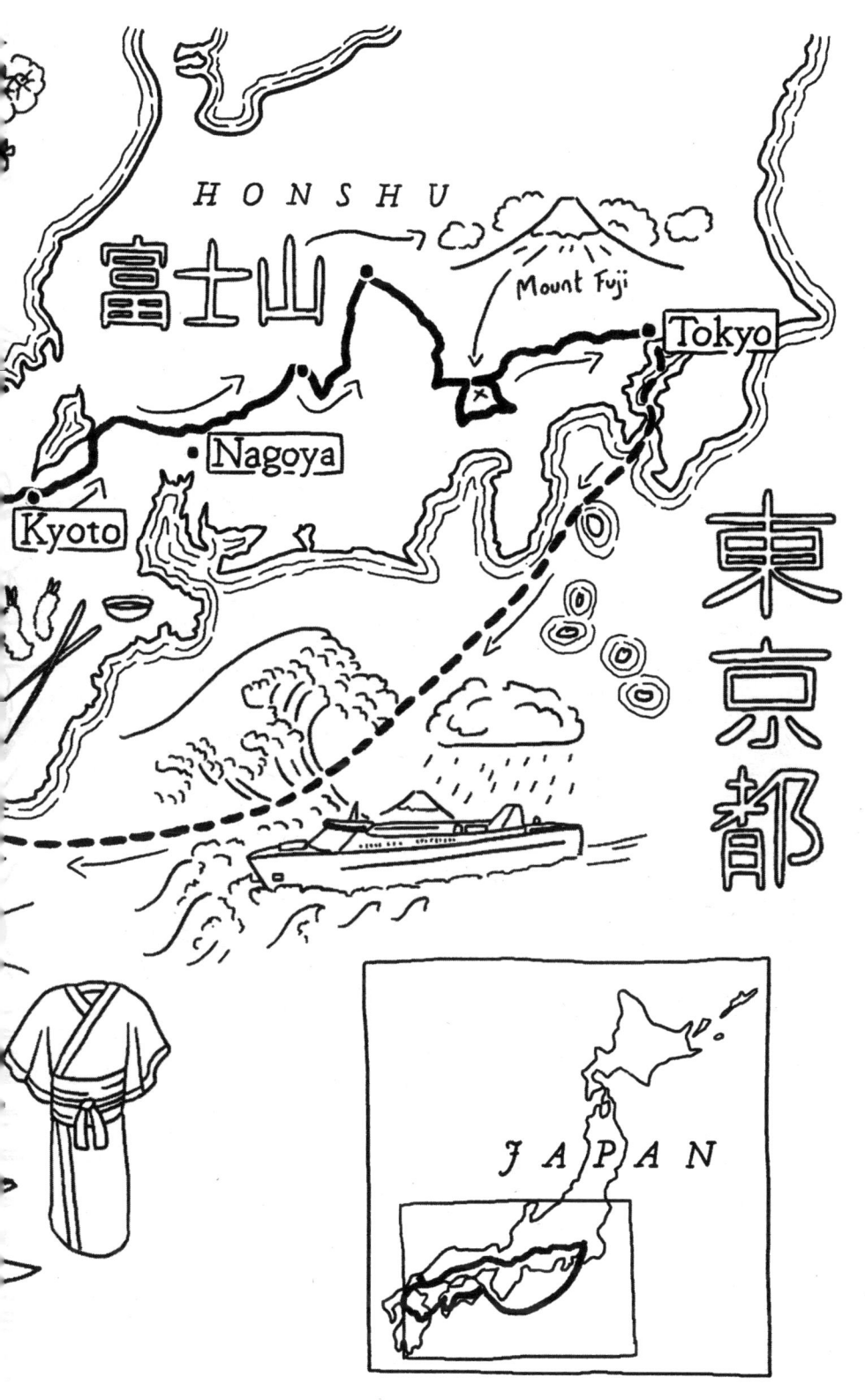

Kyoto and the obvious places. Leave it with me, Miles. This'll be a challenge, but I'll work out a good trip."

He got back a week later with his proposal. Japan has four main islands: Hokkaido in the north; Honshu, the big island with Tokyo, Osaka, and Kyoto in the middle; and Shikoku and Kyushu, both off the usual tourist trail, in the south. He was sending me round the latter two islands. I would take a ferry from Tokyo down there and bike back via Hiroshima and Kyoto. I got the map out and looked at the route. I knew nothing about Shikoku or Kyushu and when I spoke to friends in London who knew Japan well, even they shook their heads.

And so one Friday in March 2012, a year after the India trip, I found myself biking from downtown Tokyo to the port for an overnight ferry from Tokyo to Tokushima, 600 kilometres to the south, on the island of Shikoku, the second most southerly of the four main islands. I was to bike along its southern coast and then catch a much shorter ferry to Kyushu Island, the toe of Japan, its Calabria. Days of long riding through places I had never heard of finishing in the big city of Fukuoka and back, using the bridge which connected Shikoku to Honshu and "mainland" Japan. Then onwards north through Hiroshima and other places which were then no more than names, and finally Kyoto, for two days in cherry blossom time, and back to Tokyo.

I had no idea what to expect. I didn't speak a syllable of Japanese. I was laughably clumsy with chopsticks.

Japan Bike Rentals had booked me into hotels along the way. After the two-star Indian hotels last year I felt I deserved an upgrade, so I was going to be staying in some quite up-market places and I had put in a request for country *ryokans*, Japanese traditional inns.

I didn't want to commit too many social faux pas, so I had been reading up about Japanese customs and etiquette. Apparently, the Japanese were tolerant of foreigners and innately polite. No surprise there. There was one place however where you had to tread carefully. The bath. Baths, or *onsen*, were a big deal in Japan. I read up in detail how to conduct myself on the Japan Tourist Board website. These were not places where you skulked by yourself; they were communal, usually single sex, where everyone got in together. Many were out of doors fed by hot springs.

I now knew how to behave. If you were to step into one of these baths without scrubbing your skin raw first the people in the bath would be so outraged they might well assault you. Japanese baths were not for washing in. Before getting in, you had to strip naked, squat on an upturned bucket, and spend as long as it took hosing, soaping and scrubbing. You were advised to make a lot of noise and draw attention to yourself while doing this. Finally, after fifteen minutes of sluicing and rinsing you could step into the pool. You would be provided with a towel the size of a dishcloth for modesty. Under no circumstances, said the Tourist Board, must you let it touch the onsen water. Instead you folded it and put on top of your head while you sat in the pool.

I had arrived in Tokyo at my skyscraper hotel looking like a garbage collector: slept-in on the aeroplane shirt, jeans, Belstaff biker leather jacket, and hung with five bags, three BMW pannier bags, an army surplus rucksack (which was to be strapped onto the pillion with wet weather gear inside), and a tank bag. Instead of sending me round to the tradesmen's entrance, two, then three, and finally five, hotel greeters, dressed like the papal guard, snatched my biker bags and bowed me in with cries of pleasure.

"O Mr Morran, welcome to Tokyo, you had good flight? Please this way."

A special elevator sped us to the lobby where even more senior members of the papal guard took charge and whisked me to another lift to the 53rd floor where I was installed in a corner room overlooking the whole panoply of Tokyo with Mt Fuji in the distance. I was overwhelmed. This trip was going to be special.

I did not know my way around Tokyo, but I loved just walking and the wandering. I spent a happy day poking around in wonder, enchanted by the zip and elegance of the city. I loved a culture where everything was stripped down to its essence, a culture where minimalism and simplicity of form was worshipped, the opposite of Chinese or American culture.

One of my godsons and his wife were living and working in Tokyo. They took me to one of its legendary teppanyaki places for dinner. My only previous experience of teppanyaki had been Benihana in the Kings Road in London, a tourist trap. This could not have been more different. We were the only non-Japanese there. We sat at the counter where we were served countless courses magicked up by a knife-genius in front of us. Rice was thrown onto the hot surface and sprinkled with garlic, tranches of foie gras were grilled to melting-point, shrimp, abalone, more garlic, and unidentified molluscs were deftly thrown onto a flat grill, a copper dome was put over them for a minute or two, and they were flicked onto a board. Knives whirred and chunks of the finest, tenderest and most delicious things appeared on your plate with a shower of chopped broccoli, onion strings, and unknown vegetables. I went to bed that night literally drunk with pleasure and anticipation.

Next morning after breakfast I popped out to buy myself some food for the ferry ride. It would be nineteen hours in total and Jonathan had warned me that there was no restaurant on the boat, just vending machines selling noodles and ready-cooked food. Picnic bought, I returned to the hotel where the papal guard helped me put my five bags in a cab. I would have liked to have tipped them. They certainly deserved it, but the Tourist Board website had told me that offering a tip in Japan would cause grave offence so I had to content myself with effusive thanks and much mutual bowing.

The cab somehow found Japan Bike Rentals in a tiny mews. An exact twin of my London BMW 1200RT was lounging on a side-stand in the street outside. The 1200RT was a big bike, perfect for long-distance touring. My bikes in London never had names but my trip bikes, except for the Enfield Bullet, always did. You couldn't go on a long journey with an anonymous piece of metal. This one was easy. She was instantly christened Beemer-san. The 'san' suffix is gender neutral, a term of respect for people of either sex. I gave Beemer-san a pat, as you might a horse. I had a feeling she was going to look after me just as Bertha and Spike had.

Jonathan gave me a lengthy briefing, warned me that one drink on the Japanese road could put you in jail for life, gave me a GPS with my route already loaded on it, and sent me off to catch the ferry to Tokushima, nineteen hours away in the distant south.

I found the ferry-port. Or rather the GPS did. Driving in Tokyo was easy after India. No cows on the road here. The Japanese must be the most law-abiding drivers in the world. The good news was that there were lots of port signs; not so good was that not one was in English. A ferry-port marshal caught sight of the lost *gaijin* (foreigner) and leapt from behind a giant truck waving the kind of light batons five-year-olds favour for birthday parties. He ran ahead of the bike. Everyone in uniform in Japan seemed to run everywhere.

I parked Beemer-san where indicated and five minutes later the marshal came over smiling and grunting in an ominous way. He grabbed my sleeve and led me off to a dark and empty hangar behind parked trucks. I was starting to get worried. I wanted to pick up my ticket for the ferry not find myself cornered in a gay sex rendezvous with a grunting Japanese bloke with a luminous wand. To my relief I saw a well-lit office the other side. "Ticketu, ticketu," said Mr Light Baton, pushing me in.

Half an hour later having exchanged endless words with two smiling and bowing Japanese ladies in our respective languages, I emerged, ticketu in hand. Waiting to board I noted Beemer-san was almost being blown off her stand by the screaming wind. This was not meant to be the typhoon season but, as I later discovered, Japanese typhoons are no respecters of the calendar. This gale did not bode well for ferry-boaters. I had booked a "Special Cabin" on the top deck. That was lucky. When I got on board, I saw that everyone else, male and female, were cooped up in a giant deck-wide hall. All they had was a cubbyhole for their things and a blanket-size area on the floor with a square block of wood as pillow. My cabin at least was private and had a bed, a table and a small bathroom.

We tootled off into the dark down Tokyo bay past Yokohama. Despite the wind, which had reached gale force by now, these were sheltered waters. I was hungry. I unpacked on the bed the giant picnic I had bought earlier at Dean and Deluca, New York's finest deli, Tokyo branch. Hams, pâtés, cheeses, salads, charcuterie and three half-bottles of Californian reds. I munched and slurped away happily, glancing from time to time out of the window at Tokyo's fading lights or what I could see of them through the wind-driven spray.

Just as I was finishing the parmesan we left the shelter of the bay and entered the open Pacific. Ahead of us the next piece of land was Los Angeles. The boat reared like a startled horse. Wine, corked luckily, flew across the cabin. Everything flew everywhere, salad on the walls, salami on the duvet. If this was not a typhoon it was very close to it.

Within fifteen minutes waves were crashing green against my window five decks up. The boat shook, shivered, plunged, and even seemed to jump. I lay on my bed gripping the sides. Walking about was literally impossible. To get to the bathroom I had to crawl making sure I was holding on to things as the boat bucked and reared. For the first two hours I was terrified as I thought we should surely sink, but by and by I realised that Japanese boats were built to withstand tsunamis. The typhoon madness went on for fourteen hours until we found the shelter of the Tokushima strait. Funnily enough, when I'd got over the fear, being confined to bed for fourteen hours was strangely relaxing. By some miracle I never felt sick. I might have even slept for a minute or two.

On the boat, I read "Japanese Rules of the Road" in English. I liked "What to do when an earthquake strikes". Pull your car over to the left, stop, and wait for orders.

Finally, after nineteen crazy hours at sea, we disembarked into a peaceful and sunny morning at Tokushima on the island of Shikoku. Despite the typhoon, we were only two minutes late.

I felt like Dr Livingstone as I steered Beemer-san down the ferry ramp. Dr Livingstone had set off from Zanzibar into "Darkest Africa", which was only "dark" to Europeans as every inch of it was known to the locals and the Arab traders. I was now in Japan proper and I was about to nose Beemer-san out into what was, to me, Darkest Japan, an area about which I knew close to nothing.

On my trips I try not to read up in advance anything but the essentials about the places I am going. I want to experience them with an open mind unmarked by other people's opinions. All I knew was that Shikoku was the smallest of Japan's four "big" islands. I had looked at the map and seen that it had no big towns so I assumed it was relatively rural.

It would have been possible to cross the entire island in six hours by keeping to the big roads through the middle of the island but that would have been no fun. I was going to take small roads through the hills and along the coast and break my journey at Kochi, halfway along the southern coast. I wanted to find out what Shikoku had to offer, not tick it off a list.

Soon we had left Tokushima behind us and nosed our way out into the countryside. The good news was that my satnav was already loaded with my route. This made things much easier because trying to follow a folded paper map stuffed into the window on the top of your tank bag while you are riding at 80 miles an hour is not a god idea. Although I am usually a map fanatic, I hadn't brought any local maps with me, just one map of the whole of Japan which had little detail on it. Instead, the voice from the satnav would give me instructions. I had never relied entirely on a satnav before. While this was fine in theory, the bad news was that it turned out to be like spending two weeks shut up with the most annoying person you had ever met. I soon christened her the Satnav Harpy. She had a grating New York voice that still haunts my nightmares.

I expect in real life she was a delightful woman but if you only had her voice to go by, she had the charm of a cheese grater. When I took a wrong turning or failed to follow her instructions, I got a screech of, "Make a U-turn, make a U-turn". For long hours on the road, her harsh nasal voice was the only voice I heard. I began making up fantasies about what she was like in real life. Maybe her husband had left her five years earlier because he couldn't stand being shouted at by her? It almost sounded as if she was now taking her frustrations out on me.

The drive to Kochi was everything I had dreamed about when I planned the trip to Japan. At times I felt I was in Scotland, and at times in Corsica, and then I would putter along a village street which looked as if it was a set for a classic Japanese film and Japan reasserted itself.

Taking the coast road would have been too long. I was tired after my night in a typhoon. Instead we took an inland route and had four magic hours of twisty mountain roads taking us to the busy port of Kochi, mist, bursts of sun, vertiginous gorges, pine forests and everywhere, everywhere, the froth of cherry blossom.

The next day, on to Uwajima, a sleepy fishing port on the west coast of Shikoku after a day of heart-lifting riding, brilliant sun, tiny roads past pagoda temples and villages of wooden houses with graceful swooping roofs. For an hour I followed a wild river through valleys and fields, while later I skirted almost-Provencal beaches with umbrella pines and hawks overhead.

I was staying in a small business hotel in Uwajima, but, despite its modest size, I learned it had a bath, an *onsen*. Before dinner, I plucked up my courage and tiptoed off for my first-ever Japanese bath. The hotel, which didn't often get *gaijin* and regarded me in an affectionate way as a giant, pink joke had found a Triple XL kimono. Wearing this and hotel slippers I made my way to the baths led by a giggling hotel girl. There were three Japanese men already in the bath, something the size of two double-beds pushed together, squatting on tiny stools like Sumo wrestlers and chatting. They looked at me, hid their surprise, and bowed their heads without moving from their stools.

I bowed and said, "Hello."

They turned their heads away from pinko-san and said nothing.

Determined not to give offence I threw off my kimono and strode over, stark naked, to a small, upturned plastic bucket which served as a stool and began to sluice and soap and spray. Finally, after fifteen minutes of sluicing, I joined them in the bath. You could perch on a ledge running round the bath with your bottom half submerged or push out free-form into the middle. The three Japanese men were gathered at the far end, chatting, having apparently decided it was best to ignore the foreign invasion. In between chatting, they grunted. I had not read up about the grunting but it was obviously de rigueur. Soon I was sitting in the middle with only my head above water, grunting like a hippo.

Half an hour later I was back in my room, pink as a valentine, and ready for a dinner whose highlight was two huge fish-heads, one cooked, one raw.

What an introduction to the real Japan Shikoku was turning out to be. Now I knew I was in *le Japon profond* as the French say about the deep heartland of France. I had not seen another *gaijin* since getting on the ferry in Tokyo. I had drifted through some of the most beautiful scenery on earth, not grandiose and spectacular, but ethereal and beautiful as I crossed Shikoku. I had somehow communicated with the people at the hotels with whom I had no language in common. They, unlike me, made an attempt at speaking English. I wished I had done enough homework to repay the compliment. My trip was just beginning. Another ten days of wonder and discovery lay ahead.

After a night in Uwajima and the bath experience, I was up early the next day to catch the Yawatahama to Beppu ferry. Beppu was the nearest port on Kyushu, the most southerly of Japan's four main islands. I had left the Uwajima Kokusai Hotel at 8.00 am hoping to be guided by the satnav to Yawatahama in time for the 10.15 am ferry.

I had gone no more than a hundred yards before the Satnav Harpy screamed at me, "Make a U-turn". I did and followed her instructions only to find myself back at the hotel. Whichever way I went she screamed "Make a U-turn" and took me back to the hotel. I badly needed to make my way to the ferry. She clearly didn't. After the third "Make a U-turn" I could have sworn I heard her say, "Schmuck". She kept on bringing me back to the hotel I was trying to leave. I suspected that Jonathan had not cleared last night's destination when he had loaded the satnav. I turned off the harpy and followed my nose.

Despite her efforts we caught the ferry. This time, no men directing me behind trucks before getting a *kippu* (I'd learned the proper word for ticket). Beemer-san and I strolled on to a much grander ship than the hamster-cage Tokushima ferry for the three-hour crossing to Beppu.

What followed arrival in Beppu was like a dream. Satnav Harpy kept quiet. She was probably sulking because I hadn't let her stay in Uwajima. Three hours through Wagnerian pine forests interspersed with stops at little Japanese villages straight out of Kurosawa movies.

It was a perfect day for biking, the sun shone, geysers puffed steam into the clear air, Kyushu being a mountainous and volcanic island, narrow roads wound sinuously round the flanks of wooded hills and, if I had not had my iPod on, I'm sure I would have heard larks. Then, thank you, Satnav Harpy, for excellent navigation and no shouting, in mid-afternoon we coasted to a halt in a wild grove on the slopes of Mt Aso-san, the most sacred and revered mountain on Kyushu. We had reached the Takafue Ryokan, my first *ryokan*, or traditional Japanese country inn.

Two graceful maidens in traditional dress popped out from behind a rhododendron and bowed to me. How long had they been waiting on the off-chance a large pink Englishman might turn up?

"Hai, Morran-san, hai," they chirruped in unison. I felt large and hot and sweaty next to these tiny butterfly-like creatures.

They grabbed my five bags and trotted down the hill through a grove of fifty-foot bamboos to reception while I clump-clumped behind. I was ushered to a low stool in reception to shed the Beemer-boots and, after ten minutes hunting for slippers big enough for the over-sized *gaijin*, they gave up and gave me highly uncomfortable wooden clogs instead. A new team of bowing maidens now showed me to my room, or rather my own little house. It was set by itself in a bamboo grove. Indoor bath, outdoor bath, tatami mat-on-the-floor bedroom, living room with sit-on-the-ground cooking square. I felt like Jack the Giant in Tom Thumbland. My room had indoor and outdoor private baths, fed from a natural geyser.

I booked a 45-minute private slot in the much larger main hotel rock pool, by myself, no other grunting naked men, turned down a massage, and at 8.30 pm a flock of young women floated into my room with course on course of exquisite *kaiseki* cuisine for pinko-san sitting, kimono-clad, on the floor in his living room.

The food looked exquisite but what it was was a mystery. Two of the women remained behind to cook titbits on the brazier, light the spirit-flame to heat shabu-shabu, to warm rice, and then to instruct me with an elaborate mime punctuated by delicate behind-the-hand giggles as to what raw fish bits to dip into what sauce and in what order to eat them. Finally, at 10.00 pm the maidens shimmered noiselessly off with graceful bows and the most discreet of giggles into the bamboo grove. I went to wallow in my private pool for half a pre-futon hour.

That was a day and an evening as harmonious and peaceful as could be imagined. The deeper I got into Japan, the better it got.

The next day, the Japanese god of forest and mountain was out for revenge. At 8.00 am there was a monsoon. And a thunderstorm. And a banshee wind. And cold. A day to bring a smile to the face of Lady Macbeth.

By 9.00 am I had put on my rain gear over every layer of clothes I had, and trudged slowly up the hill to Beemer-san behind five smiling maidens who were bent under my pannier-bags and fighting to keep their kimonos from being blown over their heads while trying to get protection from the streaming rain under their gaily-coloured paper umbrellas. As I brought Beemer-san to life and blipped the engine, they bowed and smiled and waved to give me the kind of farewell you might give a warrior off to a war from which you knew he would not return.

Satnav Harpy had been programmed by Japan Bike Rentals to take me on a sight-seeing circuit of Aso-san's biggest-in-the-world 128 kilometre caldera, or active volcano crater, before she would allow me to head North to Fukuoka. The trouble was that the mighty Mt Aso-san was shrouded in fog so thick you couldn't find your nose in it. Circumnavigating it in this weather would have been suicidal madness. I had to ignore the Harpy but I knew no way of reprogramming her so she would take me straight to Fukuoka without first going round the volcano's crater. I skulked off in the opposite direction hoping that would bring me to Fukuoka.

She was outraged at my disobedience. "Make a U-turn, U-turn, moron," she screamed. She was determined to send me plummeting in the fog over the caldera's edge and into the bubbling lava. I needed to be strong.

I switched her off leaving me guideless in a terrifying gale. According to my only map Mt Aso, Fukuoka, and Beppu appeared to be clustered together in the same location, as useful for navigation as Borat was for Kazakh history.

Luckily I have a famed sense of direction. Using this I found I had gone in the wrong direction through the impenetrable fog and retraced an hour of yesterday's route without even knowing I was going backwards. I was now further from Fukuoka than when I left the *ryokan*.

Eventually, after ninety minutes or more of skidding along tiny country lanes, I stumbled onto an expressway by mistake where, peering through the fog on my visor and the blinding rain, I saw the wonderful words 'Fukuoka 132 kms' on it. I was frozen, soaked, and terrified. The wind was blowing the windsocks rigid and horizontal at motorway bridges and then suddenly the gale would hit from another quarter. The wind was so strong that it distorted my helmet visor if I stuck my head far enough above the windscreen to see where I was going. My knowledge of physics was insufficient to work out how a bike, hit by a 100 kph side-wind can stay upright. Why was I not blown flat into the fast lane? Must have been something to do with momentum because of speed. Was that the gyroscope effect? Did that mean go as fast as possible to just stay upright?

Every nerve and instinct was alive and working to keep the bike upright and straight ahead, trying not to tense too much, crouching for a smaller wind profile, and ignoring the rain-bullets penetrating my neck and my visor. Through it all, I could feel my heart going pump-a-dump.

I stopped for half an hour to gather myself at a service area. I stripped off layers of clothes and peeled the sodden stuff out of my tank bag. Soaked, all soaked. Puzzled Japanese slurping noodles stopped to look at pinko-san sorrowfully separating sodden banknote from sodden banknote while he munched a Japanese pastry.

Back on the bike. Had the wind diminished from typhoon to mere gale force? Even Satnav Harpy had given up trying to hurl me into the foggy caldera and now graciously pointed the way through the storm to the Fukuoka Grand Hyatt.

Just before I got there, the rain stopped and the road dried. I cruised up to a nice modern hotel happy to have survived as bad a day as I ever hoped to have on a bike. The hotel was warm and comfortable. I checked into my room, stripped off my clothes and spent half an hour under a warm shower. Unlike the sodden tank bag, the pannier bags were totally dry. Thank you, BMW.

I dressed in crisp, clean clothes and strolled out into the warm Fukuoka night. I was dry and tomorrow the sun would shine. Fukuoka was a buzzy modern city. I found an Italian restaurant where I ate a sublime dinner, better probably than any I had eaten in Italy. I was so happy to have survived the day.

Next morning, I almost choked on my breakfast when I saw the front page of that day's English-language *Japan Times*: "Strong Storm Wreaks Chaos Nationwide. Many killed, airplanes and trains disrupted, ANA cancelled 83 flights, winds of 143 kph recorded," ran the summary. These "143 kph winds" had been recorded in the middle of Kyushu, right where Beemer-san and I had been fighting the storm.

If I'd known what was in store I would have been mad not to have stayed put at Takafue even if it might have disrupted the whole itinerary. As it was, Beemer-san and I had set off into the maelstrom in cheerful ignorance. Better to have travelled ignorantly and to have arrived than not to have travelled at all.

I googled 'typhoon' on my phone and discovered two things. One, unlike the hurricane season in the Caribbean, there was no typhoon season in Japan. Typhoons occurred all year round. Two, a typhoon was any Pacific tropical storm where the wind exceeded 118 kph. If, as the paper said they were recording 143 kph not far from where we were biking, then I had spent a day of lunacy motorbiking through a full-blown typhoon. I'm not sure I felt good about that but I did feel thankful. I said a quiet thankyou to Om Banna. Zander had told me about Om Banna, the god of motorcyclists. There was a statue to him in Jodhpur where people, especially bikers, went to worship. It was in the shape of an Enfield Bullet.

After breakfast, I packed up, put on nice dry biking gear and burbled happily off with the sky as blue as a very blue thing and a gentle breeze blowing.

"Hai" is the Japanese for yes. The Japanese say it the whole time. I had been listening to the graceful female concierge in the Fukuoka Hyatt booking me into my choice of restaurant after I arrived. "Hai," said she, nod-nod on the phone as if she'd just been chosen to marry the Emperor's son, adorable smile. "Hai," more nodding and shy with an irresistible smile directed at pinko-san, and after fifteen more Hai's she put down the phone and flashed me another smile, this one as wide as Wyoming.

"Thank you, thank you, how do I get there?"

"Ah, yes, very sorry, Mr Morran, not possible, restaurant full. Hai."

How do you get a Japanese to say no? The word for no is "ie", pronounced, they say, "i-yeah", but how would anyone know how it's pronounced as no-one's ever heard them use the word? Saying no would be rude.

No is one of the many things the Japanese don't have, most of which made Japan a cheery place to be, at least for a biker. I'd done so far a thousand Japanese kilometres and had yet to see a road bump or other "traffic-calming measure". Or a speed camera. Or a strutting policeman in a Hi-Viz jacket. Or a surveillance camera. Or a traffic cone. Or hear a police siren. Or worry about where I parked.

The Japanese police treated people like responsible adults. How nice that was. As a result, you found yourself thinking it would be bad manners not to keep to the rules. Crossing the road when the pedestrian sign is at red would be like blowing your nose into your napkin. By the way, don't blow your nose in public in Japan. They think putting your nose-blow in a rag in your pocket for later use beyond disgusting. Instead, they sniff.

I left Fukuoka into a sunshine and cherry blossom day with a short 220 kilometre drive. That was lucky as I had had so much adrenalin in my system from fighting the storm that I hadn't got to sleep till 5.00 am. After Fukuoka, we had a gentle drive along the seacoast. It was a rocky, jagged coast. Japan doesn't have smooth rocks, or round, weathered, mountains like, say, the

Pyrenees or the Rockies. Everything is as sharp and jagged as in a Japanese woodcut or watercolour. Gothic. It out-Alps the Alps.

Sunny it may have been, but the sea was still raging from the previous day's storm. Spume was everywhere with waves crashing angrily against the sea-wall and over the road as I slalomed along, visor up, jacket open and the smell of kelp in my nostrils.

Halfway to Hagi, a mediaeval samurai warrior town, I crossed the high bridge over the straits that separated the southern island of Kyushu from the big, main, island of Honshu. No more ferries. It was only half a mile wide and you could stop at the service area on the Kyushu side to watch the busy marine traffic under the bridge, boats with Honda and Sanyo painted on them, hurrying on their way to keep Japan Inc going. Since modern England makes nothing apart from Celebrity Big Brother, it gave me a jolt to be in a manufacturing nation. Throughout the trip I'd rounded bends on idyllic sea-coasts and been confronted by factories the size of Sheffield belching steam.

And, unlike at a service area on the M4, with its burger and chips, you can stop at the Kokura crossing to Honshu and eat fresh "uni", sea urchins.

The ride to Hagi was like an easy rest day.

Behind was the typhoon and ahead, after Hagi, was … Hiroshima.

Hiroshima…

I'd tried to stop myself thinking about it in advance. Humankind's biggest single act of violence against humankind. Executed at the order, not of a Hitler or a Genghis, but a mild haberdasher from Missouri, Harry S. Truman. The dead had been civilians, not combatants. I was going to try to arrive there with an open heart and an open mind to stand below the place where Enola Gay's pilot pulled a lever to send Little Boy, as the USAF called the first A-bomb to be dropped in wrath, hurtling to earth, detonation and death. I didn't know what my feelings would be but it would be the heart, not the mind, that dictated them.

What we *gaijin* knew of Hiroshima was one thing: a mushroom cloud, a black and white image of death, destruction and 1945. Auschwitz, Pol Pot and 9/11 are names for terrible modern events but they were posting-points in the grim catalogue of the massacres of innocents. Hiroshima was different. Hiroshima was the opening of the door to the end of our world.

I spent a quiet night in a *ryokan* in Hagi and set off the next morning for Hiroshima.

I biked in through squally clouds and found not a monotone Armageddon but a city as cute, colourful, stylish, and appealing as a MacBook Air. Young people were everywhere, shiny shops, a buzz in the air, laughter, courting couples, youth, fun, giggling. A torrent of positive energy. Good-looking.

I was on the 30th floor of a chic modern hotel. Once more I had been greeted like royalty despite my scruffy biker-boy appearance. No tradesman's entrance for the travel-worn *gaijin*. Beemer-san, now honourably road-stained, was parked immediately next to the main hotel entrance for the admiration of visitors. People looked at her as if they had never seen a bike before. I had reflected several times on the road how strange it was that in the country that made more motorbikes than everyone else put together there were so few bikers. Biking in Europe, I was constantly saluting my fellow bikers. So far in Japan, unless you counted scooters, I had found no-one to salute.

Wherever I went people smiled and came over to stroke the flanks of the mighty Beemer-san and make comments.

"Where from?"

"London. England."

"Hai! Rondon! Ingurando! Hai!"

Much smiling and bowing.

I had a tea-time sake in the 33rd floor Sky Lounge and looked out to the south, the opposite side to my room. Hiroshima is on the coast of Japan's Inland Sea and has many rivers and canals running through it. Half a mile away, in the arms of two rivers between the neat Toronto-style street-grid of sparkling modern buildings, I could see the green and gravel of the Peace Park. Half an hour later I walked over to it.

The bomb had been detonated 600 metres above where I was now standing and directly above what was then a hospital on the west side of what

Dawn start for my first ever trip (p 16)

Europe crossed, we pose at the Blue Mosque (p 23)

Spike in Bariloche (p 40)

Heading for the Puyehue Pass (p 44)

Wild descendants of the Conquistadors' horses (p 49)

Bullets, ready to explode (p 57)

The wondrous Vijay (p 58)

Pinko-san goes the full Kaiseki (p 88)

Cherry blossom chap (p 97)

I meet the Ducati Boys (p 108)

Brenda and
empty Oz (p 124)

Where's John Wayne?
(p 148)

This here is the key to mah gun safe (p 146)   I leave Biking Viking (p 159)

was now the Peace Park. The entire centre of the city, an area the size of Oxford, was with two or three exceptions vaporised. The first people to go in there after the atomic blast had remarked that everything was covered in an inches-thick talc-like dust, all that remained of the buildings, the people, their possessions, and their toys.

In the words of the Memorial Museum leaflet: "At the instant of detonation, the temperature at the centre exceeded a million degrees Celsius generating an enormous fireball. The blast pressure 500 metres from the fireball was 19 tons per square metre. Buildings were crushed. The heat rays and blast burned and crushed nearly all buildings within 2 kilometres of the centre. In an instant the city was almost entirely destroyed."

Counting the dead was difficult. It was said that 80,000 died instantly. But, back to the leaflet, "The special characteristic of atomic bombs is nuclear radiation, something which conventional weapons never produce. The acute effects that appeared immediately after the bombing manifested in a wide range of symptoms, including fever, nausea, diarrhoea, bleeding, loss of hair ,and severe fatigue. After-effects began to appear about two years later and continued appearing for more than ten years. These include keloids [huge bumps under the flesh], leukaemia, and various cancers that continue to plague survivors to this day."

By the end of 1945 a total of 200,000 people had died as a result of the bomb. And many more since. And many permanently crippled in body and in mind.

The Peace Museum had narrative, photographs, and objects from 6th August 1945. Unlike, say, the Ho Chi Minh US War Remnants Museum, it made no judgements and took no sides. It stated its abhorrence of nuclear weapons but indicted no-one. That made it the more powerful.

After a minute looking at the early photographs of blistered bodies and torn school uniforms I had tears sliding down my cheeks.

After an hour I had walked out into the Peace Park, a tranquil place of fountains, water, trimmed evergreens, blossom, and an air of tranquillity. Every minute a deep gong sounded.

I decided to follow the example of the Peace Museum and make no judgements. Did the end justify the means? How many lives were saved by shortening the war? Was the murder of 200,000 civilians, most of them living wretched lives in the last days of the Japanese Empire, justified?

Harry Truman, who gave the order, was a decent, brave man, no vainglorious megalomaniac. The US, encouraged by Churchill, developed the bomb because it feared Hitler was ahead of them. If Hitler had really had it Piccadilly Circus would probably have been the epicentre for what Hiroshima became.

When the US bomb was being developed in 1944 there was talk of dropping it on Munich. By the time the bomb became reality, Munich was occupied by American soldiers and Japan was the only option. Kyoto, where Beemer-san and I would be the day after Hiroshima, was high on the list of targets but, thanks to General Marshall, he of the Marshall Plan, it was struck off because of its cultural significance. The list had been shortened to four cities with urban areas at least 3 miles in diameter: Hiroshima, Kokura, Niigata and Nagasaki. Hiroshima had been chosen first as the only one without an allied prisoner of war camp. The second bomb, on Nagasaki, killed allied PoWs.

The strategy had been to tell the Japanese that the US would go on dropping atomic bombs on random Japanese cities until the Japanese surrendered. It had been a bluff. The US had only had three bombs. The first had been test-detonated at Alamogordo in the New Mexico desert; the second, a uranium atomic bomb, was dropped on Hiroshima; and the last, a plutonium atomic bomb, was dropped four days later on Nagasaki.

Emperor Hirohito, whose voice had never been heard by his subjects, had gone on the radio for the first time ever: "This war has not necessarily been going to our advantage…" was how it is normally translated. A cease-fire was declared a week later.

It was 6.30 pm when I left the Peace Park. I walked for an hour through mid-town Hiroshima, had a snack and a couple of sakes. I was struck by the yawning incongruity of the sheer horror of the Peace Park and the chirpy cheerful modernity of Hiroshima now. I had never been anywhere that touched me as deeply as Hiroshima.

A week had passed. I was now passing from the *Nippon incognita* of Shikoku and Kyushu, the southern islands, to Honshu, the big island, and places of which the world has heard. I'd survived gales at sea, gripping a bunk-edge for fourteen hours, a full-blown typhoon, freezing rain and forest roads dressed with sodden and slippery pine needles. Then the day I left Hiroshima, the weather forecast sunny with scattered cloud, as we banked around the tight hairpins in the mountains on the run in to Kyoto, I found white stuff blodging my visor and for twenty minutes we were in an Alpine blizzard. Snow and large motorbikes are a bad combination, but Beemer-san shrugged and danced through with hardly a skid. What next, I asked myself? A plague of frogs?

We were arriving in Kyoto in cherry blossom time. What more could anyone have asked? The Japanese have a word, *hanami*, that means cherry blossom madness. During this time they throw their inhibitions aside and Go Silly, although one of the endearing discoveries for me about the Japanese had been that they go silly a lot of the time. I had seen this in Tokyo. Far from it being a place of sober suits and demure women, I kept on seeing people in clothes that would have made a Californian surfer jealous: wild sneakers, and crazy bomber jackets.

The trip so far had exceeded expectations in every way, the charm of the Japanese, the beauty and emptiness of the countryside, the astonishing food, and even the bad stuff, the gale on the ferry, and the typhoon, had been things I would always remember with affection.

Kyoto, everyone's favourite place in Japan, where I had just arrived, fell short. I know. That is like saying Florence falls short. To me Florence does too. I'm sure if I had had the time to get to know Kyoto it, like Florence, might have taken my breath away, but if you were an exhausted biker after a week on the road who had used up his reserves of energy and was looking forward to his one rest day and you had turned up at a very expensive *ryokan* where they were too busy with Japanese package tourists to help you find your room in a hotel where all the signs and numbers were in Japanese, you might have wished that you too were back at one of the seven smiley places you had stayed in so far.

The biggest surprise was to discover how big Kyoto was. I had been expecting a graceful, leafy little town the size of Cheltenham. Kyoto was huge, three times the size of Manchester, Google told me. Its centre was another square-grid hustle-bustle Japanese mega-city, stylish, yes, but far less so than Hiroshima and with fewer parks and trees than London. The leafy parts, and there were plenty of them, were largely round the perimeter. Fortunately, that was where I was.

My snooty *ryokan*, the Kadensho, was in Arashiyama on the western edge. That was 8 kilometres and a £25 cab ride from Gion, the famous geisha district. Not wanting to have dinner in my unwelcoming hotel, I had taken a long cab-ride to Yoshikawa, a famous and highly recommended downtown tempura restaurant. Up till then I had seen no other foreigners since leaving Tokyo. When I arrived at the Yoshikawa, the other nine people at the counter were all *gaijin*, English, Australian, or American. It was nice having a chat and comparing notes but a shock. I was just another tourist in a tourist town.

The good thing about Arashiyama being on the western edge under the hills where we got blizzarded on the way in was that it was well located if you were looking for gardens and temples. I spent my rest day visiting them.

I shall expose myself to ridicule from Japan-lovers when I say that, unlike, say, early gothic cathedrals and their wondrous variety, Japanese temples, to my ignorant eye, have a samey quality about them. The gardens were without parallel. But here was the paradox. Japanese gardens with their gravel raked in swirling patterns, their spiky trees wizened with age and pruned with infinite care, were the natural habitat for Japanese temples, and both were places that existed for silent meditation. There is no place better for that outside a Trappist monastery. They were above all about solitude.

When I left the hotel to head for the temples I saw Japanese blossom-fans marching ten deep across Arayashima bridge from the railway station to the temples. Seeing the gardens and temples in company with 10,000 Japanese blossom-lovers did rob it of the solitude angle although you would not find a more respectful and better-behaved group anywhere.

The care the Japanese took over detail was astonishing. I watched eight gardeners kneeling or lying on the moss in an area the size of a bedroom picking out blade by one-inch blade grass that was trying to grow in a moss bank.

After Kyoto Beemer-san and I would be on the way home. We would be leaving snooty *ryokans* and tourist hordes behind and heading for the hotel Kisoji, literally in the middle of nowhere, between two ancient towns on the post route between Tokyo and Kyoto. Getting there was a long day, seven or eight hours riding through the southern Japanese Alps. However, when we arrived there, said Japan Bike Rentals' briefing notes, we could look forward to an all-you-can-eat steak dinner, no thirteen-course kaiseki menus. Bring it on.

I had been anticipating a thick wodge of delicious wagyu. What bliss that was going to be. Sad to say the steak was thin and leathery, the kind of thing you might have found at an American diner. My first bad meal in Japan.

The next day was to be the last on the road before Tokyo. I found myself on the shores of Lake Kawaguchi. Outside my room I had a little private garden with a six-foot round personal bath for wallowing in. The *ryokan* also had a giant communal *onsen* but the mama-san who had checked me in had discouraged me from using that. I suspected it was a mixed-sex bath and she worried that 6ft 1in of naked pinko could have made the natives restless. She had a point.

I had caught a sight of Mt Fuji, or Fuji-san as the Japanese call their senior mountain, much as if we were to call the river that goes through London Lord Thames, from my hotel in Tokyo almost a fortnight ago. And as Beemer-san and I were swerving and sliding through the Japanese Alps on the way to Lake Kawaguchi, in some places finding snow on the roadside, we had rounded a bend and there, filling a V in the forested skyline, had been the great Lord Fuji once more. The world has many iconic natural features, the

Matterhorn, the Grand Canyon, the Victoria Falls, and other bits of postcard fodder, but Fuji-san must be the world's most iconic bit of geography.

It embodies a place and a nation; it has a perfect truncated triangle shape; it has charisma. And, from Tokyo, the red-ball Japanese-flag sun that rises in the Pacific sets behind Fuji-san. The next day, on leaving Lake Kawaguchi, we would do a circuit of Fuji-san and then head for Tokyo to return the faithful Beemer-san.

Every time I made one of these trips I wondered if it would be the last. I was a late biker, not taking it up till my forties. Long bike trips are not like long car trips. In a car you don't think of getting hurt. If you have an accident the car may get hurt but unless you're unlucky you should be all right. If a biker has an accident, he gets hurt. I'd had two accidents in twenty-five years' biking and, although I had been trickling along at 20 mph both times while an idiot car-driver (to a biker all car-drivers are idiots) decided to turn right across the road without looking, I had broken bones both times while the car-driver had hardly noticed the dent.

I have never ridden horses at speed but biking and galloping a horse in open country, such as I had seen on the pampa in Argentina, have much in common. Both are highly physical activities where the adrenalin pumps hard when you get going and in both the cost of an accident is high. The physicality and the adrenalin is why we do it. The scream of a 1200cc BMW as it banks into corner after corner for two hours of sweat-drenched mountain riding gives a high you will never get in a car.

If you are my age, you pray that if one of those mountain bends leads you into the flank of a turning lorry that you fly off into the sayonara, not the paraplegic ward. Bikers are always aware of it. That's why biking makes you grateful for being alive.

I woke for our last day on the road looking forward to a gentle circumnavigation of mighty Fuji-san. I was also looking forward to another sparkly clear spring day. I slid back the door panels preparatory to taking a steamy morning plunge in my personal *onsen* and saw it was so windy that there were tiny waves on the *onsen*. Trees were bent double. Horizontal rain.

Not again. And last night had been so peaceful. Had I not paid my dues a week earlier in the typhoon on the road to Fukuoka?

I had a choice. I could forget paying my respects to Lord Fuji, take the highway, and just belt into Tokyo, 90 kilometres away on the expressway, or I could head off uphill into what looked like a mini-typhoon. This was my last day on the road; it seemed feeble to chuck it in and do a runner for Tokyo. I could hear my old Wall Street boss from the 1970s, a graduate of the Virginia Military Academy, saying, "You pussy". I decided to procrastinate. I would try the first bit of Fuji-san's flanks and see what it was like.

Wharoosh! This wasn't Macbeth, it was Lear. When Beemer-san climbed away from Lake Kawaguchi, whose surface was white with blown spray, towards Mt Fuji, I remembered being in King Lear at school. Here we were in Japan with him on the blasted heath, "Blow, winds, and crack your cheeks! Rage! Blow! You cataracts and hurricanoes, spout till you have drench'd our steeples, drown'd the cocks!". Blow wind, indeed.

But Fuji-san gave the *gaijin* a break. After a bit the wind dropped a little, the rain went from horizontal to diagonal and we found ourselves cruising round the snow-streaked god-mountain with angry black clouds crowding its brow. No-one else was on the road. It was a dramatic way to greet Fuji-san. We never got high enough up the god-mountain to reach the snow level, but we did climb high enough to get a feel for its majesty.

The rest of the ride to Tokyo was uneventful. I was even feeling almost regretful at my impending divorce from Satnav Harpy. She had calmed down. Or maybe I had been getting better at following her instructions, so she no longer needed to scream at me to make U-turns. She took me faultlessly back to Japan Bike Rentals. Jonathan looked pleased to see me.

"G'day Miles," he shouted in his Australian twang as I biked up. "I'm pleased to see you. I figured you were OK cos you didn't call but I was worried about you, mate."

"Oh, why? I've had a fabulous trip and the bike never put a foot wrong."

"Yeah, but we had six bikes out last week and none of them biked the day of the typhoon. And you were in Kyushu then, in the thick of it. We had to reschedule hotels for the other guys. What did you do? Did you reschedule yourself and ride a double day to catch up?"

"Nope," I handed him back the keys and patted Beemer-san on the flank. "I didn't know there was a typhoon coming so I hit the road as scheduled. I did dip out of going round Mt Aso, but I made it to Fukuoka. It was pretty hairy."

"Good on yer, you crazy old Brit."

He shook my hand and gave me a big grin.

6

AUSTRALIA: ROO DODGING WITH BRENDA

Almost a year after I had said goodbye to Japan, Beemer-san, and the Satnav Harpy I found myself on a plane to Australia. I was not going there to bike. Perhaps because of my connection with Africa, I had been asked to join the board as a non-executive director of SABMiller, then the world's second-biggest beer company. We had just acquired the company that made Foster's lager in Australia and consequently SABMiller decided to have a board meeting in Melbourne and fly all its directors out there.

However, I didn't see the point in going all the way from England to Australia just for three days, so I had made plans to take advantage of being there. The board meeting would end at 3.00 pm on a Thursday. At 4.30 pm I had arranged to pick up a 1600cc six cylinder-in-line BMW GTL. I was going to shoot off for two weeks of biking round this immense and unknown, to me, land.

First I'd be on the overnight ferry for the famously rough crossing of the Bass Strait to Tasmania, three days round Tasmania, then back across the wild water to Melbourne and off for ten days riding along, first, the Great Ocean Road to Port Fairy, then north to the Grampian Mountains, on through the old gold mining towns, up through ski country, and down to the Pacific Coast to finish in Sydney.

Everyone I had spoken to had warned me of Ozzie Things Waiting to Kill Ya. One friend had told me that Australian truckers hated motorbikes and would squash me like a cockroach under their mammoth road trains. Others cautioned that deadly Australian vipers, saltwater crocodiles, and plate-sized venomous spiders would be forming a queue to sink their fangs into me.

The big danger though, or so I learned, was not these horrors but the cuddly old roo. I had done some research and discovered that kangaroos, for a biker, were one of the most dangerous creatures in the animal world. The reason was that they could not go backwards or do a U-turn. They could only move forwards. Of course, if you had a tail the size of a python attached to your bum you would find turning round and reversing a problem.

From a biker's point of view, you learned that a roo came out to feed at dusk and dawn on the tender green grass by the roadside. When it heard a car or motorbike, it panicked but it couldn't do what a normal animal would do, turn tail and flee into the woods. The only direction it could move was forwards so it bolted, boing-boing-boing, straight across the road and boing into any approaching motorbike. I had a mental image of something the size of Donald Trump hurling itself at my bike while I was bopping along listening to Chuck Berry.

Cars survived roo-attacks fine. They had roo bars bolted on to the front which tossed roos into the ditch like snow from a snow-plough. My Beemer didn't have roo bars, just a front wheel and a not very bouncy old Pom on the saddle. Roo-dodging was going to add spice to the Outback roads.

What was it about me and ferry crossings? A year earlier I had been clutching my bunk for nineteen hours on the way from Tokyo to Tokushima in a typhoon and now as I boarded the Spirit of Tasmania I had just heard that there was a full gale warning for the Bass Strait. This stretch of storm-tossed emptiness was whipped by the Roaring Forties, the incessant wind that blows round the southern globe, a wind we had last seen in Patagonia.

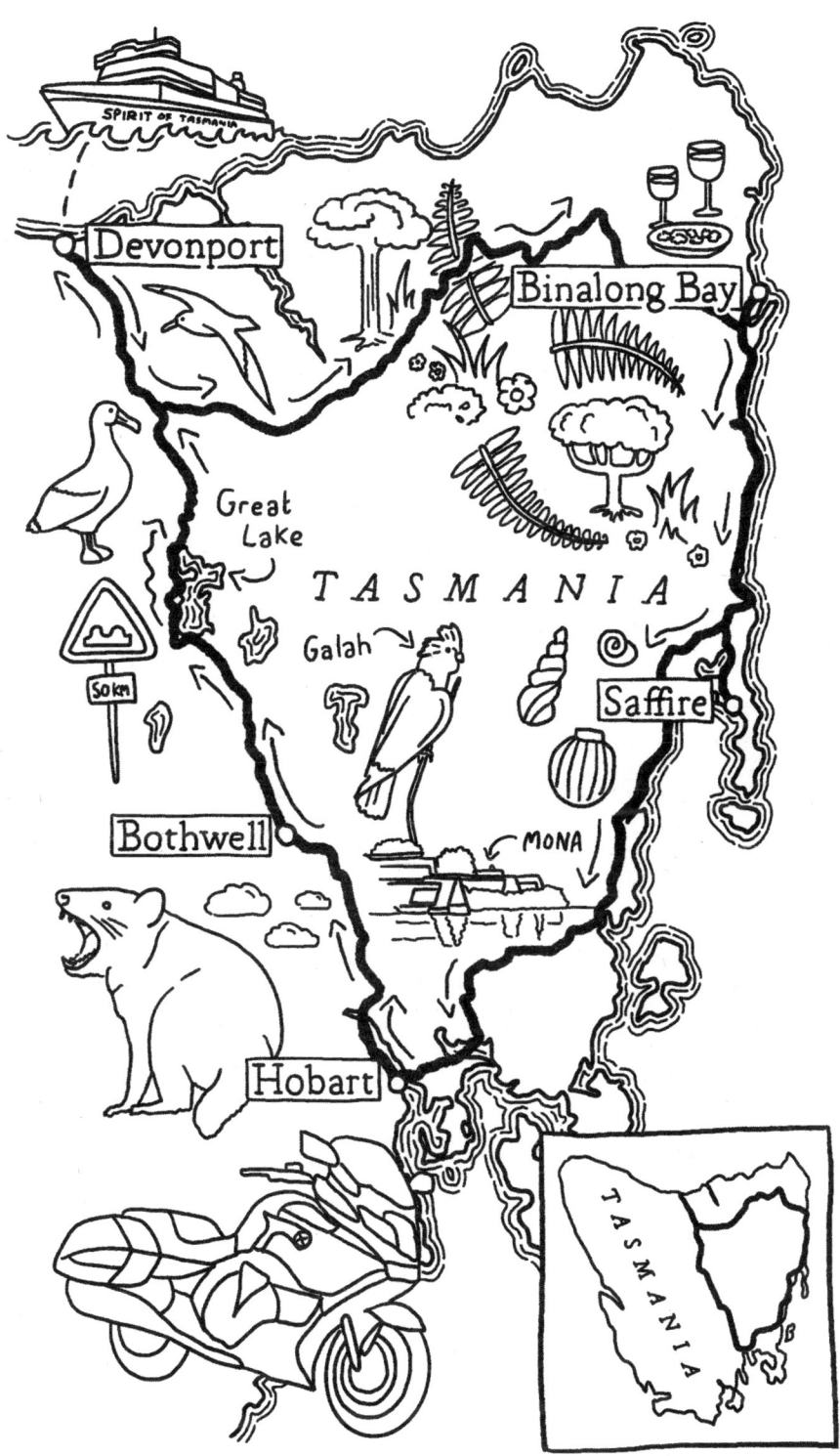

On that morning's Melbourne weather map a black vortex had been heading straight for the Bass Strait. "Winds of 100 kph plus expected by 7.00 pm this evening", which just happened to be when the Spirit of Tasmania was going to slip her moorings.

I made mates with three Australian bikers in the queue for boarding. They had sleek Ducatis. "Hey, mate, swap bikes?" said one, looking at my Beemer, "talk about easy rider." Ducatis are the Ferraris of the bike world. But after two hours in the saddle of a Ducati, bent low over the bars, weight thrown on your wrists, legs tucked up like a jockey, you needed to visit an osteopath before you could walk again.

If a Ducati was a Ferrari, my 1600 GTL Beemer was a Bentley, smooth, over-powered, long-legged, and supremely comfortable. I could ride it for ten hours, get off and stroll away with hardly a tinge of stiffness so relaxed was the upright riding position. But I felt like a traitor riding it. I'd been riding bikes for almost twenty-five years and had had six of them, every one a Beemer, but not just any old Beemer. They had all been Boxers, possessors of the world's most iconic bike engine.

The boxer engine had been first developed by BMW in the 1930s. It was so called because its two pistons were arranged in a horizontally-opposed fashion so the piston heads, if you could see them at work, would look as if they were punching each other, or boxing.

BMW had been making boxers with their horizontally-opposed pistons sticking out like ears each side of the bike for seventy years. They had tweaked them and breathed on them and finally fifteen years ago they had said they were discontinuing this ancient architecture and would only produce the K series of ultra-modern engines with cylinders in line, not horizontally-opposed, a much more flexible and up-to-date design.

For the legions of boxer fans it had been as if the Pope had announced he was giving up wine and wafers at communion and serving confit de canard and a raspberry coulis instead. Enraged Beemeristas all but stormed BMW's Munich headquarters. The K engineers had to be given bodyguards. The K design with its big square engine was designated the "flying brick" as opposed to the stylish boxer.

BMW quickly backed down and said there had been a misunderstanding. Yes, the K was a great bike but, *naturlich*, they would go on producing boxers as long as they drank beer in Munich. After owning six boxers, I was a committed boxer man. Just about every great long-distance bike trip ever made had been made on a boxer. Ewan McGregor had gone "round the world" (well, sort of) on a boxer. My old Oxford friend, Jim Rogers, did 60,000 miles, genuinely round the world, for *Investment Biker* on a boxer. The British police had been pulling you over for speeding on their boxers for sixty years. The only other people I knew who made boxers were a car company called Porsche. They too liked this antique design and had even called one of their vehicles the Boxster.

A month earlier I had owned two Boxers, an R1200RT, the long-distance tourer, on a rented version of which I had been round Japan, and an R1200 GS Adventure, the off-road bike favoured by Ewan McGregor like the one on which I had done the Motorcycle Diaries trip across the Andes.

My R1200RT was seven years old and I had felt it was time to retire its aging joints and shafts so I had trotted off to BMW Park Lane to get a new boxer and somehow, when I left, found myself astride, not a boxer, but a ... Flying Brick, the despised K1600 GTL. Despite being the size of an upturned bath-tub it was as light on its feet as Michael Jackson. Its six cylinders in-line made it feel as if it had literally unlimited power.

Not only had I just traded in my R1200RT Boxer for a Flying Brick in London I had just rented the Brick's twin from Garner's Bikes of Melbourne. That was what I'd be riding round Oz on, a Flying Brick. I may have been embarrassed but it certainly impressed my new Ducati friends.

"Awesome bike, mate."

"Thanks, mate."

Who was I to say what a traitor I was feeling after twenty-five boxer years?

Tasmania must be one of the world's most underrated and little-known destinations. I was so ignorant about it that, for once, I had been doing some online reading up on it in Melbourne, having followed my customary policy of no homework before getting there. It had not been easy reading. The first thing that struck me was how the most effective destroyer in recorded human history is Western European man. The Mongols and the Huns had done their share of destroying, but they hadn't pretended it was for anything other than greed and aggrandisement. Mr Western European on the other hand liked to say how he was bringing civilisation, godliness, and salvation to the people he enslaved and exterminated. Nowhere had been worse than Tasmania although North America had run it close.

Tasmania had been populated with aborigines who had walked across the Bass Strait before global warming 5 million years ago had turned Tasmania into an island. The aborigines lived in harmony with nature and with all the strange and wonderful animals that had been cut off with them when the land bridge to Australia went under water. They had survived in a primeval state for millennia until Cook, Tasman, and the rest of the colonising rabble turned up.

Van Diemen's Land as it was first called had been deemed a good place for the Brits to incarcerate people who had stolen a few apples or poached a couple of the squire's pheasants. They were transported in conditions not much different to a slave ship, first to Sydney and then on to Hobart in Tasmania. It was ironic that the British imprisoners should have chosen places now considered among the most beautiful city locales in the world for their grim jails.

Shortly after the prisoners came free settlers. Tasmania was like the West Country of England writ large: smiling, fertile, scenic, and over-flowing with natural goodies. The first free settlers thought that everything was perfect but for a couple of minor annoyances. First, there were these naked aborigines who kept on getting in the way of honest English settlers there to make the land productive. They had to go. And go they did. In less than a century the gentle, nature-wise, earth-friendly Tasmanian natives who had so long lived in harmony with the land and its creatures had been exterminated by settlers. Many had been shot, like pheasants in Devon, for sport. The rest were exterminated for expediency. By the beginning of the 20th century the grisly job had been done. No aborigines remained. Not one. We God-fearing Brits had exterminated an entire race. All that were left were a number of mixed-race people, because the British liked raping the women after they had killed the men, but no aborigine of unmixed heritage exists in Tasmania today.

Then there were the wild animals. They harried the sheep. They too had to go. Saddest was the demise of the thylacines, the Tasmanian tiger, a stripy, wolf-like animal which was too shy to do any serious damage but that too was finally extinguished about fifty years ago. The Tasmanian devil, a beast the size of a Welsh terrier, still exists. It makes a noise so fearsome that early settlers threw themselves in the sea rather than face it. Today the devils still live but are blighted with a face cancer that covers their face in lesions and leads to death. Who knows what brought that on?

Tasmania was one of the most beautiful places I had ever seen. Some twenty years earlier I had watched Jurassic Park with people meeting prehistoric creatures frolicking through the primeval jungle until some of them turned out to be velociraptors. Tazza was like that but without the velociraptors. Open plains, ferny woods, majestic trees, vistas over valleys to the sea beyond, eagles, funny birds with crests, and beaches emptier and more beautiful than any you had ever seen.

We docked in the early morning and I had biked from the ferry port at Devonport, after a quieter than expected crossing thanks to the giant size and powerful stabilisers of the Spirit of Tasmania, to the Bay of Fires Character Cottages on Binalong Bay. These were set on a small hill overlooking 3 miles of white powder sand beach, empty but for me, a lone jogger, and what looked like a pair of albatrosses wheeling over the long breakers.

Marian, the landlady, had given me the key to Burgess, a character cottage halfway up the hill with chintz curtains and other appurtenances of 1950s England. I had a fridge and a balcony overlooking the miles of the powder-sand Bay of Fires. No-one seemed to know whether it was so called because the Brits had seen the aborigines' fires or, more likely because of the orange-red lichen that grows on its rocks.

The Character Cottages only did breakfast, so I walked a few minutes to the five-table Binalong Bay Café for dinner. I had a plate of tiny Tasmanian scallops, each no bigger than a sugar cube, and a quail stuffed with something delicious. And three different glasses of sublime Tasmanian white wine. Happy to bed.

The next day Brenda and I set off for a short ride south along the coast road.

Brenda? Did I say Brenda?

Once again, I couldn't ride round Australia on an anonymous bit of metal. Naming cars is sad but, bikes, well, bikes, like boats, are different. Everyone names a boat. Bikes and boats are travelling companions, not mere vehicles. I had crossed the Andes on Spike, and last year the faithful Beemer-San had taken me round Japan. Not to mention, my first love, the noble Bertha who had swept me to Istanbul and back. I had to admit that the Flying Brick lacked the grace of the boxers. Thanks to the huge fairing, there was something big-breasted about a K1600. If ever a bike were a Brenda, this was she.

The Freycinet Peninsula turned out to be a National Park almost empty of habitation apart from Saffire, a minimalist but luxurious resort set in the Tasmanian jungle a short crocodile-trot through the bushes from Wineglass Bay. This was a pristine beach so stunning that the Queen and Prince Philip had gone ashore there from the Royal Yacht in the way-back-when for a beach party. I had googled this important historical event. Her Majesty had sipped a Tasmanian sauvignon blanc while Phil had tossed some shrimp on the barbie. Nothing had changed since but the food. The first course of my Saffire dinner was typical local bush tucker: Freycinet oysters with a sorbet of ginger and champagne.

Getting to Saffire had been a short drive giving me almost the whole day to laze, swim, pick up shells on the beach, and sit on my balcony with my feet up.

The next day, Brenda and I pushed on to Hobart, the capital. Getting there was a beautiful ride along the unspoiled east coast. Well, beautiful, yes, but there was one problem which I hesitate to mention: the wind, which seemed to follow me around the globe. I had become a wind-magnet. On the drive into Hobart I had memories of Kyushu's horizontal rain-bullets. What had I done to offend Aeolus (God of Winds as every biker knows)? There was a causeway 5 kilometres long approaching Hobart. The wind was so strong that waves were slopping across it and I had to bike at 100 kph (slower and Brenda would have not had enough momentum to avoid being blown over) while tilting her into the gale. Enough. You had too many wind stories in Japan, but I did wish this hurricane would stop following me around. I was starting to feel like Ahab and the white whale ... Brenda and the black hurricane.

No-one would readily confuse Sunday in Hobart, the capital of Tasmania, with market day in Marrakech. Once a year Hobart came to life for the survivors of the notorious Sydney-Hobart yacht race who were so grateful to be alive that they took strong drink and threw each other into the harbour. The rest of the year Hobart suffered from narcolepsy.

From my lunch table at "Mures, the Seafood Peoples' Restaurant" where I was quietly polishing off a lobster with a glass of excellent local champagne, I was able to see the Town Hall. I couldn't quite make out the legend beneath Hobart's Coat of Arms but I think it said, "Chill, Dude".

Daughter Tasha, who knows a thing or two about art, had told me that if there were one thing I should do in Hobart it was visit Mona. This was the creation of David Walsh, a Tasmanian who had made a billion dollars inventing gambling algorithms. Mona was the Museum of Old and New Art. It was so outlandishly successful that Walsh had just been named the fifth most influential Australian on the planet, ahead of ex-premiers and important cricketers.

Walsh said Mona was a subversive Disneyland. He had thrown together Sidney Nolan's biggest work, *Snake*, Damien Hirst's *Beautiful mis-shapen purity clashing excitedly outwards* painting, Chris Ofili's *Black Madonna*, the one that had been banned as blasphemous in New York, rooms full of Pacific bark paintings, men with female genitalia, machines making excrement, castrations, African beadwork, Victorian paintings, mummies everywhere, cascading water forming words, and a lot more. It was burrowed three cellars deep into the sandstone earth.

There were no labels or signs or directions. You were given an iPod and headphones when you went in and this gave you information on nearby art works. The whole was set in a park on a bend in the river 10 kilometres north of Hobart. Mona was unquestionably the art creation of which Australians were most proud and Walsh so admired that he transcended the Australian art scene.

After an hour I couldn't wait to get out. There was something horribly smug and self-congratulatory about it, but criticism was impossible as Walsh had got there first. On your iPod entry for each work was a Summary Description and then something Walsh called "art-wank". Smirk, smirk. How could you criticise him for being a wanker if he's pointing at himself saying "Look at me. I'm a wanker." Trust me, he is.

Mona is the most annoying, irritating juxtaposition of art works, some individually brilliant, which by themselves, or better curated, would be worth spending many hours with.

And what is to be done about Australian cuisine? At home I have a much-loved cookbook by Raymond Oliver, the owner of Le Grand Véfour, one of the grand three-star restaurants of Paris in the sixties. He devoted a thousand pages to French cuisine (his), three pages to Italian cooking, a page to Japanese and Spanish. Nothing to English, but, curiously, he gave a paragraph to Australian cooking, in the 1960s. "Australian cooking," said monsieur Oliver, "is a matter of how many fried eggs you can get on a steak".

Sometimes I longed for the time when Australian cooking was steak'n'eggs, Texas, not California. Now nothing goes un-kissed by a jus or coulis; no chicken leg goes without confit; ginger, wasabi, and white radish drift like confetti across your plate while a slaw of pumpkin, bayberries and fennel anoints your salad. Ozzies are lovely people and astonishingly good cooks, but Australian cuisine no longer has corks hanging from its hat.

Leaving Hobart was a morning of such good-to-be-alive gloriousness that the world seemed a bright place indeed. Aeolus had gone to blow his cheeks out elsewhere; hardly a breath stirred the blue gums. Three white puffy clouds inhabited an otherwise pure-blue sky.

Hobart had been left behind to Elvis singing Blue Suede Shoes. Brenda had a six-speaker sound system big enough to fill a stadium to which I had hitched up my iPod. Its big lack though was a Shuffle feature. Brenda, probably her German heritage, only played music in strict alphabetical order. After three days I was now on track 242 and had reached the Bs with Blue Moon giving way to Blue Suede Shoes. There was something agreeably crazy about cruising through Jurassic Park, the trees flicking by whoosh-whoosh-whoosh, with 130 decibels of Elvis stirring up the kookaburras.

I had to press on. I had stopped for a coffee in Bothwell, a tiny village in the Black Tier Mountains before descending to the Weasel Plains. After Weasel Plains I was a bit nervous. I was taking the shorter and more scenic route to the ferry at Devonport that night, this route recommended by Dave the hotel man, himself a trail-biker.

"Awesome route, Miles. It goes by the Great Lake in the central highlands. You mustn't miss that."

"Thanks, Dave."

"Hey, mate, you don't mind a bit of dirt, do you?"

Later map study revealed that this "bit of dirt" was 50 kilometres long. How Brenda was going to handle that I didn't know. She hadn't got her skirts dirty yet. Hardpack dirt is fine on a big bike. Gravel is skiddy and nasty. Sand is fun on a trail-bike but tricky on a big tourer, and ruts are death. There would be little traffic on the highland road and almost certainly no mobile coverage. By the time I hit the dirt the iPod should be on to the end of the Bs. Buggered, probably.

Three hours later, I had survived the dirt, but it had been hard work. It had been 50 kilometres of what (you may recall) the Argentinians called rip-rap, hard corrugated washboard baked mud, last encountered for seventy nightmare kilometres from Bariloche to the Chilean border three years earlier. Poor Brenda almost had her fillings shaken out. I had been standing on the foot-pegs for most of the way to ease the drumming and better to spot the pot-holes.

The highland road had been what I imagined Finland must look like, a lonely lake surrounded by a lonelier moor without tree or bush in sight. Not a good place to break down. In two hours on the high plateau I had passed two other vehicles both driven by evil-looking men with backwoods beards. They probably had banjos under their seats and a rifle-rack behind. Memories of Piggy and the mountain men in *Deliverance*. Not a place to be after dark.

I had passed a cackle of crows hopping about and feasting on what looked like a poor dead Tasmanian devil, the only one I had seen. Otherwise the roadkill score so far was Wallabies 10, Wombats 3. A wombat looks like a fur-covered duffle bag with tiny legs sticking out at each corner. I should add that I had been responsible for none of this slaughter. Brenda's front wheel remained unbloodied. Hotel Dave had told me to avoid hitting wombats, particularly dead ones, despite their small size.

"Christ, mate, it's like hitting a bag of cement. Curtains."

Tasmania crossed, I was sitting on the Devonport beach watching the Spirit of Tasmania waft in. Meanwhile I was being attacked by giant Tasmanian seagulls who wanted a bit of my caramel slice just purchased from the Nice n Eazy Bakery, which had won three prizes for its pies. Now two things that looked like gay pigeons in pink aprons with pink ruffled chef's hats on their heads had joined the gulls.

"Gosh, mate, what do you call those?" I asked a passing local.

"Mate, we call them a lot of things. Bloody nuisance mainly. Or dickhead birds. But their real name is galahs. That's galah with an h."

"Thanks, mate." I liked the galahs. What was not to like about a gay pigeon in a chef's hat?

No-one could have called it a quiet crossing on the Spirit of Tasmania. The sea was calm, the moon was out, unfamiliar stars lit the sky, but my chances of a restful night were scuppered by the three Ducati boys, Greg, Tony, and Justin whom I had met on the trip over. They seemed amazed I'd made it round the island and back and even impressed when I told them in a nonchalant fashion how I had breezed over the dirt road by the Great Lake.

"Awesome, mate. Surprised your bike was up to it." Brenda was too heavy and lumbersome for the Ducati boys. Anyhow they decided to sit me at their table for shipboard dinner and to tutor me in fine Tasmanian wines while telling me tales of the awesome Tassie Sheilas who had thrown off their clothes and hurled themselves at the lads wherever they stopped in their three days on the island. The girls of Hobart, Greg reported, were particularly voracious.

None had hurled themselves at me, so I was a bit jealous, though less so when Greg showed me a photograph of an elderly Asian lady wearing a flapping raincoat and not much else.

"What d'you think of this one, Miles? Aw, she went like a truck, right, lads?"

"Too right, Greg."

"And look at that rack. Awesome," added Justin.

Fortunately, the boys' wives didn't enjoy biking.

Anyhow, when we docked in Melbourne we had exchanged cards and I looked forward to seeing the lads when they stopped off in London on their way to the Isle of Man for the T.T. Races. I supposed I would have to round up a posse of Asian grannies in flapping raincoats to keep them happy.

Meanwhile I had stopped off 100 kilometres from Melbourne for an egg on toast brekky (sourdough, of course) at Vic's On The Beach in Torquay, the start of the Great Ocean Road and self-proclaimed Surf Capital of Australia. The Torquay beach was indeed impressive, wide and long with packed yellow sand. Stern-jawed lifeguards in one-piece swimsuits and rubber bathing caps like 1950s bathing belles scanned the horizon. It lacked only one thing. Surf. I'd seen bigger waves on the Serpentine.

Vic's at brekky-time was packed with surfer dudes, most wearing T-shirts commemorating Surf Championships of yore. The average age of the six Surfer Dudes and one Surfer Dudette at the table next to me was seventy and most were bigger round the middle than up and down. The Torquay Sexagenarian Surf Gut was indeed a thing of awe. I felt right at home.

Later I stopped 50 kilometres down the Great Ocean Road at a beach where there was real surf. Here, fifty Australian teenagers were being tutored in the finer points of surfing. Unlike my Torquay brekky-neighbours these surfers were so fit and young and good-looking that I was reduced by jealousy to silent but enthusiastic cheering whenever one fell off.

The Great Ocean Road lived up to its billing. There was only one word for it. Awesome, mate. Some might say it reminded them of the drive from L.A. to San Francisco. Well, they are both fine, sinuous roads skirting a boisterous surfy ocean and both have hill and mountain on the land side. But, for me, the G.O.R. was in a different league. Its sheer variety enchanted and amazed.

Thirty kilometres of surfer heaven with no buildings, just majestic clumps of unfamiliar Mediterranean-looking bushes between you and the beach. Then, suddenly you jinked inland for a stretch of primeval forest while the road took high-speed bends through the towering gums. For 30 frantic kilometres I was chasing a guy in a convertible Porsche, never quite managing to get past him, while his girlfriend whooped and waved her cap in the air to egg me on. Chuck Berry and "Johnny Be Good" were blasting out of all six speakers.

Then, we screamed round a corner with the Porsche seventy metres ahead of me and there were three stern members of the Victoria Police in uniform. The Porsche was waved to a halt where strict punishment and a large fine must have been meted out while I swooped innocently past with a cheery "Hello, Officer" wave.

I was spending the night in Anchors, one of three bungalows on a hillside by Port Campbell, near the end of the Great Ocean Road. It had taken me half an hour to find the owner to give me the key. I eventually located a man in dungarees in the middle of a field doing something intimate with a cow. He fished around in a dungaree pocket and handed me the keys. Unlike its owner, the bungalow was spotless. Jacuzzi, verandah, modern furniture, and a view over forest, sea and cow-pasture. I biked into Port Campbell and bought a steak, a bottle of merlot, a couple of zucchini and when I got back threw them on the barbie. The sun was setting, the steak was delicious, and the merlot had more punch than a Ballarat barmaid.

Cruising along the Great Ocean Road in brilliant sunshine had been soften-you-up time. Next day as I headed inland from the sea, the wind was back and rain was spitting from an angry sky for the ride up to the Grampian mountains and Hall's Gap. The sheer effort of concentrating as the wind first from the left and then from the right tried to hurl Brenda into the ditch left me drenched in sweat despite the cold. My helmet felt as if it was about to be blown off taking my head with it. On stopping for tea and a Kit-Kat at a roadside post office in the middle of cow country, the owner admired Brenda and asked where I was going.

"Hall's Gap."

"Hall's Gap? Take care, mate. The Roos are bleedin' criminal that way."

"Oh, but I'm OK if I don't drive at dawn or dusk."

He guffawed.

"Yeah, that's what they tell you in the city. Don't you believe it. I was driving up there on Monday and I just missed one that bounced into the road and then another threw itself at the side of the car. And that was at lunchtime."

"Thanks for the warning."

These roos sounded more wayward than the Hobart Sheilas.

Despite the warnings I made it to the Kookaburra Motor Lodge, without seeing a roo. Talk about multi-tasking. In addition to trying to prevent Brenda being hurled over a Grampian cliff by a screaming williwaw, I had been on constant alert for bounding roos. The only one I saw was lying flat and very dead in the road.

However Peggy, proprietress of the Motor Lodge, assured me that the open fields behind her motel would be aswarm with feeding roos that night.

"Where you going tomorrow, Miles?" asked Peg.

"Daylesford."

"Whoopsidoo, Miles. That's the gay capital of Australia. Erm, you're not staying in the Lake Hotel, are you?"

"Ahem, why yes, Peggy."

Peggy, who did not appear to have read the memo on diversity, gave a little giggle, looked me up and down, possibly surprised at not having spotted me straight off as a gay-boy, handed me my keys and said, "I expect you'll have a bunch of fun there tomorrow, Miles. I'm told they don't have locks on the doors there if you know what I mean. G'day, Miles."

Later at 6.00 pm Peggy banged on my door. I had just had a shower and opened the door with just a towel wrapped round me.

"Oh, hello Miles, you boys do like to shower don't you?"

She had a good look over my shoulder to see if she could spot any fit young men hiding behind the sofa.

"Miles, Stephen's feeding the kookaburras and I thought you might want to watch."

"Indeed I do, Peggy, let me just throw something on."

She gave me a wink and retreated.

A kookaburra turned out to be an amiable bird in a fluffy white suit with stripy dark wings and an enormous beak, just right for catching the small chunks of meat that Stephen was tossing them. There were three lined up on top of the sign saying Kookaburra Motor Lodge.

"Hey, look," said Stephen, and, bang on cue, a roo and her daughter came bouncing through the motor court dodging their way through the parked cars. I was just about to take a brilliant photo when a four-year-old boy ran up screaming and frightened them off. So I retreated to the balcony outside my room, poured a glass of pinot gris, and sat there for an hour watching scores of happy roos bouncing around the cow pasture. Three had just bounced off my verandah and over a four-foot fence without a hiccup.

I asked Stephen in between his tossing morsels of deceased wallaby to the kookaburras what the two hundred-strong flock of birds looking like pure white rooks were called. They were making a noise like a Justin Bieber concert audience.

"Ah, Jesus, Miles, we just call them Nuisance Birds."

"Oh, I thought that was the galahs?"

"Mate, I tell you they're all a bloody nuisance. But the white ones are called Corella birds."

As he said this a streak like a technicolour torpedo shot through the air.

"Wow," said I, "what's that?"

"Bloody nuisance if you ask me, mate. It's a parakeet. Place is crawling with 'em. Make a godawful noise."

Roos, wallabies, Bloody Nuisance birds, I was feeling like David Attenborough.

Arrival in Daylesford, the gay capital of Australia, was a disappointment. My lakeside room, well, more of a balcony suite, sweetie, at the Lake Hotel about which Kookaburra Peggy had got so excited didn't, it was true, have much of a lock on the door, but if you didn't want to be disturbed you only had to put a wooden duck outside your door with a label round its neck saying 'privacy duck' and no-one would bother you.

The village of Daylesford seemed to offer more in the way of diversity than my hotel. I had to elbow my way into Le Larder for a late lunch of deli platter and local gewürztraminer as it was already heaving with fit young men in Levi's and tight white T-shirts, not a surfer gut to be seen.

One of the good things about being in rainbow country was how well dressed the men were. What a relief that no-one was wearing those bizarre Australian baggy short-long trousers that have been cut off at mid-calf length and have unexplained bits of cord hanging from them.

Daylesford was not always Daylesford. This part of the world had been the centre of the Australian gold mining boom in the 1850s and for some time thereafter. Ballarat, where I had stopped off on the way to admire the Victorian wedding-cake buildings with their wrought-iron balconies, was the Australian Klondike. In gold-mining days, Daylesford had been known as Wombat Hill.

Later, when the gold ran out but the mineral water springs didn't, the city fathers realised that some re-branding was in order as rich Melbournians were not going to take the waters in Wombat Hills. So Wombat Hill was re-christened Daylesford and grizzled miners replaced by spa goers in towelling dressing gowns.

And a very jolly place it was. How nice to see deciduous, leaf-shedding trees. So far just about the only trees I'd seen were Australia's most successful export, the ubiquitous gum, or eucalyptus, tree. Two hundred years ago they existed only in Australia. Now Africa, India, South America, Arabia, and everywhere else are infested with these greedy arboreal bastards, voraciously leaching all the goodness out of the soil and leaving their better-mannered native competitors to die. Nothing lives in the shadow of a eucalyptus. When you drive through Oz all you see are eucalypts. In the Outback they are handsome trees, but they don't shed their leaves in winter. Instead they make, so Kookaburra Steve informed me, a godawful mess shedding their bark once a year.

I'd now done eight nights on the Australian road and ferry and had four more to go before Sydney. Barring some awful intervention by Allah, this had been the easiest and most pampered trip I'd made with charming places to stay, absurdly good food, and astonishing wines. It'd also been the first where monoglot Milo had been able to chat away with the locals.

Last night at the Lake House between the smoked local eel, green beetroot and wasabi starter, and crisp duck breast on a bed of pickled cabbage, I found myself talking to Jeff and Kylie. Two hours later the restaurant was empty but for the three of us, we were on our sixth or seventh different glass of fine Australian wines, most from within 20 miles of the Lake House, which Tom the sommelier kept on opening for us.

Jeff and Kylie came from Mt Isa in Queensland. They developed properties but had been going broke as Mt Isa was a uranium town and the Australian government had decided to ban the export of uranium, probably bullied by the Americans in case the Iranians should get their hands on it. Then the government changed their mind and uranium exports soared and the price doubled. Mt Isa became a boom town and property prices went through the roof, giving Jeff and Kylie an opportunity to cash in and retire.

They had a spare ticket for Bruce Springsteen who was performing down the road in Ballarat two days later. Would I like to go with them? How often do people at the next-door table in a London restaurant lean over and ask you to a Brucie concert? Sadly, I said no to Bruce; Brenda and I had to move on.

The scenery and the biking so far had matched anything on my other long trips. But if you brushed the froth from the cappuccino and looked at the colour of the coffee below ... I was hesitant to say that the trip was too easy as there were still almost a thousand kilometres to go where Providence might choose to slap me around the chops. But, so far, it had been the easiest of my big bike trips.

My first trip, London to Istanbul and back, would always be The Trip. That was when I lost my biking virginity. There was so much I didn't know about biking when I set off: how to bike in bulleting rain, how to bike at night, how to cope with diesel and donkey-droppings on the Romanian road, how to handle the wind-shear from passing trucks, how to navigate a landslide and a flood, all things no-one had taught me when I had taken biking lessons in the car-park of Wimbledon Stadium.

Argentina had been tough and long and hard but the most exhilarating trip of all. Nothing could match the beauty of Patagonia, the god-knows-what-will-happen-if-I-shred-a-tyre-in-the-wilderness-with-no-phone-signal, no Spanish, and no passing traffic, or the wild crossings of the Andes passes.

Zander's south India suicide tour had been seriously risky but wonderful in a mad way. For someone as pampered as me, five days without sight of a roll of loo-paper and almost ten without a cocktail was a challenge. Two-star Indian hotels were like something out of Chaucer. But the sheer joy of chilling with a mojito on Anjuna Beach in Goa at the end of it all, having survived the Indian road, lives with me still.

Japan was Japan. If the purpose of travel is to open your eyes and learn I started there with a blank sheet headed Japan and finished with every corner of the paper scribbled on. That had had many trials. The ride from Mt Aso-san to Fukuoka in a typhoon still scares me.

Now, Oz. Yes, it too had had its tough moments. The shrieking williwaws were no fun to bike in and if you lost your concentration you

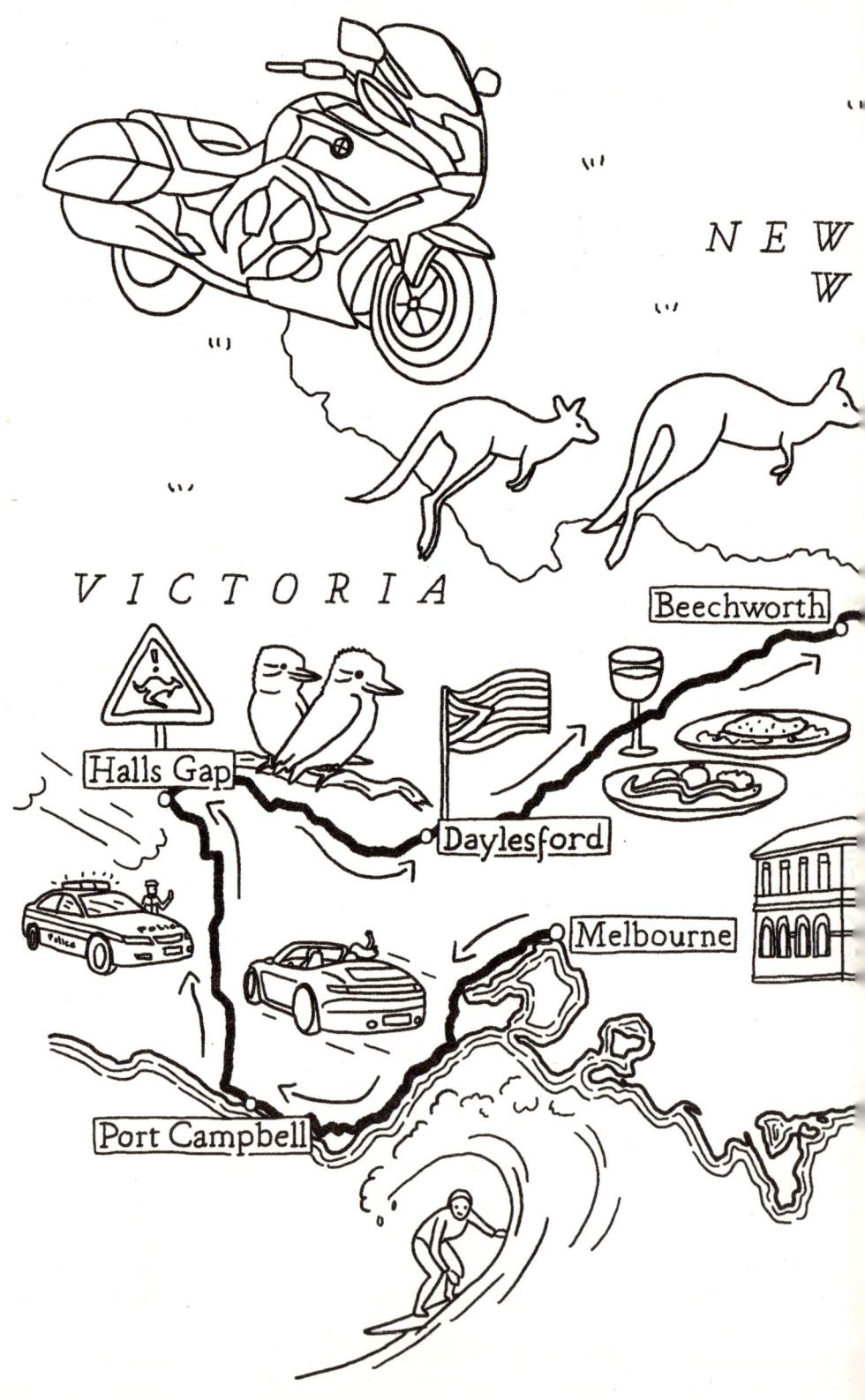

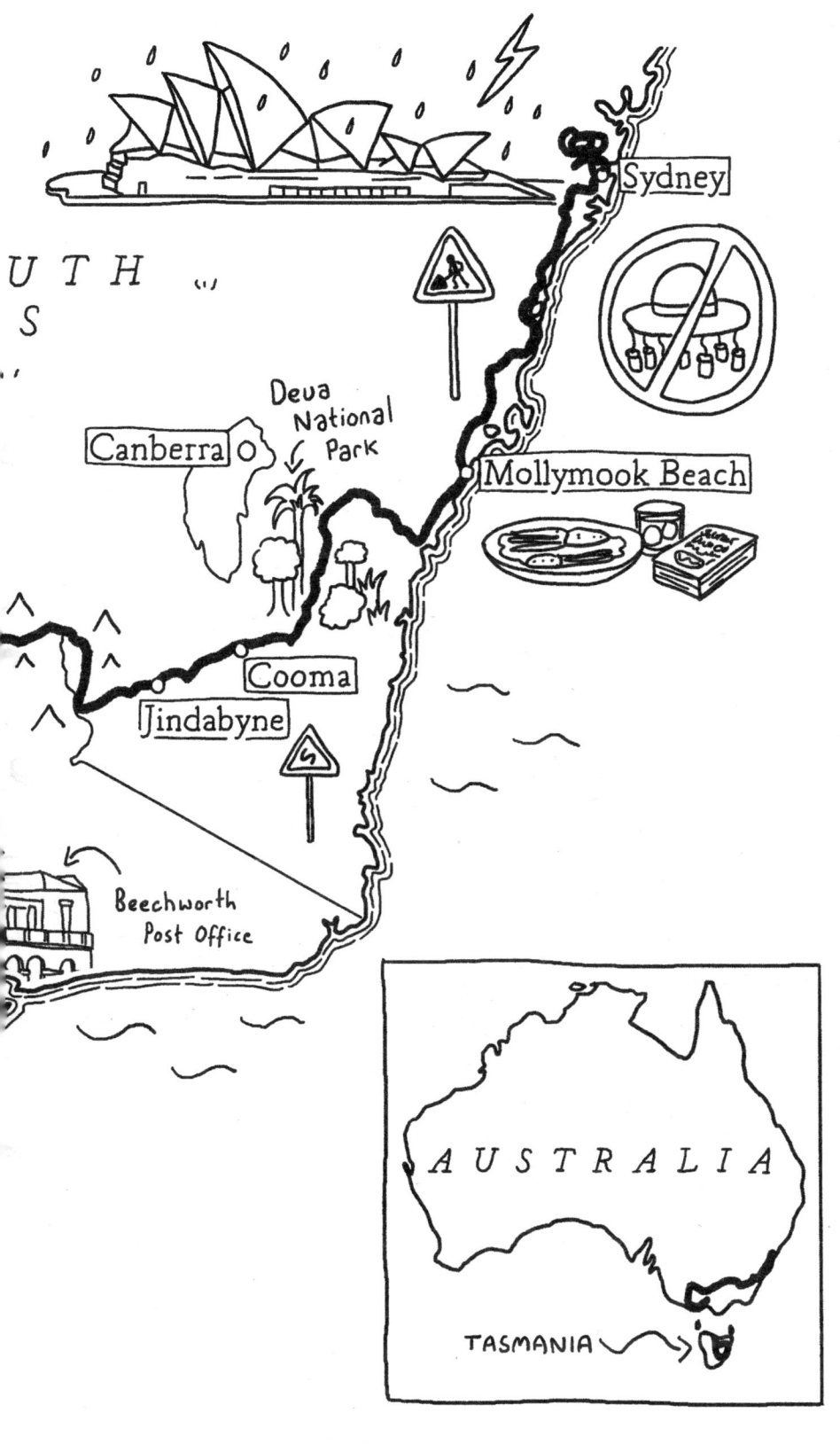

would lose the bike. And, if you hit a roo, you would do a lot more than lose the bike. But on the whole this was a country with a smile on its face. When the Australians say, "no worries", "good on yer", and "awesome", they mean it. The good fellowship was heart-warming, a heartening contrast to the empty American "have a nice day".

This is a Big Country. When people talk of the world being over-populated tell them to ride into the hills of Victoria and the emptiness beyond. The scenery, open rolling pasture dotted with gums and grazing sheep and crossed by gulches, the intensity of the light and the sheer emptiness of it are astonishing for an Englishman.

It had been not without its scary moments. Leaving Daylesford the sun was brilliant and shining straight into my eyes so I had been more or less driving blind. And when the sun was coming at an oblique angle it flickered through the roadside gums with an equally blinding strobe effect. I saw some dead tree stumps a couple of hundred yards ahead. Brenda was cruising along at 120 kph. Suddenly one of the tree stumps bounded into the air and landed in the middle of the road. Three other stumps followed it. Evasive action was useless. I didn't know whether to fall off the bike in terror at the bouncing roos, each one the size of a bear, or to laugh at how comic they were. Roos really do bounce, sproing-sproing-boing and then they were away and into the opposite sheep pasture like rocket-powered circus clowns. No-one had told these giant roos that they weren't meant to be sproinging on the road at 11.00 am but only at dawn and dusk.

After that I slowed down and concentrated every effort on squinting at the stumps and boulders three hundred yards ahead in case they too should leap into life. I saw two more roos but they didn't sproing around the road. Roos are big but about as road smart as an English pheasant. I did not want to picture what would happen to me if a large-tailed creature the size of a refrigerator boinged into me from the side while Brenda was doing 110 kph.

Despite the roos we made it to Beechworth, a story-book pretty 1850s gold town. The sun had shone all day, the gingerbread and wrought-iron balconies looked like a film set and I was staying in Provenance, a gold-era bank converted into an "ultra-modern fusion cuisine restaurant" with rooms attached. It was nice, but I was secretly longing for two fried eggs on a steak and a room with a simple shower rather than a gold-plated jacuzzi.

The next day might provide this. I had 350 kilometres of twisty mountain roads through the Snowy Mountains to Jindabyne, a ski place. Kylie, the woman with the Springsteen tickets, had marked my card in Daylesford. "Miles, you'll love Beechworth, but Jindabyne is a shitheap. How can you go there rather than come to Bruce with us?"

You did find some paradoxes in Oz. These once tough cork-hatted swashbuckling drongos had taken the nanny state to their hearts. When I had arrived in Hobart, I had seen a sign: "Hobart. Do the Right Thing". I had felt guilty as soon as I crossed the town line, and had an urge to get a T-shirt saying, "Doing the Wrong Thing in Hobart".

On the other hand, although no-one has ever accused me of being green, there were some wonderful by-products of the Australian green mania. They inhabited a country the size of the US with a tenth the population, but they wanted to take care of it. Before the unspoilt bits got invaded with Holiday Inns they had designated huge areas as National Parks and no-go areas for any development at all. Some of these had no roads or paths and were literally impenetrable, such as the one in the West of Tasmania, an area comprising almost a fifth of the island which, so the owner of my Hobart hotel had told me, had never even been mapped. That seemed to be going too far. What was the point of having a park if no-one's ever allowed to go there? It's not as if they've given the land back to the aborigines. They couldn't even if they wanted to as they've killed them all.

Other mainland parks were possible to access on dirt tracks and some even had one or two designated areas where you could indulge in the Australian national religion of putting up a tent and lighting a barbie. Sometimes lighting the barbie set fire to an area the size of Wales but, hey, that's an Ozzie barbie for you.

The road up to Jindabyne had been classic mountain biking, but Jindabyne itself was a fine example of it being better to travel hopefully than to arrive. Kylie had been right. Jindabyne was a shitheap. It probably looked lovely in the winter with piles of snow but out of season it was a sad place. I spent the night in a featureless ski condo and eventually found a Chinese restaurant where I could get something to eat, about the only place open. It was our first disappointing stop.

After Jindabyne I headed down through the mountains to Mollymook on the Pacific a hundred and 50 miles south of Sydney. The ride could not have started better. A brilliant day, crisp chilly morning, a couple of fluffy clouds in an iridescent blue sky, and NO WIND. I had just two more days' easy riding down to the coast and it would be over. Sniff. And the hard Outback stuff was now behind me.

Those whom the Gods want to destroy they first give a satnav to. I had a map bought in Melbourne, a map which refused to acknowledge anything that happened outside the great state of Victoria (capital city – Melbourne) so neighbouring New South Wales, which I was now in, was as effectively mapped as the Empty Quarter. According to the map there was no direct way from Jindabyne to my destination at Mollymook. I could have done an inland, northern loop past Canberra, a city whose very name makes people yawn, or a southern, coastal, loop. I went for the coast.

However, after 30 kilometres of brilliant driving with bendy high-speed roads and vistas for 80 kilometres, we came to Cooma. It was here that clever Bruce Satnav discovered a third, more direct way. Unlike in Japan where I had been tormented by the Satnav Harpy, on this trip I had an Ozzie bloke directing me whom I christened Bruce Satnav. We had become decidedly matey. He was never in doubt. Bruce knew the secret short cuts. Up to this moment I had considered him a good mate, a big improvement on the Harpy.

He suddenly told me to turn sharp right and then sharp left over the railroad tracks onto a smaller road. There was no sign of the small road on the map, but Bruce had found a new, shorter route. Thanks, Brucie. There were a couple of trail bikers ahead of me who also took the turn. They looked as if they knew what they were doing so I happily followed them. I sailed along, half a mile behind the trail bikers. The road was narrow and there was no other traffic but it was a beautiful drive, the speakers were blasting out "The Girl Can't Help It", and then, "Girls Just Wanna Have Fun", and all was cool (after 763 tracks I was onto the Gs today).

I was suspicious that there were no signs or buildings, but I was now 20 kilometres down the short cut with 100 kilometres to go to the next junction according to Brucie, so it was too late to go back; I was committed. Everyone knows the old joke about the difference between involved and committed … In an egg and bacon breakfast, the hen is involved while the pig is committed. By this stage I was bacon.

Then, *whappp*, the road disappeared. It turned to dirt. The trail bikers on their light dirt bikes sailed off leaving a very pissed-off Brenda and her terrified passenger skitting and skidding around a non-road in the middle of a jungle in what I later learned was the Deua National Park (an area half the size of Slovenia) entirely without habitation, sign, or traffic, let alone a mobile signal.

Inuits have a hundred words for snow, the English a hundred for rain. I now had a hundred for Australian dirt road surfaces. First I had to deal with packed corrugated mud which shook poor Brenda out of her tights. Thank God I was riding a piece of stout Bavarian, not British or Italian, machinery or all that would have been left was a pile of nuts and bolts in the road.

The corrugated washboard was the least bad surface. Then there were ruts. Ruts are a literal killer. You have no control and you are constantly on the edge of being flipped. Worst though was the gravel. This was thick, inches-deep gravel. It was like riding on ice. A bow-wave of gravel builds under your front wheel and the bike skeeters from one side of the road to the other while your heart fibrillates away in fear that the camber will throw you off the road, as you have no grip nor way of climbing back against an adverse camber. Using the front brake would have produced a terminal fish-tail. At times I slowed to 20 kph and I still had 70 kilometres to the junction. I cursed Bruce. Satnavs. They sucked you in and then dumped you. If Satnav Harpy had been there she would have told me to, "Make a U-turn, moron." I had no idea where I was.

THE HOPELESS BIKER

At last a sign. At least this would tell me where I was.

"Foot Rot Control. No Sheep Cross This Point."

I was in the middle of the jungle. The nearest sheep was probably a thousand kilometres away. And since when do sheep read road signs? Then I saw humans. The dirt bikers had stopped for a fag. I could at least commiserate with them about the plight we were in. They looked at me with amused astonishment.

"G'day mate. How's the Beemer on these roads?"

"Christ," said I, "did you too get sent down here by the fuckwit satnav? Jesus. Where am I?"

They thought this was very funny.

"No, mate, we meant to come here. It's a test of the bikes. Keeps you on your toes. But on that," pointing at Brenda who was in a terrible sulk, "you don' want to be on this road."

"Mate, don't I know it? By the way, where am I?"

They peered at the map mounted on top of Brenda's tank-bag and pointed at an area as unmarked as the Antarctic.

"Somewhere in here. Great biking. You don't find much like this any more."

"Thank God," I grunted. "How much longer till I reach a surfaced road?"

"Oh, not far, 50 kilometres, max."

Ten minutes later as Brenda and I were picking our skiddy way through the gravel at 20 kph, the trail bikers danced past. They gave me a merry wave. That was the last time I saw them.

Then, 20 kilometres before I'd expected it, we hit a surfaced road. I don't want to go into road-porn here but the sheer silky-satiny-smoothy ecstasy of a metalled road after fifty kilometres of corrugated dirt was better than three days in a locked bedroom with Scarlett Johannsen. Brenda purred.

After 3 kilometres of Scarlett we were back in gravel and tyre-shredding rocks for another 15 kilometres.

Somehow we had made it. That evening I had finally cruised into at

Bannister's, a resort-hotel for Sydney glitterati on a headland between two tenmile white sand beaches. The hotel restaurant was "Rick Stein's at Bannister". That's it, the same Rick Stein who had turned Padstow into ten restaurants all owned by him and was always appearing on your television. Apparently he had dumped his wife for an Australian girl. Hence this restaurant. Looking around it seemed that this was the place where important Sydney businessmen took their personal assistants for hard-working weekends.

Next day Brenda snoozed all day in the Bannister's garage, while I tried to banish the inevitable end of trip melancholia. I had got up at 10.30am, had a leisurely brekky, a long walk on the surf beach, salt and pepper squid by the pool for lunch, read my friend Lola Shoneyin's *The Secret Lives of Baba Segi's Four Wives* (excellent – funny, sad, and moving) on Kindle, had a long nap and was now ready for a dinner overlooking the crashing ocean waves, the previous day's corrugated washboard almost forgotten. The following day would be my last on the road, just a short 220 kilometres to Sydney and goodbye to dear, reliable, good-humoured, Brenda.

Those whom the gods wish to punish they make complacent. "Easy and short", a mere 220 kilometres, turned out to be the worst ride of the trip, a ride with no redeeming features whatever. The roads so far had been excellent, well-surfaced (no need to mention Bruce Satnav's evil detour through the trackless jungle or the Tasmanian Great Lake dirt adventure), free of traffic, no cones, jams or roadworks and everywhere adorned with hilarious road signs showing scooting wombats, charging emus, bouncing roos, and Tasmanian admonishments to 'Do the Right Thing'.

The road from Mollymook to Sydney is called the "Prince's Highway" named after the chap who later became King. He had done an exceptionally poor job of looking after his road. Almost the whole of it was being dug up, diverted, or channelled into contra-flow, this being the main road between Australia's two biggest cities. Traffic burped its fitful way towards Sydney.

Finally, in pissed-off mood, after four hours' inching along to do a trip which should have taken half that, we reached the Sydney outskirts. Bruce Satnav chose that crucial moment to go black. I stopped and prodded his screen. Dead. The petulant sod was sulking because I had been rude about him taking me off-piste two days earlier.

I stopped for petrol, restarted Brenda, and Bruce suddenly jumped back to life: "Follow me, mate, just 19 kilometres to the Park Hyatt, know what I mean". I knew he was lying but what's a guy to do? I had never been to Sydney so had no feel for the lay of the land. The evil bastard then took me so close to the hotel I could almost smell it before he directed me into a tunnel that felt significantly longer than the one under the Channel.

We entered the tunnel in central Sydney but when we finally emerged I was expecting to hear people speaking Indonesian we had gone so far North. Brucie's smug little screen, which earlier had been announcing we were 1.5 kilometres from the Park Hyatt said now: "Destination: 32 kilometres" and showed an orbital route back that may have taken in the Outback. I was tempted to stop and beat Brucie's brains out with the "Hungarian salami" that I had bought in Beechworth for snacking on en route and had hardly touched since, but I realised that, lacking a Sydney map or any knowledge of Sydney geography, I was reliant on the evil Brucie to get me to the Park Hyatt.

Thirty odd kilometres later, having crossed six bridges and seven tunnels, we were close to the hotel. The nearer we get the more kittenish Brucie became: "Turn left in 100 metres" and, when we had gone 50 metres, he suddenly said, no, "Turn right in 350 metres". I was sorely tempted to take the salami to him.

I have mentioned before my unerring sense of direction. I used this to locate a taxi.

"Take me to the Park Hyatt, I will follow on the bike," said I, and thus, ably led by an honest Gujarati, two minutes later Brenda and I arrived at the Park Hyatt. Brucie, meanwhile, was feigning sleep.

I had a day in Sydney to chill, loaf, and be a sightseer. First, though, a sad parting. I had to say goodbye to Brenda who had taken such care of me over 3,000 kilometres without putting a foot wrong. She needed to be dropped off at the local agents of Garner's Bikes of Melbourne so having scanned the map carefully as I no longer had any faith in Bruce I made my way to Sydney Motorbike Wreckers in the suburb of Alexandria. Despite Brenda being unwrecked they greeted her like family and promised to transport her mighty frame back to Melbourne. I had a thirty-minute chat with the biker boys while waiting for a taxi. I now felt one of them. I'm not convinced they shared this view, but they clearly thought a senile Pom going bikeabout in the wherever was the best laugh they were going to get all day.

Brenda returned, I was gloating over how good the weather was in Sydney as I looked out towards the Opera House from my hotel. My gloating was the signal for an unseasonal monsoon to arrive. Tropical rain poured down.

Fortuitously, Sara, an Australian friend from London where she had been a successful model had decided to chuck it in and return to Oz to do some writing. She was living with her computer in Coff's Bay, a surfy, beachy place north of Sydney, but she had used my arrival as an excuse for a trip to town to show me round. We scurried off, taking advantage of a rare pause in the monsoon, to MOCA, the Museum of Contemporary Art five minutes away. The Park Hyatt was situated on The Rocks, the first place the white man had built on in Oz, and a place that was now the centre of art galleries, restaurants, and ferry-boats.

I was curious about art done by aborigines. I'd seen a tiny bit in London and had been bowled over by its strength, optical energy, brilliant use of colour, and relationship to the world of spirits and dreaming. I'd learned a little about modern African painting and could see some kinship although the Australian aboriginal work seemed far less influenced by Western painting.

We padded happily around MOCA. This was everything Mr Walsh's Mona, which had so annoyed me in Hobart, was not: brilliantly curated, brilliantly displayed and a place to learn. I don't know where to start with the aboriginal paintings. They are amazing. Some had a Bridget Riley quality and seemed to dance in the air; others used colour with such wit and energy as to leave you breathless. And then there were the astonishing bark paintings, etched in black and ochre on big strips of bark. They were filled with symbolism, most of which in my ignorance I probably missed: snakes, birds, leaping dancers, fecund women, rivers, and leaves. What a wonderful place.

After lunch we went shopping in the local arts and crafts shops. I failed to find the thing I had set my heart on: a Waltzing Matilda-style hat with corks dangling from its brim. Hats there were a-plenty, most made from roo fur and some adorned with croc teeth stuck in the hatband, but it appeared that cork-danglers were now considered culturally embarrassing. When I asked hat shops for a cork-dangler, there was a sucking in of breath and "No, sir, we don't do that kind of thing any longer," as if I had requested a leather codpiece. Finally we found a shop with a hat in the window festooned with dangling corks. At last the quest was over.

"I'd like a hat with corks just like the one in the window," said I.

"No, sorry, sir. None left. We've sold 'em all. Too much demand."

To make up for my disappointment Sara bought me a present. It was a butter-coloured leather pouch about four inches from neck to base. This was a "sensitively harvested" kangaroo scrotum. Did sensitive harvesting entail the harvester reciting Kahlil Gibran to the roo as he snicked off his pouchy bits? The possession of a roo scrotum, said the box in which it was sensitively wrapped, assured the owner of a long life, happiness, and healthy children. For me, maybe, but not for the poor knackerless roo who was presumably sproinging around the Outback with a squeaky voice having little success with the hot roo babes.

To him, all I can say is, "Sorry, mate, I promise to take good care of your scrotum."

Australia is a huge continent and I had just scratched little bits of its surface but what a place. The rolling hills, the primeval forests, the untouched parks, the views for 50 miles with no building to be seen, and the astonishing coast where mighty surf crashed down on deserted white sand beach after deserted white sand beach.

I love England and I'm now not going to live anywhere else, but if I were in my twenties … G'day, Sheila … Where better to live than Sydney for a few years?

How little I knew when I got on the plane the next morning that I would be back. Not to live in Sydney but back for one of the greatest adventures of my life.

SOUTHWEST USA: DAISY IN THE DESERT

I have only done one trip in America and that was different to all the others for several reasons. The other trips had been personal journeys of discovery and adventure, this was more a get-together of friends for a trip around the deserts and mountains of the southwest United States. Much of it was in what became the Trump heartland, an area I hardly knew: Texas, New Mexico, Colorado, Utah, Nevada, and finishing in California. Because of that, I won't detail the trip, just the bikey bits.

My friends were in classic cars, mainly Alfa Romeos and American muscle cars while I was on a bike. Before I had even started I was confronted with a problem. I love BMWs and BMWs were all I had ever ridden but it wouldn't have seemed right to ride a Beemer through Trump country. A cultural misfit. No, I had to brace myself and sleep with the enemy. Surely, Harleys could not be as bad as I had always imagined?

Hello Harley. I had flown into El Paso on Easter Sunday, having booked a gigantic 1700cc Harley-Davidson Electra-Glide from Eagle Rider of El Paso. This had been booked online through Ad-Mo Tours. Ad-Mo Tours, whom I had found on the web and who had arranged the rental had

told me not to worry about it being Easter Sunday.

"No problemo, Miles, they're open all day Sunday," said David Meyers at Ad-Mo when I called him to check.

Being a sceptic about Texas evangelicals being open on Easter Day, I had then called Eagle Rider themselves in El Paso to confirm they were going to be as open as Ad-Mo had told me. Adrian, at Eagle Rider, said they were hermetically closed on Sundays and particularly the coming one as it was Easter and that the whole depot would be sealed with chains.

I called Ad-Mo.

"No, no," said Mr Meyers, "I've spoken to my contact in corporate, he's in Chicago, and Eagle Rider is open on Sunday."

"Dave, I've just spoken to Adrian at the dealership itself and if your definition of open is chains and locked doors, they're open."

This was definitely a problem. If I couldn't pick the bike up till Monday I'd have a 500-mile drive on Monday to catch up with my friends, OK maybe on a Beemer, but a long drive on a new and unfamiliar machine, a Harley to boot.

I spoke again to Adrian. "Miles, man, here's what I'm gonna do. It's Easter Sunday. Everything in El Paso will be closed but, send me a scan of your licence, and I'll take the bike home on Saturday night and meet you in the church parking lot opposite Eagle Rider on Sunday at noon."

I remembered then why it was that I love America. There are many things about today's USA with which I and much of the rest of the world are not in sympathy, but can you imagine an English, let alone French, rental firm employee offering to interrupt his Bible Belt Easter Sunday to hand over a bike in the church parking lot to someone he didn't know, and a limey to boot? God bless America.

Adrian had been as good as his word. He had hot-footed it out of the First Baptist Church as soon as the sermon ended to the parking lot where with a minimum of fuss he handed over the keys to a giant plum-coloured Electra-Glide, and off I went.

I was not sure what to expect about the trip ahead. For me this was more foreign than the depths of Africa. We would be stopping in Taos in New Mexico, a magical adobe-built town which I had visited when we had lived in New York on trips to Taos Ski Valley, and then on to what for me were unknown lands. Monument Valley where John Ford had shot his great Westerns; Telluride, once a silver mining town, now a ski resort; the Grand Canyon, Death Valley, and Joshua Tree National Park, before ending on the beach in Santa Monica.

The Harley was a simple enough machine to drive, although in spirit it seemed twenty-five years behind a BMW, maybe closer to an Enfield Bullet. I was surprised by its lack of punch considering it had an engine as big as that of a medium-sized car. You opened the throttle and it surged sluggishly forward, no punch in the back. It wallowed when we went round bends and if you banked hard for a sharp corner, the running board hit the ground and sparks flew.

The Harley chundered along for four untroubled hours. I was burbling along at 90 mph listening to a Las Cruces country music station on the Harley's six speakers, possibly the most impressive part of the bike, and admiring the passing mesas, those flat-topped mountains so familiar from Western films, when I went to change down from sixth to fifth. As you may know, the gear lever on a bike is a foot pedal which you push up and down with your left foot to change gear. Not today. The gear pedal was still there but it was no longer joined to the gearbox but was wheeling around like a pub sign in a stiff breeze. I stopped as soon as I found level ground by the side of the highway and examined it. The shaft connecting the gear pedal to the gearbox slid smoothly out and in while the pedal rocked up and down without engaging a gear.

I was a hundred miles short of Albuquerque, my intended destination, there was not a building in sight, traffic on the expressway was sparse and there were probably wolves in the nearby hills. I decided to phone for help until I discovered there was no phone signal in this bit of wilderness. And no exit from the expressway in sight.

Harleys, dontcha love 'em? I'd had seven BMWs over the previous 25 years, and I had once lost the horn negotiating two-foot-deep flood waters in Turkey but otherwise nothing but nothing had ever gone wrong with them. Four hours on a Harley and the gear pedal had gone doolalley. Last time I had had gear trouble had been driving an ancient Romanian Dacia around the wastes of Moldavia in 1990 just after the demise of Nico Ceausescu. The clutch cable had snapped and I had managed to drive 50 miles to Suceava with no clutch. Well, if the Dacia could be driven with no clutch, why not the Harley with no ability to change gear? We were stuck in sixth gear so I could forget about first to fifth.

I engaged the clutch and started the engine with its signature gargle gargle noise. I began easing the clutch in very slowly to avoid a stall and the beast began to inch forward. Sixth gear was the worst to start in but I was hoping that the engine had enough torque to go at a slow speed in sixth if I slipped the clutch enough. I eased the clutch out a bit further. The bike coughed and knocked. I pulled the clutch back in and slipped it again as we gathered speed. Heart in mouth, but this seemed to be working. Meanwhile I kept my left foot pressed hard against the outside of the gear pedal in case that was minded to fall out in the road. I edged back onto the freeway and was nearly flattened by a sixteen-wheeler going at 80 mph in the inside lane. But now we were doing 30 mph and I had let the clutch out altogether. Five minutes later we were bopping along at 90 in the outside lane with my foot fused to the gear pedal.

I now had a hundred miles of freeway where I wouldn't need to change gear, just keep going at a steady 90 mph. That wasn't a problem. I even dialled up the country and western again. Getting on and off slip roads in Albuquerque would be tricky, as would starting at stop lights. I'd be OK as long as I didn't have to stop on an uphill slope. If that happened I'd probably burn the clutch out as I'd have to slip it so much to get moving.

Reader, I made it. I checked into the delightful Hotel Andaluz built by Conrad Hilton in the 1940s. I was in the Zsa Zsa Gabor Room. She, you will remember, was married to Conrad, among others. I called Adrian at Eagle Rider in El Paso and he was going to arrange help from the local Harley dudes.

Scenery on the ride from El Paso had been classic American. Fluffy clouds, distant mountains, scrub bush, no trees, occasional giant cattle feedlots by the road smelling worse than a Bombay slum, sunny, 90s but dry. Strange road signs: "High Acting Deer". Could I expect a stag to prance onto the road impersonating Freddy Mercury? "Gusty Winds May Exist". Really? Who was Gusty Winds? Was he a legendary Texan R & B singer? Well, I never saw Gusty, nor a high-acting deer but maybe next time.

Grudgingly I had to admit that when it wasn't breaking down, the Harley was almost cute. But that is all it was. As a motorbike it was a disaster. Alongside Beemers, Triumphs, and Ducatis it was like an obese St Bernard trying to run with a pack of foxhounds. It couldn't corner and it had modest acceleration considering the titanic size of its engine, but for just cruisin' along straight American roads, gargle gargle, it worked. The Dr Feelgood of the biking world. The engine was a magnificent thing to look at but so was the Brooklyn Bridge. It belonged in a museum.

Daisy's swinging gear pedal had been fixed. Yes, Daisy. She had of course acquired a name. Naming the Electra-Glide was a challenge as it was about as feminine as Rudi Guiliani, but bikes need a female name. As I was pissed off at her for breaking down so soon, I had decided to give her a really feminine name just to annoy her. She'd probably have liked to have a good ol' boy name like Bobby-Jo or Big Sal. Sorry, babes, from now on you're Daisy. I was tempted by Daisy-Mae but thought that might be a step too far. That'll teach you to be so flighty with your gear pedal.

Adrian had called Thunderbird Harley of Albuquerque and the next morning a bearded Visigoth turned up at my hotel, winched Daisy onto his trailer and the three of us took off for Thunderbird Harley on the outskirts of town. Thunderbird was a Harley Vatican, a place of worship in which a hundred giant bikes were being fondled by wizened men with purple tattoos and skins like sun-dried tomatoes, and their wobbly women. Our mechanic, who had a nameplate pinned to his chest identifying him as "Tigger", had taken one look at the offending gear pedal. "Ah, that's easy, buddy. The whoopsit's fallen off". I think that's what he called it. Soon we had a brand new whoopsit and were back on the New Mexican road. I almost said that whoopsits never fell off Beemers, but felt Tigger would not appreciate that.

I met up with my buddies who had been driving from Florida in Santa Fe. They were led by an old friend, Tarik Wildman. Despite his name, Tarik was about as Arab as George Bush. His macho-loving American-in-Spain father had been an admirer of the Berber conquerors who had crossed from Morocco to conquer Andalusia in the 8th century. Their general had been Tarik bin Ziyad who gave his name to Gibraltar, aka Jebel-al-Tarik, or Mount Tarik, and later to Mr Wildman's son, my friend.

Tarik was driving a beautiful dark-blue 1962 Alfa Romeo Giulietta Spyder, a car as stylish as Audrey Hepburn. I tried to keep up with him, but he hated dropping below 100 mph and scorched round the bends with his tyres smoking, while I lumbered along behind, wallowed round the bends and was quite unable to keep up.

Bends on Daisy were not like bends on a Beemer. With a Beemer you only needed to think about initiating a bend and your bike would be banking into it. Daisy on the other hand needed a lot of coaxing to get her to bank. In addition to throwing my weight to one side I had to lift on the outside handlebar as if it were a sack of potatoes to try to haul the old girl over because if I didn't she'd be going straight on and there was a nasty drop ahead. And if I hauled her over too far, the running board would ground and send sparks everywhere.

It was hard work but after a bit I found I was enjoying learning this new biking skill. I felt like a waltz champion being introduced to line dancing. A couple of hours after leaving Santa Fe, Daisy and I lumbered into Taos, the mother of all New Mexican towns, with its Spanish architecture and large Native American population. Just out of town was the biggest Indian pueblo in existence, four hundred adobe living units piled together, and still inhabited by red men and women despite everything the colonists had done to them…

We had arrived in Taos as the sun was setting and parked ourselves in the graceful old plaza. A cop materialised from nowhere and marched, hand on holster, over to Tarik's Alfa. What now? He engaged Tarik in serious conversation. I kept my distance on Daisy as I didn't want to be arrested as Tarik's accomplice. He had already picked up two tickets that day for speeding. He was probably wanted in at least two states by now. Eventually, the cop left, leaving Tarik at liberty.

"What's wrong?" I asked.

"He wanted to give me a warning. About thieves. See that guy by the 4 x 4 over there with a hiker's backpack? The cop says he's no hiker. He's a leading Taos car-thief."

Sure enough the "hiker" was standing by his backpack and watching us intently while pretending not to. "And that dear old Mexican couple sitting under the tree in the middle of the plaza? Professional thieves."

You did have to like a town where the police came up to newcomers and introduced them to the people who were later going to steal their cars.

Our route was something of a mystery. Tarik had proclaimed this a "democratic rally". Tarik's idea of democracy was to produce a map in the hotel bar at one in the morning and, speaking very fast in the manner of a conjuror, announce a route which bore no relationship to anything we had discussed before. Alternative suggestions were dismissed: "road closed", "went there in 1983", "well, if you like boring scenery". The American Southwest was largely new territory for me, so I didn't care where we went.

Someone had told Tarik that Telluride was pretty so off we headed from Taos. So much for the desert. Telluride was an old silver mining town which, like Aspen, had re-invented itself as a fashionable ski resort. Two problems. Getting there involved an eight-hour drive and, second, I only had desert clothes and the ski season was only just ending. As Daisy climbed laboriously out of the desert the road got narrower and the temperature lower. Lacking a sweater, I stopped and put on two extra T-shirts and my raingear; it wasn't raining but I hoped this would keep some of the chill out.

Daisy was doing her best, poor thing, but she was not made for sharp mountain bends on crumbly roads. She was like a horse on roller-skates. I was hauling away like a sack-lifter on the handlebars to try to get her to bank into the corners because if she didn't bank we'd be over the cliff ahead, and then halfway round the bend we'd hit what the French like to call *chaussée deformée* and Daisy would bounce around all over the lot.

I stopped and put on a second shirt and another T-shirt. I now had seven layers on so I looked like the Michelin man, but that did not stop the cold from entering my soul. Daisy had a thermometer. It read 25 Fahrenheit, or -3 Centigrade. I could no longer hear the mighty Harley radio as my chattering teeth drowned out the noise. What, I wondered, were the symptoms of hypothermia? Delirium? Well, now you mention it...

We were finally at the highest pass, 10,000 feet. Last time I had biked through a pass this high was on the Motorcycle Diaries trip when Spike and I had crossed the barren Andes between Santiago and Mendoza, bleakest of all mountain places, but that was nothing like as cold as this.

My hands had gone numb long before. I wondered if I'd find a black frost-bitten finger left behind in my BMW summer mesh gloves when I took them off. Four feet of snow lay by the road but, thank heavens, not on it.

Finally Daisy and I reached Telluride. Our team had grown. More people had arrived on a variety of strange vehicles. We met up in one of the few places still open, as Telluride had closed a week before when the season had ended, a bar which could have been in *Gunfight at the O.K. Corral*.

I was in search of new experiences, so I abandoned my friends drinking in the bar and went next door to the Pot Shop to which the waiter had directed me and Rebecca and Jasmine, told me how good the locally grown weed was. We were in Colorado. It was legal. The shop was like an old-fashioned pharmacy with bottles of weed and exotic contraptions for getting the best out of it. I invited Rebecca and Jasmine to join us on our road trip. Sadly they couldn't. Their boss, the owner, was in Mexico "in recovery" and they couldn't leave the shop.

I bought ten Jasmine-recommended Telluride Specials for $100; they came in a cylindrical drum, just like cigarettes in the 1950s. I took the lid off and sniffed. I reeled backwards. Wow. I am no pot connoisseur, but this smelled earthy and dangerous, quite unlike the sweet, refined scent of Marrakech.

I returned to the bar. A friend of Tarik's named Marcella, who had apparently been Miss Colombia in days long gone by and had joined our group, had left to make phone calls, but came back into the bar. As she entered she picked up the scent of my Telluride Specials from twenty feet away and squealed with delight, "Ah, baby, I am back home. I LOVE that smell."

We smoked a couple. They tasted harsh and raw. I used to like weed because it was mellow. Mellow this was not.

Next morning I tried to buy a sweater in Telluride. Impossible. All the ski wear shops were packed with sweaters, but they had closed for "post-season inventory". Tarik advised me to wrap myself in copies of the *Telluride News* under my shirt as a cold-preventer. I remembered from George Orwell's *Down and Out in Paris and London* that that was what tramps did to keep warm. No, I would brave it and freeze rather than wrapping myself up like fish and chips. On the way back through the pass and on down I stopped a few times to take photographs of the dramatic scenery. When I drove off from one stop I heard a little tinkle and assumed it was just another whoopsit detaching itself from Daisy. I didn't stop to investigate; there was plenty of Daisy still left.

I stopped for gas half an hour beyond the pass. Tarik and Marcella arrived in his little Alfa. I went to put the gas in and reached for the key to unlock the tank. With Harleys you didn't have to insert the key in the ignition when you are driving, they acted as a fob, but you did have to insert them in the lid of the gas tank to open it. The key was not in the normal pocket. Soon I discovered it was not in any pocket at all. I had lost the key. The tinkle which I had ignored must have been the key falling off the bike having first been pulled out of my pocket along with my gloves. I resolved never to ignore a tinkle again.

I had enough gas for 40 miles and no way of opening the tank or locking the bike. Luckily Daisy did not need a key to start her. Tarik, the great mechanic, would have a solution. I asked him.

"Easy," he says. "We'll find a mechanic and get him to bore the lock out."

Eagle Rider would love that.

"But," he said, "even better, let's find the key."

We abandoned poor Marcella with the Navajo storekeeper and set off in the two-seater Alfa back up the mountain to find the key. Almost two hours later we were back at the gas station having crawled on hands and knees around everywhere I remembered stopping to take a photograph. No key.

This was serious. We were in the middle of the Wild West with a giant bike which would turn into scrap metal in 40 miles.

The law arrived in the shape of Rick, a US Marshal in a 4 x 4.

"Marshal, is there a Harley dealer in Cortes?" I asked. That was sixty down-hill miles away and we might just have been able to make it.

"No, sir. Nearest Harley dealer is Durango. That's 160 miles if you take a short cut through the mountains."

"Do you know a mechanic who might bore the lock out?" asked Tarik.

"Sir, you won't find anyone who'd take the legal risk of doing that unless you are the certified owner."

I was screwed. And I couldn't even dump the bike and get a lift with Tarik. The Alfa had two small seats and one was already full of Marcella.

"Erm. Know anyone who could pick the lock?" I asked the Marshal.

"Sir, I've owned Harleys. They are high-tech spec. Those locks are impossible to pick."

Well and truly screwed.

The missing key was a little cylinder with a small tongue on the side. The Marshal rooted around on his key chain.

"Waal, sir, this here is the key to mah gun safe. It ain't going to work, but…"

He showed us a small cylindrical key. He inserted it in the lid of the Harley gas tank, which sprang open immediately. Tarik has a photo of the expression on my face.

Three minutes later I had a full tank of gas and we were on our way. Tarik used sticky tape to prevent the gas tank lock from clicking closed and another bit to keep the tank lid down. I couldn't lock the bike now, but

Americans were honest people, weren't they? My opinion of US Marshals was sky-high and remains so to this day.

Our destination for the night was Monument Valley. Before that we would go through the Valley of the Gods. I had no idea what to expect. We had booked for the night in Goulding's, an old trading post in Monument Valley where John Wayne had stayed when he was making Stagecoach. The Grand Canyon to which we were headed the next night I had seen in a million photographs but what lay ahead in Monument Valley was unknown territory.

I have travelled to lots of exotic and wonderful places but never, with the possible exception of the Great Salt Desert in Bolivia, the Salar de Uyunyi, had I seen anything which has so left me gasping with amazement as the three hours from Natural Bridges, a giant stone bridge spanning a canyon the width of St James's Park, to Goulding's in Monument Valley.

When I edged Daisy up to the cliff which stood above the Valley of the Gods a thousand or more feet below us and looked over a flat valley bed of brown, yellow, and purple of wrinkled rocks, craggy spines, huge volcanic pustules, distant valley walls like weathered brown egg-cartons, I could only think Shock and Awe. Shock and Awe.

I got an even bigger shock when I realised that Daisy, a couch potato if ever there was one, was going to have to descend a thousand feet of hairpin bends to get to the floor of the valley and, just to make things worse for people not on a horse, that thousand feet was unmade gravel, a biker's worst enemy after snow, ice and sand. Riding obese Harleys downhill on gravel is a skill I had not acquired. We edged gingerly down the hill with Daisy skittering and skeetering like a drunk ever on the edge of losing her balance. Images of Daisy and me tumbling down the cliff together filled my mind.

We made it but fun, no.

The Valley of the Gods was surreal. It had a flat rocky floor with 300-foot sandstone pinnacles jutting up at random. The dirt road dipped and dived its way through the rock formations. But the Valley of the Gods was just the precursor to Monument Valley, an area of limitless boundaries, of flat, browny-green scrub as foreground to huge brown mesas, some flat-topped as if presenting UFO landing pads for Martians, and some as sharp and eroded as teeth, though in this case teeth that had long rotted in a god's mouth. Something about the Valley seemed familiar. And then it hit me with a bang. I knew this Valley. I had seen every inch of it in a thousand western movies.

Art and national spirit combine to define a country. Germany is defined by music, Holland by painting, France by philosophy, Italy by opera, Greece by tragedy, and England by poetry. America is defined by its movies. Perhaps the things of one's youth always seem better, but American movies in the middle of the last century had an appeal and a magic that captured the whole world for America. They were powerful movies that went straight to the soul: lonely High Noon heroes in Westerns, adorable Debbie Reynolds girls-next-door in musicals, tough Jimmy Cagney criminals in gangster films, and modest Jimmy Stewart and Spencer Tracy heroes in war movies. How different to American movies of today which have been affected by the infantilism which has seized America. Half the movies on show today are infantile science fiction, infantile fantasy about time travel, or infantile triumphalist military movies. Perhaps that goes with modern American politics. In the middle of the last century America was the man in the white hat whom the world admired; today it is the playground bully whom everyone fears but none respect.

Movies. Westerns. John Ford, some would say the greatest and most consistent of all American film directors, pioneered location, as opposed to back-lot-at-Paramount, shooting. Many of his Westerns, particularly the John Wayne ones, were shot in Monument Valley. *Rio Bravo*, *The Searcher*, *Shane*, *Gunfight at the O.K. Corral*, *Tombstone*, the movies that helped define American culture. I'd seen the films but seeing the reality was so different. I stopped the bike, took off my helmet, and for ten minutes sat low in the saddle taking in the view. If any of the other cars had come up, I would have said, "Howdy, Pardner…"

Daisy and I barrelled happily along into the setting sun, gravel left behind and feeling the ghosts of John Wayne and Jimmy Stewart, of Doc

Holliday and Wyatt Earp everywhere about us. It was a wonder of the world. And there was no-one else there apart from the ghosts.

From Monument Valley, we moved on the next day to the Grand Canyon. I found this less shock and awe because I had seen so many photographs that I knew what to expect, just as in India it was difficult for the Taj Mahal not to be a teensy bit disappointing, whereas the less-publicised Fatehpur Sikri next door blew your socks off.

There was one surprising thing about the Grand Canyon. Its size.

You had never seen anything so big. You could drop the Eiffel Tower, St Paul's and the Chrysler Building into it and they would disappear unseen at the bottom. The Canary Wharf complex? The Bilbao Guggenheim? Bye-bye ... lost in the depths. Until you saw it you had no idea how big it was.

I puttered round the Canyon rim on Daisy, stopping off at many of the frequent viewpoints to get off, gawp, and take photos. Impressive, of course, but no soul. Not like Valley of the Gods and Monument Valley.

We all met up at the Canyon Plaza Hotel some 10 miles away in the middle of one of those untidy American sprawls of Taco Bells, gas stations, and Travelodges. The weather had been beautiful since Telluride, clear, breezy and daytime temperatures in the seventies. I checked the weather forecast on my iPhone for the next day. Dear God. A giant storm front was about to cross America. In the morning the temperature would be between 15 and 40 Fahrenheit (that's a low of minus 5 for centigraders), and there would be heavy snow with accumulations of four to five inches. Damn. Daisy and I didn't do snow. It would be literal death for us to try.

I checked Flagstaff, 60 miles to the south and on our proposed route to see if that was better. It was worse. Our problem was that where we were at the Grand Canyon was at 6,000 feet and Flagstaff was even higher.

It was 7.00 pm and I had already biked 250 miles that day from Monument Valley. I had checked our route for the next day, we were heading for Las Vegas. That was at a much lower altitude but a long way away. According to Google, the town of Kingman was on the way to Las Vegas and 3,000 feet lower than where I now was: low enough to be below the snow line. Rain I could handle, snow I could not. If I were able to make that additional 120 miles to Kingman, Arizona, before the snow came in, it would be cold and rainy, but I would not have to face snow in the morning.

I needed to get out of town before the storm hit. The last thing I wanted to do after a long day's biking was hours more biking through a dark and stormy night, but I had no option. I checked out, said goodbye to the car-drivers who would not be life-threatened by the snow, put on eight layers of clothing, and headed Daisy out into the sunset. The man at the check-out desk had told me to watch out for elks. Herds of forty or more roamed around at night and elk-smash was a common occurrence in this part of Arizona. Memories of roo-dodging in Australia.

Soon it was dark. The wind was whipping itself up as the storm front drew closer. Daisy and I were being tossed about like a raft in the rapids. I was hoping I could reach Kingman before the snow started. Daisy was a surprisingly good night-time driver. Her powerful headlights were strong enough to spot an elk at four hundred yards. I turned up the volume on her mighty radio to ward off the loneliness of the dark road, deserted but for thundering sixteen-wheel rigs every ten minutes or so. I got a Public Radio station. It was broadcasting a BBC World Service programme about the Prophet Elijah, the hard man of the Old Testament prophets. Fire and brimstone, appropriate companions for a night like this. As we passed Flagstaff and turned west for Kingman on the interstate, Elijah was taken up into heaven in a chariot of fire at precisely the moment that the first flash of lightning lit up the western sky.

As Kingman drew nearer a plot began to form in my mind. Why spend the night in a desolate truck-stop town in a Travelodge? Two and a half hours beyond Kingman was Las Vegas. I had eaten nothing all day. I longed for a good meal and a glass or two of wine. There would be nothing open at 10.30 pm in Kingman apart from a gas station with microwaved pizza. Could I make Vegas without falling asleep? It was another 100 miles. Would the storm hit on the way? If it did at least I would be at a low enough altitude to avoid snow and would only have to battle wind and rain. And if I made Vegas, where I had never been, I could have a rest day while the others caught up.

I stopped for gas in Kingman, a sad and charmless sprawl of gas stations and fast-food joints, its only reason for existence being that this was where the road split, with Route 40 continuing on West to Los Angeles and Route 93 forking off to the north and Vegas. It was as depressing as only truck-stop towns can be. I was not going to spend the night in the Days Inn in Kingman. Decision taken.

It was now close to midnight. I filled the gas tank and Daisy and I set off down the Interstate bound for Vegas. By now, the adrenalin had started to pump as it often did on long bike journeys through difficult terrain. I was excited. We were bombing along the interstate with Daisy's huge 1700cc engine ticking lazily over at 3,000 revs and 90 mph. We wobbled as we were caught in the wind-wake of the huge trucks, lit up, as all American trucks are, like ocean liners, and then we would be past. On the radio, the prophet Elijah had given way to country and western. Dolly Parton belting out "I Will Always Love You" was the perfect companion for the stormy night.

I could see the storm approaching. The lights of Vegas, 50 miles to the northwest, reflected in the night sky. Against that reflection I could see big black anvil-shaped clouds. The wind was getting stronger. Keeping Daisy on course demanded full concentration. We had to slow to 70 mph; the wind was too strong to go faster. And then the storm hit. Rain lashed down, thunder cracked, the wind strengthened. Las Vegas 10 miles away now looked like a lit-up Gomorrah suffering biblical destruction from the flashing lightning and rolling thunder.

Then, suddenly, the storm stopped. We seemed to have come out the other side, the road dried and the wind calmed.

Half an hour later I opened the door on a spotless room in a posh Vegas hotel. It was 2.00 am. I had a shower and ordered a Thai green chicken curry and a bottle of Alsace from room service. I deserved it. What a day it had been, starting in Monument Valley, taking in a first view of the Grand Canyon, followed by a night-time ride through a building storm while accompanied by the Prophet Elijah and Dolly Parton.

I now had the wonderful prospect of a rest day while the others caught up. I wasn't tempted to gamble. Being on the bike was gamble enough.

I had a perfect day sitting by the pool in brilliant sunshine snoozing while pretending to read. That evening the car drivers caught up. I had a smug little glow of pleasure on hearing their tales of skidding around fighting the snow. We took ourselves out to a happy dinner in Andiamo, a highly recommended Italian steak house, and talked about Death Valley, the next day's destination.

Next morning we motored out of Vegas in convoy bound on the interstate for Beatty, three hours to the north. Beatty was the "gateway" to Death Valley where we would take a left, cross a mountain or two, and be in The Valley.

I don't know what it is about Death Valley that is so exciting. There are deserts far bigger in Africa and Arabia, but there is something unique about Death Valley, a place that claims to be both the lowest place on earth and the hottest. Neither of these often-repeated claims is remotely true, but its competitors are not called Death Valley. Other bigger deserts into which I have dipped a toe in Africa or Arabia are exceptionally hot and sandy places, but you always felt that things lived there, however hard to find. When I went through Death Valley I felt that nothing lived there, or could live there. In the hours I spent traversing it, the only creatures I saw were a crow and a dead rattlesnake.

On the way we stopped off for lunch at a whorehouse. This was at Roy's, a place that sold gas, had a diner and a shooting range, and was, said the T-shirts and mugs on sale in the diner, the locale for frequent visits from aliens, and UFOs, mainly from Mars. Perhaps it was the low modern building next to the diner which had a sign with letters two feet high proclaiming it to be "Roy's Brothel" that attracted the Martians in the same way that it attracted the truckers, many of whose articulated rigs were parked outside. The brothel had a neon sign advertising the wholesomeness of the girls within. Brothels are legal in Nevada.

After a disgusting lunch that involved "pulled pork", an appropriate menu choice for a brothel diner, we decided to move on to Death Valley.

While the others shot on ahead, I and my friend Robert, in a Mustang, lingered behind to admire views and take pictures as we crossed the hills and descended into Death Valley. We came to a T junction. Thanks to satnav we had not troubled to get paper maps. But thanks to no phone signal our satnavs didn't work, and we had no idea as to whether to go right or left. I sort of remembered from Google Maps that Stovepipe Wells Trading Station, our destination, was only 8 miles from the T junction and to the right.

Half an hour later we were in a place where the desolation was absolute. The only vegetation was little bunches of stubborn tumbleweed; the earth was baked a chemical-looking white and on our right were hills of evil black basalt boulders. We stopped to confer. There had been no turning. How could we have missed it? And I was very low on gas. No stations here. We flagged down a 4 x 4 going in the opposite direction.

"Stovepipe Wells?" I asked.

"Hmmm, dunno." This was their first time in the Valley.

"Wait," the passenger said, "I think we saw a sign some way back. Said Stovepipe Wells 40 miles. That way."

He pointed the way we had come. It couldn't be. We should have turned left at the T junction. Half an hour and Robert and Miles were already Lost in Death Valley.

The 4 x 4 people scrabbled around and found a tourist map they had picked up on entry. It was a rudimentary map but there was Stovepipe Wells, a long way away from where we now thought we were. They gave us the map, wished us luck and drove off.

Another triumph for my unerring sense of direction. Robert and I turned around, creeping along at 45 mph so I could preserve petrol. Finally, as the sun was lowering, we reached Stovepipe Wells, with a motel, a dining room, a bar, a general store and, yee-hah, a gas pump. Our friends had been there for hours and were about to send out a search party.

After a couple of beers we all set off to the nearby Mesquite Dunes to watch the sun set. We marvelled and drank beer as the sun slid behind the jagged mountains to the west, the desert went from white, to yellow, to gold and finally purple, brilliant stars began to pin-point the sky, and the temperature plummeted, while a rising wind blew tumbleweed across the road.

Next day was the final road trip day. After that it would just be a boring run into Los Angeles. We set out for 29 Palms, the legendary entry point for the Joshua Tree National Park, almost 300 miles of winding desert road to the South. I had gone ahead as I wanted to leave early on the bike before it got too hot. By 10.30 am Daisy's thermometer was saying it was already 100 degrees.

You might expect the desert would be monotonous. The reverse was true. The variety of Death Valley was amazing. You drove along the flat valley floor, a valley maybe 5 to 10 miles wide and on either side were high mountains. It was those that created the rain shadow. The highest peaks on the west, California side, had snow on them. The colour and texture of the valley floor changed constantly from gravelly wasteland to pure yellow sand to stripes of minerally earth. The formations in the foot-hills of the mountains were likewise all different. Evil-looking egg-box hills looking like cancerous growths fringed the harsh rock mountain behind; huge plates of striated rock jutting up at an angle from the sand; threatening black hills that should be in Kazakhstan; and then Badwater, a place where the earth was bleached white and there were pools of black water with yellow and purple oily chemical streaks. It was the most chemical place I had ever been.

Despite the harshness of the terrain, it was not bleak. This was a place of wildness that had always captured men's (it's always men) imagination, but it was not an evil place. I cursed that I had missed Zabriskie Point by 8 miles. I boppled along happily on Daisy, radio turned off, and full of new wonder at every turn in the road, stopping to take photographs every few minutes. I stopped to photograph a crow eating a dead rattlesnake, but it flew off before I could click the button.

Arriving at the 29 Palms Inn was like coming home. I had been there twice before. We had had family experiences at the 29 Palms Inn and in the neighbouring Joshua Tree National Park. They are too complicated to go into here, but it is a place both of magic and of tears for me. The Inn is famous, a 1970s-style psychedelic jumble of cabanas painted orange and purple with an equally psychedelic main block for eating and drinking. Being there you felt the 1960s had never ended. If you want to write a book check into 29 Palms for a month or two.

The next day we picnicked in the Joshua Tree National Park. There is nowhere like it. The road snaked between boulders bigger than houses, with flanks like elephants. Everywhere were the spiky little Joshua trees, trunks like a baobab with stunted branches adorned with spiky leaves. The air was vodka clear. Los Angeles friends had told me that they used to camp out here at night. On a night with a new moon and a sky lit up with stars there would be magic all around.

A day later, sipping a mojito in Santa Monica with Daisy returned to Los Angeles Eagle Rider, I had to admit that a Harley may not be much of a bike, but for cruisin' through the deserts, it rocked.

8

ICELAND WITH BJÖRK

O Iceland.

I seldom read up about places before I go there, but I often look at *Lonely Planet* and maybe some online guides after I have arrived. I do this for background reading about the history and terrain of where I'm going rather than a method of route planning. Iceland, up to my arrival an unknown land for me, was no exception. However, 24 hours after flying into Reykjavík and doing some reading up, I was ready to have Iceland as my special subject on Mastermind. Puffins, reindeer, sagas, volcanoes, geysers, glaciers, calving icebergs, giant waterfalls, trolls, elves, and hobgoblins, not to mention steam appearing from places it had no right to be.

At 9.00 am I had caught a taxi from my hotel and presented myself to Thor of Biking Viking. "Godan daginn," said he. "Bless you," said I, and he handed over the keys to a BMW F800GS Adventure.

Thor had given me an itinerary which he had loaded onto the satnav which did its best to avoid things like main roads and took me through Iceland's hidden back parts. My pathetic desire to appear macho meant that I never liked to admit to anyone, least of all other bikeys, that I was now reaching the age when I quite liked driving along a nice smooth road with a tarmac or concrete surface. Bumpety-dump is fine if you are a 28-year-old, but with age comes not only wisdom but a falling of the testosterone

"Steam hissed from the green earth" (p 160)

No Northern Lights with Nikki (p 161)

Bjork climbs away from Djupivogur (p 168)

Raise your hand if you want to puke (p 190)

The Haka Twins (p 190)

Companions of the Nullarbor (p 208)

Ozzie Leapfrog (p 208)

Priscilla, Lost in the Outback (p 209)

The Zen of the longest straight road (p 215)

The Pacific, 5946 kms, from the Indian Ocean (p 221)

Hello Baja (p 230)

Haz and I plot our
route (p 245)

Farewell, companions
of the road (p 246)

levels that make men so eager to do uncomfortable things like ride half-ton motorbikes down goat tracks.

Iceland had F "roads". This showed that Icelanders had a sense of humour. "F" they may have been, but roads they were not, unless you were a sheep wanting to find untroubled pasture. I'd seen better roads in Patagonia. These ones were like egg cartons made from ossified lava. Let's not dwell on them. Most of my first day's biking had been sublime. Iceland, a tiny country the size of Scotland (but with better-humoured people) had enough scenery for an entire continent.

I don't want to go all geological on you, but Iceland is sitting firmly, although that may be the wrong adverb, on the collision point between the European and the American tectonic plates. This means it can't stop erupting and generally throwing itself about in a most unseemly manner for such a young country (only inhabited a thousand or so years ago by people called Fork-beard).

The result of this geological turmoil was that Iceland was a lava scab sitting on top of a subterranean mound of molten magma. The subterranean stuff couldn't help itself. It popped up everywhere. Geysers. I saw the original geyser (pronounced Gay-Sir) after which all others are named on the first day. Every fifteen minutes or so it puffed a giant belch of muddy steam-water into the atmosphere. Everywhere steam hissed from the green earth. And it was a strange green. Not an Irish or an English gentle green but a violent in-your-face green, usually streaked with brown lesions of earth from down below. What was that colour? Viridian?

Every extreme film ever made, *Batman Returns*, *Lara Croft: Tomb Raider*, parts of Tolkien, *Letters from Iwo Jima*, *Land Ho*, *Interstellar*, and many more but you can find them in Wikipedia as easily as I, was shot in Iceland.

It is not only films; it is stories. I downloaded some of the Icelandic sagas on my iPad. They are up there with Homer. The Icelanders seemed literally superhuman. No wonder Gods and men mingled so easily. They crossed oceans in boats more fit for the Serpentine. They cleaved heads with their broad axes. They ravished everyone from their aunts to their nieces and the king's daughters in between. They spoke with Thor and Odin and what names they had. Not just Fork-beard, but Fair-hair, and Red-Nose, and Crook-Back, and Strong-Arm. These more-than-humans crossed a thousand miles of erupting sea in something not much bigger than a canoe, built houses from the raw earth, grew crops in weather where crops could never grow, brought along sheep and cows and dogs and hens in their canoes and went from being Norwegians to being a new race, Icelanders.

My first evening on the road had been perfect. I was staying at the Hotel Ranga, a hotel by the Ranga river, famous among fishermen everywhere, out of which wild Icelandic salmon, the finest in the world, more or less hurled themselves onto your hook.

Before dinner, I had fallen to talking with Nikki, the Hungarian bartender. She had made me an Icelandic sour, which caused a scent of citrus and volcano to drift round the bar. Then she made me another one, possibly two, while we told each other adventure stories. The hotel manager came by to tell me and other guests that later that night there would be a good chance of seeing a stunning showing of the Northern Lights. The guests and I, having read up in the guidebook that it was too early in the year for that, were dubious. He smiled. "Trust me," said he. "Starting at 11.30 pm, it will be worth watching."

After dinner there was time to kill before the great viewing so what could be more natural than to drift back to the bar and re-engage Nikki in telling stories. She introduced me to something called an Icelandic Goodnight, a most aptly named cocktail. I think this involved juniper vodka. By the time I had dealt with a couple of those it was almost midnight, so I bid Nikki a wonderful night and slipped out to watch the show. All I could see were a few green wisps in the sky. "Talk about anti-climax," thought I after ten minutes peering at this vague greenish glow so I slipped back to the bar and one last Icelandic Goodnight which Nikki thoughtfully pressed on me.

The next day when I arrived in Höfn, a friend in London, Gordon, had sent me an email saying, "You lucky bastard, seeing this." It was a link to a BBC news story. The heading read: "Spectacular Northern Lights

Filmed over Iceland". There was a video of this amazing showing. Talk about spectacular. I watched the video on my iPad. It was a cross between Pearl Harbour and the opening ceremony of the Beijing Olympics. This had actually been filmed from … the Ranga Hotel where I had been. But the film had been taken at 11.30 pm while I was engaging Nikki in earnest conversation. By the time I had stumbled out at midnight only a few green wisps remained. I had missed it. But I did watch the BBC's video twice on my iPad, so I tell my grandchildren that Grandpa saw the most spectacular showing ever of the Northern Lights.

Constant distractions, that was the trouble with Iceland. It was going to feel strange when I was back in England not to see belches of sulphurous steam popping up out of the earth. (To be fair you do see that in New York; never quite understood what's going on under the Manhattan pavement, troll activity, possibly?)

Not to mention the Icelandic dangers. The online guides had been scaring me silly. This place, said they, was more dangerous than the Congo or even Australia. Here were some of the things to watch out for if you ventured out into the country, on a motorbike for example:

- Fording a river in a vehicle, as you often had to do owing to the lack of bridges on country roads, was highly dangerous. You should get out of your car and wade across first. If you drowned, don't attempt to drive across. Even in summer, rivers could swallow you up owing to the dreaded glacial run-off.
- If you did get across the river, watch out. "High winds can create vicious sandstorms." Sandstorms? Iceland?
- Don't cross dangerous quicksands at the end of glaciers.
- Avoid thin crusts of lighter-coloured soil around steaming fissures and mudpots.

I certainly would. I have never been a fan of steaming fissures, let alone mudpots. The guides had some other interesting stuff to tell me. Iceland has, apparently, the world's most welcoming people. I'd always thought that the world's most welcoming people were the young ladies to be found in the bars of Lagos, but apparently they take a back seat to Icelanders. And it is the world's most peaceful country. Whoever said that had clearly not read the Icelandic sagas and heard what Fork-beard and Broad-axe got up to. It has the most writers per capita of any country, one of whom, Halldór Laxness, won the Nobel Prize for Literature in 1955. Not bad when you consider about the same number of people live in Croydon as Iceland.

What else? It is the country where women are most equal. Everyone knows that Iceland was the first country to elect a woman President, Vigdís Finnbogadóttir in 1980, just a year after Maggie Thatcherdóttir became Prime Minister in the UK, and, more importantly in 2009, Jóhanna Sigurðardóttir, who had started her career pushing trolleys up airline aisles, became Iceland's first female Prime Minister, and also the world's first openly lesbian head of government.

For once naming my bike was going to be easy. When I had arrived at Biking Viking, "Hyperballad" had been playing on their music system. Bingo! Iceland's best-known and wildest singer was going to take me on my trip.

Hello, Björk.

Discussing gender these days can be more dangerous than larking around on the edge of a mudpot, but I had been doing some thinking in advance about Icelandic women. Curiosity about them was one of the reasons I had made the trip. Like Björk, Icelandic women seemed to be super-achievers and up for anything. Just as you can't bike around Los Angeles without encountering gangs of leather-clad Hell's Angels, I wondered if I would be pursued on this trip by their Icelandic equivalent, posses of blonde women clad only in lipstick and leather. Possibly riding Harleys. A man can dream.

Well, after four days in Iceland I was now something of an expert on Icelandic women. Reader, or should I say, male reader, I hate the dream to die, but so far I had remained totally unpropositioned by women of any sexual preference. There was worse. Icelandic women may be Scandinavian, but they are not blonde. All I had seen were dark-haired brunettes. I finally made a breakthrough in my hotel in Höfn. I spotted a blonde at the bar. I'd never seen anyone blonder. Lilja was her name, a name as pretty as she. I bought her a drink; it was the least I could do.

"Lilja," I said, "I'm so happy to meet you. You are my first Icelandic blonde."

"Miles, I have news for you," she pointed at her eyebrows which were darker than a badger's brush. "But it's fun to be blonde for a bit."

The day after not seeing the Northern Lights, Björk and I had biked happily along the south coast. It was as if a Hollywood locations scout had got together a portfolio of outlandish places for *Lord of the Rings* on acid. On the right had been the sea not looking at all friendly as it crashed giant waves against jagged black rocks while on the left were green escarpments, that viridian colour again, rising up out of the sheep-lands like a cross between the Dolomites and the Grand Canyon. Through fissures in the rocks at the top, waterfall after waterfall cascaded down, often dropping hundreds of feet before striking rock which jutted out below.

Then there were the volcanoes. In the distance long lines of volcanoes marched across the horizon like demented fretwork. Not all were in the distance. Close to the road on the left came up an evil, smoking giant. I looked at the map. The name seemed familiar. I checked it out on my phone. This was Eyjafjallajökull. I don't expect you to pronounce it, but you certainly remember it. This was the thing that five years earlier had gone berserk and blown such a large chunk of Iceland into the air that flights throughout Europe and the North Atlantic had been cancelled for a week because of the continent-sized ash cloud. And don't think it's done yet. It was sitting there sulking just waiting for an opportunity to throw another square mile or two of molten Iceland up into the ionosphere. A smell of sulphur pervaded the air. People had built guest houses and visitor centres near its base. Well, no-one had ever accused the Icelanders of being sane. I thought about turning left down one of the tracks leading to the base of the smoking giant and decided straight ahead was better.

Between the crashing angry sea on the right and smoking evil volcanoes on the left was a strip of gentle pasture, maybe a mile wide that could have been transplanted from County Limerick. Sheep, a few cows, hay-bales and the occasional red-roofed farmhouse (God help anyone who did not put a red roof on their farmhouse in Iceland; they'd have Fork-beard from the council round the next day).

Then everything changed. Gentle pasture disappeared to be replaced by something more bleak and desolate than any desert: the black-lava flats of Mýrdalssandur. They were not actually flat but a bumpy jumble of boulders and scree and they were not black either, more a dark grey-greeny colour as if they were covered in a toxic mould. Nothing grew. I stopped for some water. No bird sang. Nothing could have lived there. I also noted that for the first time in Iceland I had lost my phone signal. Not a good place to break down. You would not want to spend a night alone on Mýrdalssandur. It was scary enough by day, but God knows what stalked its flats at night.

Iceland being Iceland was not finished with me yet. The strip between road and sea narrowed. On the left, through the gaps in the mountains was glacier, glacier, and more glacier. This was the southern edge of Vatnajokull, the biggest ice cap in the world outside the polar regions. It was, I had read, twice the size of Luxembourg and probably a lot more fun. Seeing these vast rivers of ice trapped and frozen between the mountains was a humbling sight.

Then, we cruised round a bend and there wham-bam was Jökulsárlón. I may have seen more dramatic and beautiful sights in nature, but I don't recall them. A giant lagoon a-jostle with icebergs. These were not towering sink-the-Titanic Arctic icebergs but huge ice-floes and building-size chunks of ice that had calved from the glacier and were waiting in the lagoon before floating out to sea. The lagoon was a bluey blue while the icebergs seemed irradiated with a shimmering darker blue. Some were streaked with multi-coloured volcanic ash that had been frozen into them centuries ago. For all I know Henry VIII was having Anne Boleyn beheaded when the snow had fallen high up on Vatnajokull to be pressed into ice and covered by subsequent centuries of snow as it inched its way down as glacier towards the sea.

I biked Björk up as close as I dared to the edge of the lagoon, where

I dismounted, propped her on her side stand on top of a chunk of lava, took off my helmet, and stood there open-mouthed in wonder. I took photographs but as so often with scenery the photos can't quite capture the reality. Monument Valley had been like that. After half an hour watching the tumbling icebergs I reluctantly slid my helmet back on, skidded Björk through the boulders, and went on our way to Höfn, a tidy little port and the "lobster capital" of Iceland. Here I checked into a modern hotel and, um, ate a lobster. No Icelandic sours there.

The next day turned out to be a long one. A day of two halves. Morning had been skirting the coastline to the little harbour of Djúpivogur and then in the afternoon up into the mountains. "You're OK on gravel?" Biking Viking had asked when they handed me the keys to Björk. "You'll find some on the way up to Hallormsstaður. Can be a bit tricky if you're not used to it." That sounded ominous. But not as ominous as when I checked the weather forecast over breakfast. There was a gale warning, and when Icelanders talk about gales, they mean gales. You have probably heard enough about Miles biking in gales but they do seem to follow me around.

The wind when I had set off from Höfn may not have been as strong as it had been in Japan, but I soon found myself a very frightened man. Björk was a lighter bike than Beemer-san had been and had a higher centre of gravity. The height and lack of heft created less momentum and less inherent stability.

The road to Djúpivogur skirted the sea with black mountains to the left and spray from the crashing waves being blown onto the road from the right. This was the emptiest part of Iceland. The population of East Iceland, an area the size of a couple of English counties, was 11,000, no more than that of a small town. There were long stretches with no houses or signs of humanity. Traffic on a Saturday was as scarce as sunshine. The scenery was dramatic, but I was paying no attention to scenery, preferring to pay attention to staying alive. In a car with its four wheels you are planted on the road. If you stop, you are safe and stable as a table. On a bike you are planted on nothing, two wheels with no inherent stability kept upright only by moving forward with enough speed to create a gyroscopic effect which disappears when you stop moving. I expect you remember when you were four spinning a little wooden top and watching it wobble as it slowed...

Most of the time the gale was coming in over the sea from the northeast and I was having to tilt the bike at an angle of what seemed like 15 degrees or more into the wind to stay upright. But then we would pass a valley between the mountains on the left and the wind would suddenly whack us from the other side and I would have to reverse tilt or be blown flat. I was crouched low over the tank in an attempt to reduce my wind shadow. I stayed in the centre of the road where it was flat as the last thing I needed was camber to add to the tilt but when the occasional car came, I had to edge over to the side of the road to let it pass and pray I could crab my way back up the slippery incline to the level centre. I was scared. I was travelling at about 100 kph in the belief that the extra momentum from the speed would help keep me upright. Slowing would have been dangerous while stopping and waiting for the storm to blow itself out was not an option. I had no reason to believe that the wind would diminish any time soon. I did know from the forecast however that if I could reach Djúpivogur that the wind there was forecast to be less strong.

I was also frozen. God, I was cold. I had put on four layers of T-shirt, shirt and sweater but none of them were the kind of thing you would take skiing. It was August, it had no right to be cold. My frayed old Belstaff leather jacket, companion on so many bike trips, was no parka. The centre of my chest was literally aching with cold. Thank God for heated handlebars.

Somehow, I limped into Djúpivogur with back aching, feet like blocks of ice and hands like claws from clutching the grips. I found a cafe. I warmed my hands on a coffee mug. The shivering began to subside. I had two bowls of deliciously warm mushroom soup and felt it make a growing point of heat in my stomach. I stayed in the cafe for an hour and a half watching the little fishing boats rocking at anchor in the harbour. Circulation returned. Things got better. The wind was dropping from gale to strong breeze, a nuisance but no more than that.

Björk and I struck inland to the highlands. Iceland was more or less devoid of trees. Bushes yes, trees no. It had one natural forest, and that was where we were headed.

Soon, the road petered out and we found ourselves on the threatened gravel. Hard-pack gravel is easy to handle, but quite a lot of this was soft-pack muddy gravel where streams and springs had run across the road. Mud and bikers are sworn enemies, but the wind had dropped and that was so wonderful that I didn't give a toss what was happening between the tyres and the road. A bit of skidding here, a bit of almost over the edge of the cliff there, but I was so glad to be sitting upright I felt I could handle anything the road threw at us. I was soon frozen again but I was frozen and cheerful now as I knew I would soon arrive at my hotel, so much better than being frozen and frightened in the morning.

The Hótel Hallormsstaður was a jolly place set in the midst of Iceland's only forest just above a lake which could equally easily have passed for a loch. How glad I was to arrive. To stand under a hot shower for ten minutes while blood began to flow to frozen parts. People touring in cars can never know the joy a biker feels when he has had a day like we had just had, and he has checked into his room, had a long hot shower, and then crawled under the duvet to doze and dream and feel warm while the afternoon sun filters into the room. In the evening, dry, warm, and happy I strolled down for the celebrated Hallormsstaður Icelandic buffet. Little plates of smoked fish and pickled vegetables followed by local lamb. I decided against the dried horse and the rotted, six-month buried shark, Iceland's most celebrated delicacy. That was on display in an air-tight mason jar. I was told by a German at the bar that when the jar is open the ammonia-laden stench drives non-Icelanders running from the room. To my disappointment, pressed rams' testicles, another local delicacy, were off the menu that night.

The next day was a doddle. How often this seemed to happen on my trips that, after a day of terror, I would have one of gentle calm. Memories of biking along a sunny coast in a gentle breeze the day after surviving a typhoon on the way to Fukuoka in Japan.

We had a short 250 kilometres through gentle and empty highlands. No cloud, hardly a whisper of wind, Thor and Odin were rewarding us for surviving the trip to Djúpivogur. This was sulphur country. I stopped for lunch at a place whose pillars of steam had drawn my attention. Bubbling mudpots everywhere and next to the restaurant was a giant natural pool, twice the size of an Olympic one, with happy Icelanders gambolling around naked in the sulphurous haze.

The last night on the road was spent in Akureyri, the second biggest town in Iceland, a town with half the population of Abingdon. It may have been small, but knowing that you were hanging on by your fingertips to the edge of the Arctic Circle seemed to give the inhabitants the feeling that they had better party today, because tomorrow the elves might get you. Akureyri could well be the Happy Hour capital of North Europe. The streets round my hotel were packed with galleries, restaurants, bars and more music venues than Shoreditch. Although I was feeling exhausted by this stage in the trip, I was tempted to join the queue to get into a rock concert at the buzzing "Græni Hatturinn", or Green Hat, but decided that oysters and fish soup at the next-door restaurant were a better option.

I was sorry the next morning to set off to complete our circuit of Iceland with the ride back to Reykjavík. It was a long 400 kilometre ride. If this had been my first day in Iceland I would have been awe-struck by the scenery. As it was, I was becoming blasé. Giant steaming volcanoes – seen them. Crashing waterfalls and eerie basalt deserts – done that. Little red roofed dockside restaurants with the scent of rotting fish in the air – old hat. Out in the country in Iceland you got the feeling that nothing much had changed since Fork-beard shared his wife with Broad-axe.

It felt like re-entering civilisation as Björk and I nosed closer to Reykjavík and began seeing real buildings and shops and villages. Reykjavík itself is charming, a smiley town. Wooden buildings painted surreal colours. Every third building a bar. Sudden vistas to the sea at the end of the street.

I had specially left myself a spare day to explore Reykjavík, but when the time came I found I had run out of puff after a week on the road. I felt drained and strangely short of energy, so I spent the time sitting in bars and talking to locals, most of whom turned out to be Hungarians, Germans, or Serbians, a surprising number of whom were not tourists but people who had emigrated to Iceland. After a week biking round the island I could see why they loved their new home.

There are, it is reported, two countries where over half the population believes in elves. Ireland is one; Iceland is the other. You have to like a country where elves are real.

> READER WARNING ... The rest of this story might fall into the Too Much Information category. Anyone who is squeamish or has no interest in medical matters should skip to the next chapter.

The last couple of days in Iceland had been made more exciting by the fact I had been doing some Dr Google self-diagnosis. I couldn't understand why I had been getting so out of breath that I could hardly walk a hundred yards without stopping for a rest. I had been fine in Ranga, where I hadn't seen the Northern Lights, but by Akureyri, a week later, I could hardly walk back up the gentle hill to my hotel after dinner.

After fifteen minutes' consultation with Dr Google I realised that this exhaustion was an early-warning sign of an impending heart attack. Not wanting to spend the next couple of months in a Reykjavík hospital bedbound with a dicky ticker, I decided to get back to England rather than consult an Icelandic doctor who would rush me into a Reykjavík hospital and not let me on a plane. With difficulty on the last morning I lugged my bags to a taxi to the airport. When I saw that the flight home was leaving from a distant Gate 30 I had to ask for a wheelchair to take me out to the departure gate as I didn't have the energy to walk there by myself.

Once back in London I hurried off to see my GP and informed him I was about to have a heart attack.

"I'll be the judge of that," said he in that annoying manner doctors have. He did a bit of poking around and announced that my heart had seldom been in better shape.

"You have anaemia," he announced. "Have you lost any blood?"

Having already crossed the Too Much Information line I don't want to go further by disclosing that I had noticed the possibility of internal bleeding during my time on the road. But I had. If you have ever looked in the loo after eating beetroot you will know what I mean. He took some blood tests and told me he'd call me the next day.

"You're not going to have a heart attack, but you do have one big problem," he said when he called. "Your blood count. That measures the haemoglobin or red cells in your system. They carry the energy to your cells. The normal blood rating for a man of your size and age is fifteen. Eleven is dangerously low and a rating that requires treatment. At six your body closes down. You are at seven."

"Cor, doctor," said I. No other comment came readily to mind.

Two hours later I was in hospital. The nurses were charming, dinner was not bad at all, and they even rustled up a bottle of Côtes du Rhône. I was drinking it with a tube in my arm, four hours into a nine-hour blood transfusion. It was a slow business. They were giving me three pints of the fresh red stuff. Each pint took three hours.

What a relief to find out that there had been a good reason for the Icelandic energy failure and what an even bigger relief to find out that it had been nothing to do with my heart. I was able to leave the hospital in the morning. With energy restored by three pints of fresh new blood I was unusually Tiggerish. If you saw a large fair-haired object bouncing down the Kings Road that morning, it was probably me.

9

KIWILAND WITH COOKY

Everyone, including me, knows that New Zealand had, in some unimaginable prehistoric era, broken away from Australia, like Madagascar from Africa, or indeed Britain from Europe. Musing on this subject in Qantas somewhere over Sri Lanka, it struck me that there was a problem with this idea. Australia was filled with large jumpy marsupials with pouches for their offspring, ones with an alarming knack of springing out from roadside undergrowth and knocking over passing bikers.

But, as I had recently learned, there were no roos, wallabies, or indeed other pouchy-tummed creatures, bouncy or not, in New Zealand. Odd that. My exposure to a website called "Ozzie things that want to kill ya" which proudly featured so many snakes, spiders, crocs and other horrors that it was a wonder anyone was left alive in the land of Oz, had taught me as much as I wanted to know about Australian fauna. But, as I began reading up in preparation for a trip to New Zealand, I thought how strange it was that none of their cousins had survived in Kiwiland. It seemed that I would be able to ride in carefree fashion round the South Island, my destination, without anything the size of Donald Trump bounding out of the bush and whacking me.

Here was the weird thing. Everywhere you have ever been is filled with mammals.

THE HOPELESS BIKER

Apart from birds and the odd reptile, almost everything we see every day is a mammal: cows, dogs, sheep, mice and all the rest of them. And so, we imagine, it is elsewhere. Well, not if you are a Kiwi. Until Europeans trotted up and colonised New Zealand, bringing along a boatful of sheep, pigs, and horses, there were no mammals in New Zealand, nothing with warm blood apart from birds. New Zealand did not have one native mammal.

I was gob-smacked. Actually, that's not strictly true. It had two: *Mystacina tuberculata* and *Chalinolobus tuberculatus*, that's the short-tailed bat and the, er, long-tailed bat, New Zealand's only native mammals and they were probably blown there by a typhoon. There are lots of mammals in the Kiwi sea, whales, dolphins, walruses, porpoises and all that lot, but nothing on land.

How could that be? When New Zealand got split from Australia why did all the Australian animals die out? Here is the reason, and my apologies if you already know this but I found it fascinating. New Zealand was never joined to Australia. When Gondwanaland, the giant land mass of which Africa is the sole survivor, split up and places like India and America broke away, so did Australia and another completely separate continent, known as Tasmantis or Zealandia. That continent was not joined to Australia. As the millenniums passed most of Zealandia slipped under the waters leaving just New Zealand and an assortment of islands like Tonga and the Cook Islands sticking up.

New Zealand … so I really was arriving in the literally Lost Continent. No wonder they had shot the *Lord of the Rings* movies here. And no wonder that the continent of Zealandia, the most isolated place on earth, missed out on the mammals. I never did find out the reason for this but supposed that mammals had developed after other life forms and by that time Zealandia had already broken away.

I had hardly checked into my lodgings at the Commodore Airport Hotel in Christchurch, after thirty hours on Qantas, when there was a bang on the door and six foot six of Wayne loomed up.

"How do, Miles, I got your bike."

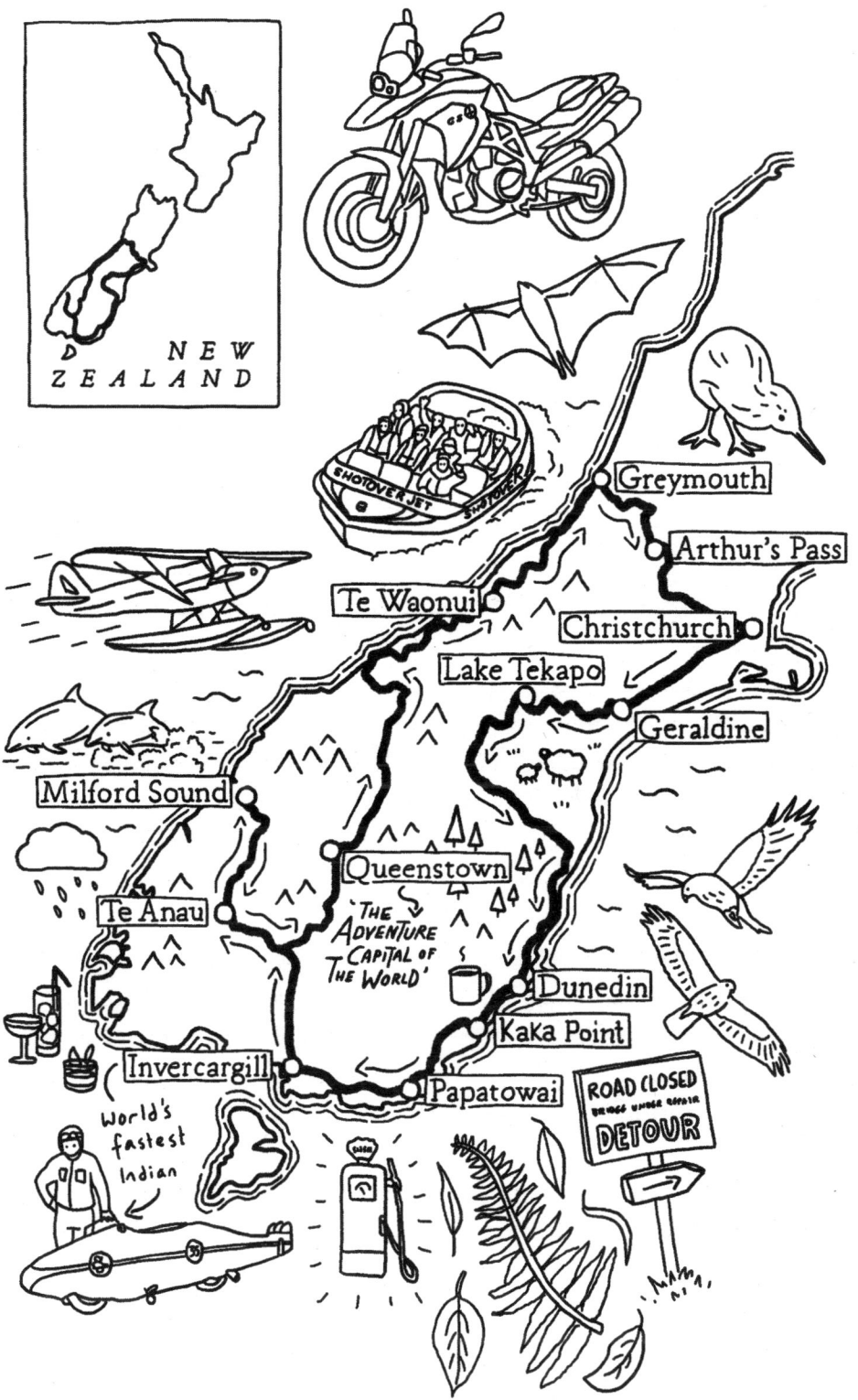

We stepped outside, and there, leaning nonchalantly on the side-stand, was a gleaming F800GS BMW, a near twin of Björk who had taken me so faithfully around Iceland the previous September. In fact there are many similarities between Iceland and New Zealand. Iceland sits on the friction point of the American and European tectonic plates, effectively making it a patch of magma on a sea of boiling subterranean lava, while New Zealand straddles the friction point between the Australasian and South American tectonic plates.

A feature of occupying one of these zones, as any San Franciscan will tell you, is that you live in a place where the earth is going to move. One-third of the city I had just flown into, Christchurch, the biggest city in the South Island, had been destroyed by an earthquake only five years before my arrival in 2011. What had made the quake one of the most devastating of the last fifty years was not its Richter scale score, a relatively moderate 6.5, lower than the 7.1 of Christchurch's previous mega-quake in 2010 which had done only modest damage, but its depth. The big 2010 quake had been deep under the earth's surface; the 2011 quake centre was close to the surface. The whole city shook for a minute, Wayne told me.

"Miles, it was like trying to dance on a waterbed."

I mused for a second how the giant figure of Wayne knew so much about dancing on waterbeds and decided that was not a sensible avenue of enquiry.

"Wow, Wayne, that must have been scary."

"Then, Miles, we had the aftershocks. They went on for days. And a few months later we had another big 'un but there wasn't much left to fall down by then."

"Erm, Wayne, what about here, the Commodore Hotel? Safe?"

"Well, I dunno, Miles, we're quite a distance from the epicentre of the 2011 quake so there wasn't much damage then round here. It was downtown that got the hit. So I couldn't say how safe you are, but, yeah, you should be OK here. I guess."

The F800GS was nothing like as powerful as the K1600 BMW I had in London, a behemoth with its six in-line cylinders, but it was nippy. The F800, light on its feet and with a high centre of gravity, was ideal for throwing around Kiwi bends. In two days' time we would be in the high passes of the Southern Alps, the great glacier-capped mountain range that ran down the spine of the South Island and we'd see how Cooky performed. Björk, her Iceland near-twin, had been brilliant so I had high expectations.

Cooky. James Cook was the first man to sail round both islands of New Zealand and to map it. He wasn't the first white man to "discover" it. Abel Tasman, the Dutchman had bumped into the South Island when a storm had blown him there from Tasmania, which he had also just discovered. He had named it after the province of Zeeland in Holland and decided it was part of Argentina.

He had then gone ashore at a spot on the northwest corner, where I would be biking in a week's time, and promptly had four of his men speared by Māoris who were unimpressed by their first sight of these pale ghosts covered in dead skins. Tasman had called that spot Murderers' Bay and sailed off to discover Australia, never to see New Zealand again.

To be fair, Captain Cook wasn't trying to discover New Zealand either. He had been sent to the Pacific, near Tonga, by the Royal Geographic Society to observe the Transit of Venus across the face of the sun. That was an era when the world was there to be discovered. When he'd done that he opened sealed orders he had from the Admiralty, who had given him a naval vessel, which said "Go and discover New Zealand. And Australia too while you're about it." So he did.

Cooky and I were going to go round the South Island clockwise. We would head south through farming country, no shortage of mammals in the South Island these days, and then up into the Southern Alps where I would find mountain lakes of glacial blueness, or so said the flier in my room.

Two days on the road later and 700 kilometres covered, it was dawn in Dunedin. Dunedin and Invercargill, next on the itinerary, were the two most southerly cities in the world outside South America. If you forget Ushuaia and Punta Arenas, an easy thing to do, these two cities were nearer to the South Pole than anywhere else on earth. You would have thought that would have made them all raw and Wild West-y, with big-boned men packing fearsome weapons in the main street, louche women with low-cut dresses hanging out in dodgy bars, and the wind blowing tumbleweed down the road.

Well, no. New Zealand may be the last frontier in the sense that it is the place furthest away from everywhere else, but you couldn't imagine anywhere less Last Frontier-like. It was tidy, clean, and well-behaved. Kiwis are, and there were surveys to prove it, the best-behaved people on earth. They make the Germans look lawless.

You would think New Zealand and Australia would be similar. They are both on the bottom of the world and both were settled by people from the British Isles. Having ridden a motorbike round bits of Oz a couple of years before and now having done the same in New Zealand I was struck by how different they are. Australians are loud, braggy, restless, funny, and genuinely curious; Kiwis are polite, quiet, well-mannered, mind-your-own-business, and self-reliant. If both countries were cities, Oz would be Dublin and New Zealand would be Edinburgh. Dunedin, into which I had just biked, was indeed the Gaelic form of Edinburgh.

Everywhere I had been in Oz people asked you questions about where you were from and what you were up to. Admittedly that may have been so they could tell you that where they were from and what they were up to was twice as interesting as what you'd just told them, but it made for many happy conversations and cold beers.

"Hey, Miles, where you from, mate?" an Ozzie would ask as soon as you opened your Pommie mouth.

"London."

"Jeez, yeah, I've been to London. Yeah, it's OK, mate, but lemme tell you, you wanna go to Bogaballoo, that's where I'm from. Now that really is something. Forget London. Lemme buy you a beer and I'll tell you about it."

After two days on the road in New Zealand and quite a bit of contact with locals, no-one had asked a question or shown any interest in getting into a conversation. Everyone was polite and helpful but that was it. Maybe that would change and I'd meet some people to match the three Australian Ducati Boys on the ferry to Tasmania with whom I had spent the night crossing of the Bass Strait drinking and laughing.

The Edinburgh analogy may not be a bad one. Everything I'd seen so far was Scottish. The towns were often named after places in Scotland, apart from ones where they'd kept the Māori name. I was going to go through Invercargill and Balclutha (Gaelic for Clyde Town), Berwick and Balfour, and I'd already done Roxburgh, Ettrick, Clyde and even Bannockburn. Every town had a neat Victorian stone church, usually Presbyterian, that would have looked at home in the outskirts of Dundee or Dumfries.

If I'd yet to have any exciting encounters with people, my encounter with the land had been breathtaking. New Zealand, with Iceland as its only rival, must be the scenery capital of the world. And I'd yet to see some of the best bits. In the next few days I would see fjords and glaciers and wild mountain ranges. The biking had been sublime. I've described too many times already the thrill of riding a big bike through mountains so I won't repeat that here. I had become a mountain junky when it came to motor biking. In the past few years I'd biked across the Andes twice, the Pyrenees three times, the Alps more times than I could count, the Sangre de Cristo Mountains in New Mexico, the southern Rockies, the Adirondacks, the Japanese Alps, the Western Ghats in India, the Apennines, mountains with names no-one can pronounce in Iceland, the Vosges, the Bavarian Alps, the Massif Central, the Pindus Mountains in Greece, and the Grampians and Blue Mountains in Australia.

The Southern Alps in New Zealand were a match for any of them. They were not the highest nor the most difficult nor the wildest but they had a special magic. Nowhere matched their unique marriage of mountain and water. It was something to do with the glaciers or limestone, no geologist I, but the lakes were a shimmering icy blue not the dark broody grey-black of the Alps. The only place I'd seen lakes like this was crossing from Bariloche to Chile in the Andes.

THE HOPELESS BIKER

Cooky was light on her feet as she danced round the long bends at full speed in a way my K1600 in London could never do. It was like driving an Alfa rather than a Mercedes. These were old mountains, like the Pyrenees, with their craggy bits worn smooth by millions of years of erosion unlike the arriviste jagged Alps. As a consequence, for a biker, they were a long series of high-speed interconnected S bends, swoop, bank, swoop, opposite bank, letting the corner do the braking, unlike the hairpin bends of the Alps where you are constantly braking and accelerating. Here it was almost like gliding.

The day before coming down from the ice-blue Lake Tekapo to the South Coast the road had swooped and curved round the mountain flanks. In the higher areas there were few trees just the ubiquitous tussock grass and then as you went lower you entered pine-land where, as in Scandinavia and Scotland, pines looked natural. At times it reminded me of Greece: speeding along with the evocative whiff of pine-resin in the air, I could almost hear the bouzoukis play. I'd been lucky with the wind so far, no typhoon tales to tell, but the presence of sixty-foot-high windbreaks of pine trees between fields told you how wind-torn the Southern Alps can be.

Bat news. You may remember my discovery that New Zealand had no native mammals apart from a couple of bats, which I suspected of having been blown there by a passing typhoon. I had mentioned this to a friend in an email, Catherine Arnold, at that time Our Man in Mongolia, having been appointed Her Majesty's Ambassador there a few months earlier at the age of 34. Catherine knows everything. She had emailed to give me further bat information:

"One of those two bats you mention is actually learning to walk and, if the evil Western Imperialist *rattus norvegus* doesn't wipe it out (which is possible), it will turn into a rat in another few thousand years. Equally interesting is that the kiwi bird is beginning to evolve its feathers into fur. And, finally, in response to your comment about the ubiquity of mammals, there are actually comparatively few species of mammal worldwide, way fewer than reptiles, birds, fish and oodles fewer than insects. But, over 20% of mammals are bats, by far the largest group of mammals in the world."

Thanks, Your Excellency. The things you find out while ambassadoring around in Mongolia. Scary about there being all these bats though. Who'd have thought it?

No-one goes to the South Island to see its towns, of which Dunedin was one of the dreariest. I was happy to leave it and head for Te Anau, a lake in the fjordland, some 400 kilometres away.

For me motor biking has two great joys: biking through mountains, and biking along seaside roads that skirt beaches, sprinkled with sand and bordered by marram grass, roads which climb round headlands and dip into hidden fishing villages, roads always with the scent of the sea. And that is what I found beyond Dunedin.

It was an epic drive along almost the whole length of the South coast of New Zealand. This was special. I have had many epic mountain rides but those along the beach were rare, a couple of times in Japan and that was about it. The Great Ocean Road in Australia had been memorable but that was a mighty highway not like this, the Taleri Mouth Road, the didgeridoo little lane I was gently cruising along which had its toes almost in the sand.

There was hardly any traffic, that was all taking Route One which ran 5 miles inland, parallel to the coast. On this tiny coast road 50 kilometres went by without finding a village and when I did it was five ramshackle wooden houses, three fishing boats, and a pub where you could stop for a coffee, sit outside in the sun and smell the wind from the Antarctic. This I did at Kaka Point.

After Kaka Point I had reluctantly left the Southern Ocean and turned inland but still avoiding anything that looked like a main road. Half an hour later I passed through the small village of Owaka and was bopping happily along when the 'low petrol' light came on. Wayne, who had rented me the bike, had warned me that the gauge could stay looking fullish for a long time and then suddenly dive towards Empty. "Can be a bit tricky," he had said. Prophetic words.

Luckily I only had about twenty kilometres to Papatowai, a place big enough to feature on the tourist map of the whole of the South Island that

I had been using for navigation along with the GPS. If it was on the map it must have a petrol station. The fuel gauge was now very low although I had no idea whether that meant I could go another 50 kilometres or would sputter to a halt round the next bend. Papatowai was only six kilometres away said a sign. Phew. And then, disaster struck. "Road closed – Bridge Under Repair – Detour" and a sign pointed off into the wilderness. I had often been deceived by unnecessary "Closed" signs before. Surely I would be able to sneak over a bridge under repair on Cooky even if a car couldn't get over it? I'd just dodge the barrier. God knows how long the detour would turn out to be as the map showed no proper road going in the direction the arrow pointed.

I decided to chance it. Ten minutes later I got to the bridge. Its middle third had collapsed into the river. Cooky was not an amphibian. With a feeling of dread I turned back, having just wasted unnecessary petrol getting to the fallen bridge and back. From what I could see from the useless map the detour would take me on a 30-kilometre journey through a nature reserve with no known habitation before it looped back to Papatowai. I considered going back to Owaka, at least that was on the main coast road if I ran out, but, blind rashness always being the best policy, decided to press on.

The surfaced road now disappeared. It turned into a biker's nightmare of gravel and ruts. Poor Cooky was very unhappy and skidding around all over the place. If I had been in a 4 x 4 with a full tank I would have been admiring the astonishing scenery, primeval forest, probably looking much as it did in the Jurassic Era. Here the primeval forest was made up of pines and ferns, ferns of extraordinary variety and beauty. However my eye was fixed firmly on the fuel gauge, not the ferns. Was it now reading Empty? No cars passed. No houses. No farm animals, let alone a farm, just virgin forest. And no phone signal. How long till they found my skeleton, picked clean by the giant buzzards that floated overhead? What a way to go in the ferny forest.

Suddenly, there were signs of farming activity … Ta-da. Fenced fields and three houses which looked as if they belonged in one of the more incestuous parts of the Appalachians. Someone must have a can of petrol they could sell me? I stopped the bike outside one of the falling-down shacks thinking to go and bang on the door. I did. No answer. Back to the bike when I heard a noise, and an ancient tractor clanked out of the forest. Astride it was a Māori, possibly the most fearsome man I had ever seen. He dwarfed the tractor. He was so terrifying he had probably been banned from playing rugby for New Zealand because it wouldn't have been fair on the others. He stopped, peered at me from eyes hidden under a low brow, and dismounted. I was back astride the bike. He looked at me intently. He was probably deciding whether to eat me or feed me to the pigs.

"Hello, hello," I said cheerily, "Bit low on petrol. Don't s'pose you could, ahem, sell me some?"

He opened his mouth displaying his four remaining teeth. I wondered whether to counsel him against eating sugar but decided not to.

"Ee Jit," he hissed.

Oh God, he only spoke Māori, a tongue in which I was even more deficient than French. It must have been some kind of greeting.

"Ee Jit," he repeated and made a noise that sounded like geese cackling.

That was a good sign. I was about to return the greeting with a merry "Ee Jit to you too," when I realised he was speaking English. He was calling me an idiot. Fair comment under the circumstances.

"Didn't they till you? Niver, niver pass a pitrol station without filling up. Ee jit."

I laughed nervously. "Good advice. I certainly won't in future. But do you have any pitrol you could sell me?"

"Pitrol I don't have. Dizel I got. But, cin you do ten kims?"

I wondered if this was some kind of Māori challenge and then registered that kims were kilometres.

"It's ten kims to Papatowai. Cin you mek it?"

"We'll see," said I and with a cheery "Thanks, mate," Cooky and I skidded off down the gravel.

I nursed her along at 30 kph in sixth gear, finger featherlight on the throttle. Twenty tense minutes later we glided into the forecourt of Ma

THE HOPELESS BIKER

McDonald's General Store in front of which stood a single petrol pump, one of the finest sights I have ever seen. When the stooped and ancient figure of Ma McDonald shuffled out of the store I had to restrain myself from giving her a big fat wet one right on the lips.

An hour and a half later, I took another detour, this one intentional, into Invercargill, another charmless town but here I was on a mission. In 1967 a 68-year-old pensioner called Burt Munro had had a hardware shop in Invercargill. He liked tinkering around with motorbikes. He had a forty-year-old Indian Scout bike, an American bike from the days when Americans made good bikes unlike the Harleys they now make, a Harley being to biking what a codpiece is to sex.

Burt had read about the speed trials on the Bonneville Salt Flats in Utah. He fiddled around with the old bike, built a stream-lined body for it, cadged money from his mates, and put himself and the bike on a cheap cargo boat to America. Somehow he made it to Bonneville where he was told he couldn't take part in the speed trials as he hadn't filled in the form in time and who the hell was he anyway and would he please go away and stop making a nuisance of himself.

Luckily some of the other bikers were so amused by this mad doddering old Kiwi pensioner and his absurd home-made contraption that they persuaded the officials to relent. Burt was allowed to compete. The other bikers helped him with fuel and getting him ready as they had never seen anything quite like him. Who had ever heard of a man born in 1899 turning up at Bonneville in 1967 with a forty-year-old machine? Everyone else was backed by professional teams.

Burt chuntered out to the start, crouched low in his streamlined cockpit and hit the throttle. The course was 8 miles long and he fell off at the end of it. But on the way he shattered the world speed record for an under 1000cc bike by averaging 180 mph with a top speed of 205 mph. Burt was 68 years old and the bike itself was 47 years old. When the bike was new it had had a claimed top speed of 55 mph. And anyone who hasn't seen the film, *The World's Fastest Indian* with Anthony Hopkins should download it tomorrow.

I knew Burt's bike was in a museum in Invercargill and assumed there would be signs everywhere to it as Burt, along with Edmund Hillary, was rightly one of the great Kiwi heroes. Not a sign or mention of this great man anywhere … Eventually Google Maps led me to it. It wasn't a museum. The bike was back in Burt's old hardware shop though it was now a bit bigger than in his day. There, in the back of the shop wedged between the chainsaws and the electric drills was the World's Fastest Indian.

This had been a lovely day's ride, starting with the ride along the Southern Ocean and then paying homage to Burt Monro. Ahead of me I had a treat, a rest day, two nights in the same hotel. What a luxury that was, particularly as the hotel was the Te Anau Lakeside, staffed by the nicest people I had met so far, chiefly of Indian origin, a staggering view over the lake, fantastic food cooked by a Japanese chef, and Miki from Piedmont behind the bar making me cocktails.

My rest day was indeed a day with no scheduled travel, but it was not a rest day. I had for once being doing some reading up. I needed to be at Milford Sound to catch the 11.10 am sight-seeing boat round the Sound. That was 120 kilometres there and 120 kilometres back. In the rain. Through the forest. Milford Sound was the pearl at the centre of Fjordland, the southwest quarter of the South Island, which is a jumbly mess of fjords, and sounds, and inlets, and bays, and lakes, and islands, and no roads. Looking at the map only one proper road penetrated this geographic marvel, an area the size of Wales.

What an amazing 120 kilometres it turned out to be. Yes, it did rain and I had to put on my rain gear, but who cared? The road for the first half skirted the lake and dived in and out of the forest. This was rain forest, not Congo-style, Tarzan-on-a-vine rain forest, but Kiwi-style pine trees and ferns. Ferns bigger than you had ever seen, ferns greener than Ireland, ferns wavier and more delicate than first communion lace. In the 120 kilometres there was never a kilometre of straight road, just bend on bend. I was constantly on alert because in some parts the road was good grippy granular tarmac but in others it was shiny, slippy, concrete.

As a biker you become hyper-sensitive to road surfaces and heaven forbid you are keeled over sideways round a sharp, long bend when the surface changes from grippy to slippy. Heart in mouth, exciting biking. Then came the last 30 kilometres. We entered a spooky tunnel, 3 kilometres long, with a twenty-degree downward angle so you came out several hundred feet lower than you went in. The tunnel had been built in the thirties and was hewn from raw rock. No lining or fancy stuff, just leaking rock, and when you popped out at the far end you were at the top of a long, windy valley with scenery such as you had never seen outside a Spielberg movie. Sharp cliffs, some bare, some covered in pines, and ferns growing out of the rock, floaty clouds misting the mountains, bounding waterfalls from every ledge, and primeval rock.

No wonder they had chosen this place to make so many films. I arrived at Milford Sound just in time for the boat. Off we went down the four-kilometre-long sound to the Tasman Sea and back. I learned that this was not a sound because sounds are carved by rivers; this was a fjord because fjords are carved by glaciers. The fjord walls were sheer. We were hugging the side of the fjord on the way out, but our captain told us that we had four hundred feet of water underneath us, so precipitous was the drop. We nosed up to waterfalls, everywhere there were waterfalls, and scurried under cover while tons of water cascaded onto the deck.

The rain had stopped, mist and cloud played around the flanks of the mountains while a lemon sun cast luminescence through the clouds. We stopped not just for waterfalls. We stopped to admire bottle-nosed dolphins playing with us in mid-fjord, we crept over to look at primeval vegetation, we nosed out into the open sea, the rolling Tasman Sea where the next stop to the West was Argentina, and on the return we cosied up to some rocks which had tiny seals the size of dachshunds on them. These were full-grown seals. They lay on rocks and hammed it up for us by waving their flippers in the air, rolling over and pretending to fall off the edge and generally being unbearably cute.

Then at 2.00 pm back through the forest to Te Anau. The rain had more or less stopped, the road had more or less dried, and Cooky sped along, sure-footed and confident through 120 kilometres of high-speed bends.

I was hurrying back to go flying. Parked in the lake by the hotel was a small four-seater float-plane bobbing on the lake. I had arranged to go for a spin over the fjords and islands and through the clouds at 4.00 pm. I had invited Miki, the Piedmontese cocktail mixer from the hotel bar, along as my guest. She had been in Te Anau for six months but had yet to go up in the seaplane. And I had never been in a seaplane but I had always wanted to. Excitement all round till Adam the pilot, who looked about twelve, said the cloud ceiling was too low.

Curses.

The forecast was good for the next day when I had a shortish ride, so at 9.30 am, before I biked off to Queenstown, Alan had agreed to take Miki and me, weather permitting, for a forty-minute spin over Doubtful Sound. The floatplane had been tantalising me at anchor in front of the hotel since I arrived. The idea was that we would do an aerial tour of Fjordland. Despite its enormous size, Fjordland had only one road in it. The rest was water and mountains whose faces rose vertically out of the fjords and which were covered in vegetation as dense as anything in the Amazon. Somehow the trees put their roots in moss which could be four feet deep.

I trotted off at the agreed time to speak to Adam, the pilot, a friendly Kiwi who assured me he was 34, not 12. "Yup," said Adam, "Forecast is good, not too much wind, we're good to go." We would start out over Doubtful Sound, the most spectacular of them all, so called because Captain Cook got to its entrance and didn't think with the wind where it was that he'd ever get out if he sailed in, so he called it a doubtful harbour. And then we'd cruise on out over the Tasman Sea and back over other mountains and lakes. Adam was a man who inspired confidence. So, at 9.30 am Miki and I presented ourselves on the jetty to which Adam had brought his tiny plane.

I was excited. I have always thought that seaplanes are the last word in romantic travel. We climbed aboard, untied the moorings, and off we went, thrum thrum thrum across the ripples and then we were airborne. What a sight as we rose up. The clouds had blown away, we were cruising over fjords hemmed in by towering mountains on either side. The scale of everything was unimaginable. Adam pointed down at what looked like a pond almost at the top of a mountain. "That's a kilometre long. We could land and take off on that." From where we were it looked no bigger than the Round Pond in Kensington Gardens. Doubtful Sound was dramatic, a wide fjord whose entrance looked as if a giant had thrown a handful of islands into it. Everywhere apart from the very top of the mountains was covered in an impenetrable green of dense pine forest. I asked Adam if it would be possible to trek through that. "Not a chance, too thick."

I asked the inevitable Tolkien question. "Yup, this is where they filmed most of it," said Adam, "remember when Frodo said goodbye to Bilbo? That was down there." I do remember thinking, when I saw the film, how wonderful the natural scenery was and how it lost impact as soon as it switched to computer-generated imagery.

We were up for forty minutes. When we got out of the plane and were back on the jetty I looked admiringly at the neat little plane, sparkling in the sunlight.

"Looks new," I said.

"Not quite, Miles. It was new in 1967."

Our plane was over forty years old, six years older than its pilot. I was glad I found that out after we landed.

Two days later I was having another two-night stop. I was gazing out over one of the most beautiful views I had ever seen, Lake Wakatipu, an ice-blue lake on which sat Queenstown. Queenstown spent part of its time being a ski resort. The rest of the time Queenstown, or so said the glossy book in my hotel room, "is recognised as The Adventure Capital of the World".

I leafed through the book. Here were some of the things I could do:

- Take the Thunder Jet Boat and hurtle over 'peaceful' Lake Wakatipu at 85 kph doing some 360 degree turns en route.
- Get a jumbo race quad-bike and scream up the Nevis Mountains at 100 kph.

- Pile into a 4 x 4 and shoot off into the wilderness on a "Discover the Rings" Tour.
- Jump into a 4x4 Off-Road Buggy with which to churn up the virgin wilderness.
- Take the Jet Boat, Two Rivers, Twice the Excitement followed by a trip to the Underwater Observatory where you can see Diving Ducks, Massive Trout, and Slinky Eels.
- White-Water Rafting. "Are you game?" asked the book. No.
- Embrace the Fear and hurl yourself out of a plane strapped to the front of a bearded Jumpmaster (I'd seen the Jumpmaster's picture in the book, it was Rolf Harris … did I really want him strapped to my back?)
- Jet Ski anyone? No, definitely not.
- An Exhilarating Zipline Eco-Adventure where you flew down a mountain through the trees strapped to a wire? Bring closed-toe footwear and minimal personal belongings.
- A cruise on the lake in New Zealand's last coal-powered steamer seemed a bit tame, though unlike the Zipline it did have a bar.
- Highland Motorsports. Screech round a racetrack in a V8 muscle car or a Lamborghini.
- Highlands Jurassic Safari Tour? Over the Top Helicopters? A Jawsome Thrill Ride in a mini-submarine painted like a tiger shark which could dive and jump out of the water.
- The Shotover Jet, the "world's most exciting boat ride". You shot up the narrow but spectacular Shotover River Canyon at 95 kph in depths of less than a metre while executing helicopter turns.

I was going to give The Shotover Jet a go. A bonus, it only lasted twenty minutes. The Shotover River ran along a gorge. It opened out in places to a width of maybe thirty metres but between that were long, twisty bits where the river was no more than the width of a country lane. The river walls were formed by hundred-foot-high cliffs of jagged black rock and boulder.

I checked in for the boat ride. They gave you a life-jacket and a waterproof black rubber wet-suit. "Gets wet out there, mate. You'll see…" We were lined up to have our photo taken looking as if we were off to a fetish-wear party and then herded into a boat. The boat itself was a twenty-foot-long RIB, effectively a rigid rubber dinghy. It had four rows of seats and a solid steel bar in front of each one for you to hold on to.

Keith, our pilot, looked as if he had not yet started shaving. He gave us a safety briefing in which we learned that we would be doing some 360-degree helicopter turns. And we would hit speeds of 95 kph. And the river was only ten inches deep in places but as we had a flat bottom and no propellers, hey, no worries. And, a special tip, shout if you're going to be sick, said Keith, so "I can stop and you can puke over the side. Can get messy if you throw up in the middle of a helicopter turn." And off we went.

Keith threw the boat straight at rock faces in the twisty bits and then somehow flicked by with four inches to spare leaving you with a blur of granite almost on your nose. Then a more open bit and Keith did a whirly with his hand above his head to indicate a 360-er coming up. The boat suddenly stopped dead, stood on its nose, threw itself sideways, accelerated, stopped, accelerated, water went everywhere and off we screamed at 95 kph.

"Hey, all OK?" yodelled Keith. I did shut my eyes a couple of times when I knew we were going to hurtle into the rock face but somehow we didn't. My wet-suit was drenched. No-one vomited. I can't offhand think of twenty more exhilarating minutes.

Next day we were off early in a sky-clear, frosty dawn to cross the Alps, descend to the Tasman Sea, and cruise up the coast to the Franz Josef Glacier. New Zealand, so the book said, had glaciers closer to the sea than anywhere other than the polar lands. Well, that's what the book said: whoever wrote the book clearly hadn't been to Iceland, but we'll let that pass. A day of incredible biking through deserted mountains. More of the long swooshy bends, no traffic, nothing for company but dead possums on the road. Kiwi possums appear to be even more accident prone than Ozzie wombats. I stopped at Lake Wanaka, another impossibly blue lake with absurdly picturesque mountains as a backdrop. Cooky posed coquettishly for a photograph by the lake, I ate a muesli bar, and on we went through Makarora and past Mount Aspiring. More long S bends as we crossed the Haast Pass and followed the Haast River down to the Tasman Sea.

The topography here was very different to my last sight of the Tasman Sea in Fjordland a few days earlier. There it was all cliffs and fjords, here it was a hundred-mile-long deserted beach of black sand and dead tree trunks. I found myself biking along in the midst of a car rally. The cars were covered in mud and grime and soon left me behind as they screamed off into the undergrowth and I pottered along the long straight highway that bordered the sea, stopping only for a tea-time whitebait patty at Mike's Whitebait Shack.

I was getting excited as I saw Glacier-land appearing on the signs. Would I be biking through snow? I remembered the last glacier I had seen in Iceland where huge chunks of iceberg were breaking off and heading out to sea. Would this be the same? By now it had started raining. Hard. Visibility was much reduced and the mountains to my right were in mist and cloud. We skidded past the signs to Fox Glacier, but the signs said that we'd have to bike 14 kilometres inland to see it so on we went to our destination, the Franz Josef Glacier. What a disappointment to find that the town of Franz Josef Glacier was at sea level while the glacier itself was actually out of sight inland. All that way to New Zealand and I never saw a glacier...

However, compensation came when the Scenic Hotel, a simple Holiday Inn type of place, said yes they did have my booking but unfortunately they were over-booked so would I mind going instead to the Te Waonui luxury hotel, spa, and eco-lodge just up the road. No, no extra cost. It was owned by the same group. The Te Waonui had the same restrained luxury that the Saffire had had in Tasmania. It was in the middle of a Jurassic forest of pine and fern. I kept the sliding door to my room closed in case a velociraptor got in.

Next morning the forecast was dire, "heavy rain" and when they say heavy rain in NZ they are not fooling about. The South Island has climate schizophrenia. Its west coast is one of the wettest places on earth. Milford Sound where I was a couple of days previously has had 26 inches of rain in one day. By way of reference that is what London gets in a whole year. Meanwhile the east coast has a mild climate similar to England. It was going to be chilly when I got up in the mountains. I had to head north for 120 kilometres then turn inland and climb to Arthur's Pass, the main way through the Alps, before heading down to Christchurch and the end of my journey.

I put on six layers of clothing including tracksuit bottoms under my biking trousers. The BMW biking trousers were waterproof, but my faithful Belstaff twenty-year-old leather jacket was not. And once it got wet it took a week to dry out. Luckily I had an impermeable black BMW rain jacket to put over the top of the Belstaff. Off we went into the howling monsoon.

You may wonder how you see anything on a bike in the rain as helmet visors do not have visor-wipers on them. I've been biking for almost forty years and I'm still trying to find the answer to that. How do you see in the rain? The combination of solid rain on the outside and steam on the inside of your visor makes for tricky navigation. If you go fast enough the wind blows the rain off your visor, but if you go that fast in heavy rain you won't be around long to care about whether you can see or not.

It was bad enough going up the coast road but when I turned in towards the Alps the rain came down twice as hard. So hard you couldn't see the surface of the road under a layer of bouncing water. I now made a discovery. My BMW biking trousers were not waterproof after all. Nor was the bit between my neck and the helmet. Water was seeping in everywhere. Trickles of water invaded different parts of the six layers of clothing covering my top half. And meanwhile I was desperately trying to see enough through the visor to get round the next bend.

It was at times like this that you needed to remind yourself that you were doing this for fun. When conditions got really bad I resorted to singing the hymns I remembered from prep school. "The Church's One Foundation" had brought me safe through the Japanese typhoon three years ago. The only problem with belting out "Dear Lord and Father of Mankind" as you tried to get round the next blind bend in the Kiwi Alps was that the singing made the fogging of the visor even worse. I stopped for a meat pie at an Alpine cafe and had to spend a minute trying to separate the sodden Kiwi dollars from each other in the pocket of my "waterproof" trousers.

We biked on. I tried to remember if there was a hymn starting "How long, O Lord," but finally we were at Arthur's Pass. This had been hard work. Two bends after Arthur's Pass we suddenly shot out of the mist, rain, and cold into the sort of weather you might find in Juan-les-Pins on a nice day in June. Ahead was only cerulean-blue sky, without a cloud, a bone-dry road, and when I raised my visor an inch to see where we were going a balmy breeze of warm air came floating in. I have never been anywhere where the climate changes so abruptly. Annual rainfall in Milford Sound where we had just been was 250 inches, ten times London; Christchurch, a scant 150 miles to the east, the other side of the Alps had 25 inches, the same as London.

After that it was a breeze. My clothes dried. I put on Ray-Bans and raised my visor. If I lost a few kilos I could have been mistaken for Tom Cruise. I stopped for a flat white and a Manuka honey-cake at a roadside café. Sitting outside it in the warm sun I began to strip off surplus clothes and felt myself drying. The hard bit was over.

Back to the Commodore Airport Hotel in Christchurch. Wayne came to pick the bike up.

"Nice trip, Miles?"

"Yeah, thanks Wayne, nice trip."

I loved New Zealand. The scenery was some of the best on earth, the high points of the biking were as good as it gets. But, Kiwiland could be a bit Scottish and dour. I thought back and realised that all the conversations I had had on the trip had been with non-Kiwis, mainly Asian and European hotel staff, not one with a native New Zealander. Australia was more laughs.

10

AUSTRALIA: PRISCILLA, QUEEN OF THE DESERT

Journeys. Journeys are different to trips. On trips you stop and look about, do some sight-seeing, check out a church, and have three-hour lunches; trips are things where getting there is often less important than arriving. I love trips and have taken many of them. A journey is different. A journey has a beginning and an end. The point of the journey is the journey. Scott didn't go to the South Pole to have a three-hour lunch, Speke didn't go to Lake Victoria to admire the bougainvillea, and I don't remember mad old Thesiger taking any detours to admire a wadi when he crossed the Empty Quarter.

For much of the previous year grannies with walking sticks had been overtaking me in the street. After seeing a doctor or two I learned that this was due to a dodgy aortic valve. Not enough energy-carrying haemoglobin was being pumped into my arteries. Memories of my near-collapse on the return from Iceland, but this was not something that could be solved by a transfusion. To remedy it I had to have open-heart surgery, the Full Aztec.

I went into the Royal Brompton where my breastbone was sawn open and my heart taken out while I was put on a heart-lung machine. The offending valve was then replaced with pig tissue. Lucky that I'm not Muslim. The operation took eight hours. It took a few weeks for things to heal up but

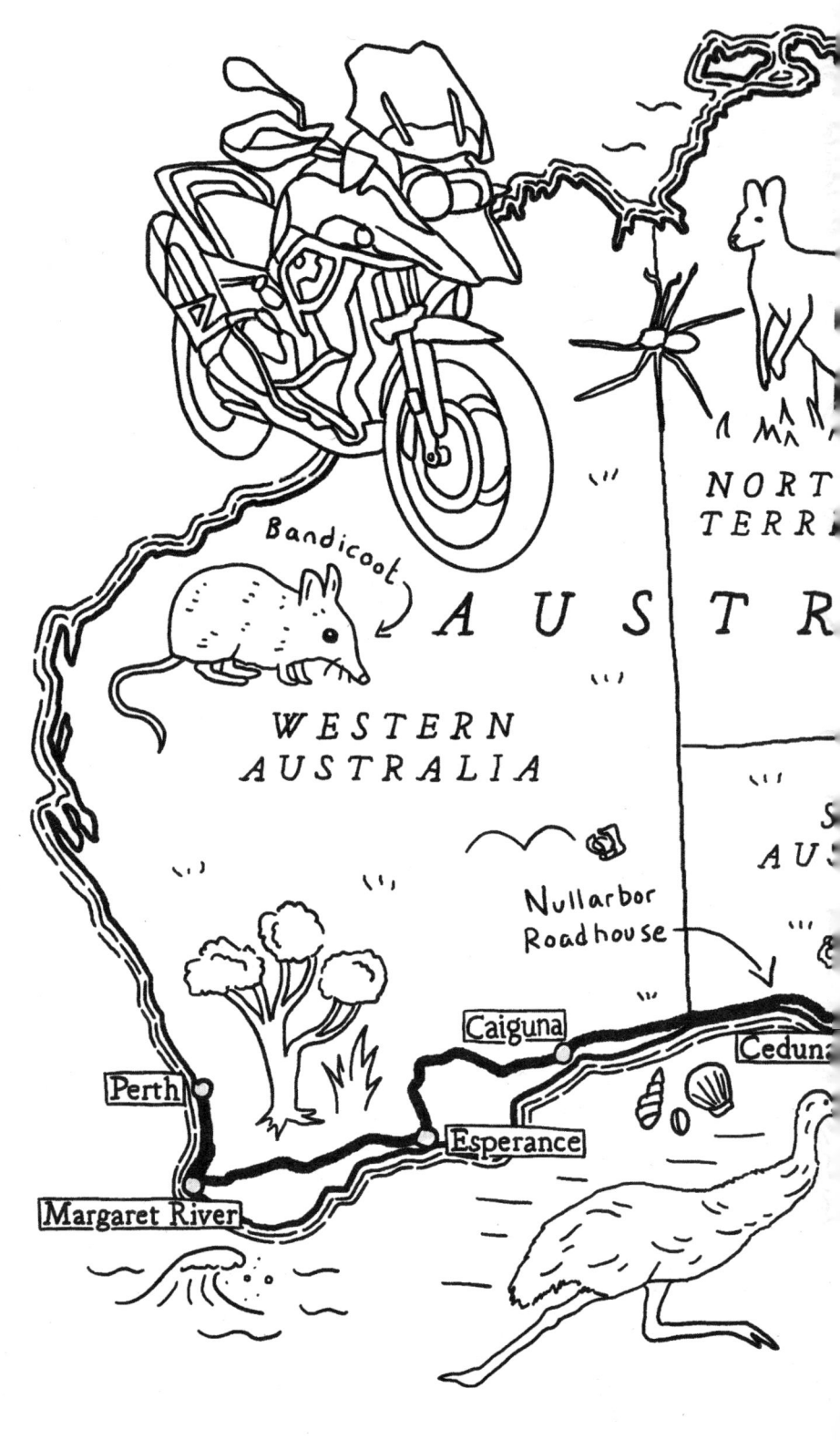

soon I was leaping around like a teenager on a pogo stick leaving grannies gasping in my wake. The year before the operation the longest journey I could plan had been from a taxi to a restaurant. After the operation it was let's see what's the other side of the mountain, over the horizon, in the way-out-there. There was only one way to celebrate. A bike journey.

For many years there had been two special bike journeys I had wanted to do. One, I didn't have the guts to do. The other one was about to start.

They were both classic journeys, ones where the beginning and the end were what counted. The one I was too chicken to do was the Ruta Cuarenta, Route 40. This started in the tropics at Argentina's border with Bolivia and ran all the way down the spine of Argentina, skidding and swirling through the eastern part of the Andes, till it stopped in Tierra del Fuego where after 5,000 kilometres you staggered into Ushuaia, the world's most southerly city.

Twelve years earlier, when I was doing the *Motorcycle Diaries* trip, following in the footsteps of Che over the Andes, I had criss-crossed parts of Ruta Cuarenta and very seductive they had been, but I had only been on the easy-peasy paved part.

The last third of Cuarenta, the southernmost part was gravel. Gravel is no fun on a big touring bike but it's do-able. Cuarenta, in addition to being gravel, could be badly rutted, or so I had read. Ruts are a biker's worst enemy. In a 4 x 4 you can fight your way out of a rut. It may be bumpy, but you can escape. On a bike you are trapped with no way out if it's a deep rut of hard-dried mud. To make it worse, the southernmost part of Cuarenta was also the domain of the Roaring Forties, the worst wind in the world, the one that made Cape Horn so dangerous, a screaming westerly that shrieks its way round latitude 40 south with no land but Tasmania, the South Island of New Zealand, and the tip of Argentina to interrupt its fury. Riding 1,500 kilometres on rutted gravel with a near-hurricane trying to flatten you was more than I had the guts for. I'd ridden gravel, lots of it last time I was in Argentina, as well as in Iceland, India, and Tasmania, and I'd ridden in scarily strong winds including the insanity of the typhoon in Japan, and survived both the gravel and the hurricane, but the combination with added ruts …

I was now closer to eighty than seventy in age; I would leave Ruta Cuarenta to the younger and braver.

Because I didn't have the guts for Ruta Cuarenta, I was setting off to do the other legendary long-distance bike journey of which I had dreamed. I could think of no better way to celebrate the gift of energy my heart operation had given me.

Consequently, I found myself in Perth, on the west coast of Australia, the most isolated city in the world, and the only major city in Australia settled originally by free men. Two weeks later, I was hoping to bike into Cabarita Beach, just south of Brisbane, having crossed a continent the size of the United States. That would be a journey of around 5,000 kilometres but I'd chosen to make it longer, 5,900 kilometres in all, by starting with a detour round the heel of Australia, through the Margaret River wine country to the south of Perth, and, later, another detour through the Blue Mountains just north of Sydney. Much of the in-between was the Nullarbor Plain. Nullarbor means no trees. No people either. In fact, no anything apart from arid desert with spiny bushes and every few hundred kilometres a lonely roadhouse with a corrugated iron roof flapping in the wind and a close relation of Tony Perkins in Psycho behind the desk, and God-knows-what sinister creepy-crawlies in your sheets.

This was not a trip. It was definitely a journey, a journey from ocean to ocean, the Indian to the Pacific. Nerding around on Google Maps had told me that my journey would be 200 kilometres further than London to Baghdad, and over a thousand kilometres more than New York to Los Angeles, in fact the equivalent of New York to Honduras.

I had flown in non-stop from London, at that time the longest non-stop flight in the world. Perth was the nearest thing I had ever seen to a perfect city. It had grown up where the majestic Swan River flowed into the Indian Ocean. It was surrounded by yellow-sand surf beaches and little islands. Along the riverfront were art galleries, boutiques, bars, and restaurants, most of them crowded with impossibly fit, good-looking young people. The whole population were well-dressed and prosperous. Riding around I never saw any ugly or depressed areas. This may sound odd but the only place as cute, modern and buzzy I had seen on my travels was Hiroshima.

This however was no time for sight-seeing. I was not on a trip. My first morning I hopped on a train to Armadale some 50 kilometres from the city centre. There Alex, from BikeRoundOz, picked me up and drove me off to his house in the bush. Parked outside it was a blue and grey BMW 1200 GS Adventure, a near-twin of the bike I had ridden round Argentina. It gleamed in the sun while its mighty steel panniers positively glistened. It was like meeting an old friend. There was something very reassuring about a 1200 GS Adventure.

Before handing over the keys Alex gave me a briefing about how to repair a puncture in the middle of the Nullarbor. As I find locating the petrol cap a mechanical challenge, I wasn't sure how useful that would be. He showed me long wormy rubber plugs and strange tools like mutant corkscrews with which to ream out the hole. I thought it best not to tell him about my mechanical incompetence.

He also gave me a briefing on Ozzie fauna. I had had these before, the old "Ozzie Things That Wanna Kill Ya" routine when Australians boast about how their continent has the world's most dangerous and venomous spiders, snakes, and jellyfish, the hungriest and biggest crocodiles and sharks, so that you were ready to congratulate yourself if you could cross the road without being chewed, stung, and bitten to death.

I was starting to tell Alex I'd heard the spiel before but he said, "Hey, listen, Miles. You've not ridden the Nullarbor. That's different. Mate, forget the snakes and the spiders and the crocs. They're not going to give you a problem but let me tell you what will. The big problem is the roos. There's probably 10 million of them out where you are going. They're the big danger cos if they're startled they can't turn, they can only go forward."

"Thanks, Alex, I learned that when I last rode in Oz."

"Cool, no worries then, mate, but don't drive at dawn or dusk and never ever at night."

"I certainly won't, Alex," said I, omitting to tell him that most of the people I had met out in the country on my previous Ozzie trip had told me that that theory was city-boy public relations to reassure bikers.

"Remember, Miles, start after eight in the morning and be off the road by five at night. You should be OK. The roos don't come out to feed during the day."

"Thanks, Alex, I hope someone has told them that."

Alex gave me a funny look and then burst into laughter.

"Mate, you and your Pommy humour."

I was just reaching for the keys when Alex said, "Mind you, it's not just the roos."

"Oh I know, but I'm not too worried about the snakes and spiders."

"Miles man, forget them. They're nothing. But you do have the camels. You really don't want to hit one of them but at least you can see them coming."

Apparently the Ozzies had imported camels from Afghanistan in the 1870s when they were opening up the Outback, together with Afghan drivers who were made exceptions to the White Australia policy as no white Ozzie knew how to drive a camel. These days the Afghans had become accountants, and the camels had been released into the Outback when railways replaced camel-trains. The camels love it there. They have spent the time since shagging away in the privacy of the desert, with the result that literally millions of rogue camels were lying in wait for passing bikers on the Eyre Highway. Who knew?

"Gosh, thanks for the warning, Alex. I'll keep an eye out for camels. Um, keys?"

"Of course, mate, but, yup, one last thing. Possibly worse than the roos."

"Yes?"

"Emus. The trouble is the emus are so damn stupid. I mean they are six feet tall and can run at 50 kph. You'll be cruising along and suddenly you'll find an emu striding along next to you. Good, you think, it's seen me but then five seconds later the fuckwit bolts across in front of you and I can tell you, mate, they're very solid creatures. You don't want to hit one. Stupid birds."

Up till now I had always thought that the world's stupidest bird was a pheasant, which is why the roads of southern England are carpeted with pheasants too stupid to get out of the way of a car, unlike those canny pigeons. Suddenly I began thinking: imagine if pheasants were six feet tall and could run at 50 kph.

"Thanks, Alex. Understood."

He handed me the keys.

Then, in the manner of Lieutenant Columbo, "Just one more thing, mate."

"Yes," I said warily.

"The eagles."

"Alex, eagles?"

"Yeah, mate. We don't have vultures here but eagles. They're huge, with seven-foot wingspans. Trubbliz there's all this roadkill along the highway from the road-trains which blast through killing anything that comes on the road. That's a feast for the eagles. One will be tucking in to a dead roo on the road when you come along on your bike. 'Hey, mister, this is my lunch,' says the eagle, 'Get lost.' But then you get close enough to threaten its prize and it'll shoot up into the air and open its wings in front of you and suddenly you're biking into seven feet of open eagle wing."

"Alex, the keys."

Before he could tell me of killer wombats, well, actually he'd already mentioned that hitting a dead wombat was like hitting a bag of cement, but I'd heard that before in Tasmania, and other Ozzie Things Out To Kill Miles On The Nullarbor Plain, I threw my leg over the bike, kicked her off the stand, and fired her up.

What a sweet noise.

I had a lovely ride back into Perth. The bike was smooth and responsive. Despite its 80,000 kilometres on the clock it looked in good condition and Alex had fitted a new front tyre, the old one presumably having been burst

AUSTRALIA: PRISCILLA, QUEEN OF THE DESERT

by an eagle.

Now I needed to find a name for the bike. We were headed for the Nullarbor. I needed a companion. As I cruised along the Kwinana Freeway heading back into Perth I had a brainwave. This bike and I were going to cross lots of desert, well, near-desert. There was only one name for her.

Meet Priscilla, Queen of the Desert, from one of my all-time favourite films.

The next day, Priscilla and I were heading off to cross Australia.

Unlike on my trips around Japan and India where I had followed a pre-ordained route, this one was like my previous Ozzie trip, pencil in a rough route and then see which way the wind blew you.

The pencilling in went something like this: Perth – Margaret River – Albany – Esperance – Caiguna – Nullarbor Roadhouse – Ceduna. When, and if, I reached Ceduna on the sea, I would have crossed the Nullarbor. Then on to: Port Augusta – Broken Hill – Cobar – Dubbo (you have to love a country where towns are called Dubbo) – Katoomba (in the Blue Mountains) – Pokolbin – Armidale – Cabarita Beach, where I hoped to hit the Pacific and a whole continent would have been crossed – then, finally, on 18th March, God, Allah, Vishnu, and the rest of them willing, Brisbane.

This trip was going to be different, fundamentally unlike my previous bike trips. Those were about excitement and the joy of hurling a motorbike twice the weight of an adult gorilla through high mountain bends. This would be the opposite. A few of the first bits and a few towards the end in the Blue Mountains would have elements of the old thrills but the heart of this trip, the crossing of the Nullarbor, could not be more different. Hundreds upon hundreds of kilometres of unswerving road running without so much as a curve from horizon to horizon. One of the longest straight roads on earth. No excitement (although the anticipation of a night in a Guantanamo-chic Nullarbor roadhouse was enough to make anyone's pulse quicken), no throwing your weight from side to side as you screamed out of one turn and positioned yourself for the next.

It was going to be a new experience, and it turned out to be one of the most rewarding things that had ever happened to me on a bike.

The women in my family do meditation and they love it. I don't. It has never been my thing. But the days crossing the Nullarbor were days of the purest meditation, the brain empty, living entirely in the moment. A back part of my brain, it was true, was on radar alert scanning the road a quarter of a mile ahead for roos, camels, eagles, wombats, emus and dingoes, but that was done with the subconscious. The rest of my brain was empty. There was nothing to "see". Nothing external to occupy the brain.

The Nullarbor was as empty as the Southern Ocean. The name "Nullarbor", concocted from the Latin words, "nullus" for no and "arbor" for tree, was a misnomer. Yes, there was a patch of about 300 kilometres towards the eastern end where there were indeed no trees, just scrubbly little bushes and shrubs with a few patches of bare earth. Strictly speaking this was not a desert, more a giant wilderness.

Priscilla and I started off with a detour. We went due south although our destination was due east. I wanted to see Margaret River country, the "heel" of Australia. That was a good decision as this turned out to be some of the loveliest biking I had ever done. Margaret River, to the south of Perth, was wine country but not wine country as we Europeans know it because the wineries were hidden in eucalyptus forests. What a stunning place Western Australia was. If you could imagine California inhabited by normal people, you would have a good idea of Western Oz. The weather was like Los Angeles without the smog. The sun shone, there was an occasional puff of cloud in an otherwise unmarred blue sky, and the temperature was just right.

I had three full days' biking round Margaret River before starting the Nullarbor crossing. The first day I spent scooting along a coast of white beaches and thundering surf from waves which had started in Madagascar. Driving the "heel" of Australia was spectacular. First, I had had no idea how many different types of eucalypts there were. I still don't know but the answer was lots and lots.

I'd biked through forests of stunning majesty. Jarrah trees 150 feet high gave the forest the feel of a gothic cathedral; huge karri trees; the tingle tree, which can grow to a 79-foot trunk circumference; and Waltzing Matilda's coolabah tree, eucalypts all. Almost the whole of the Southwestern corner of Australia, through which I was biking, was forest, virgin primeval forest, more than a match for the Californian redwoods.

The only trouble for the biker was that when the sun was coming down through the trees from the side in the morning, the tree-trunks created a blinding strobe light effect of flashing dark and flashing brilliant sunshine, tricky if you were trying to spot Roger Roo about to hurl himself at you.

I had been keeping a wary eye open for the dangerous creatures of which Mark had warned me but apart from spotting a brace of emu trotting around with their noses in the air like French comtesses at Longchamp races, I had seen nothing alarming till a danger sign cropped up along the road to Albany. "Watch Out for Bandicoots", it said. Bandicoots? I assumed this was a sign put there to scare passing Poms. Did anyone know what a bandi bloody coot was? No, of course not. A fictional animal, an Ozzie joke beast.

I was so annoyed by this that I had refused to look it up on Google when I arrived in Esperance for my last night before the Nullarbor. I did however say to Sally, the owner of the Bayside B&B where I was staying, "Sal, tell me, is there really such a thing as a bandicoot or are they pulling my leg?"

"Oh yes, Miles, sure is. They're everywhere."

"OK, OK, I believe you. What do they look like?"

"Hmmm, lemme see, Miles, well imagine a rat the size of a rabbit. Funny looking creatures."

I preferred not to imagine a rat the size of a rabbit, but I did sneak a peek at Google after that. I will say no more but to inform you that the bandicoot, says Wikipedia, has a bifurcated penis.

After three days drifting and dreaming through the enchanted forests of Margaret River, we circled up north to Norseman, a strange little town surrounded by chemical looking stained earth and dried-up lakes that reminded me of Death Valley. This was where I had to right and head east for the crossing of the Nullarbor, something that had built up to Homeric proportions in my mind...

THE HOPELESS BIKER

The guidebooks had told me that the first three-quarters of the crossing would be through tree-spotted savannah. I wished I knew my eucalypts better, but all have grace and presence, many with fan-like lacy foliage like hundred-foot high ferns. They didn't jostle together as in a forest but kept a respectful distance from their neighbours.

On the straight I usually had Priscilla on cruise-control, set at 4300 revs or 113 kph in sixth gear. The speed limit was 110 kph and the police, I had been warned, could be fierce but 113 kph should be safe. Petrol stations were far apart, the longest gap being about 200 kilometres between Belladonia and Caiguna. When you saw a petrol station, you filled up, a lesson I had learned in New Zealand: "Niver, niver, pass a pitrol station", although Priscilla's range of about 260 kilometres gave us a comfortable margin.

There was traffic but it was sparse. Every ten minutes or so a car, always a 4 x 4, would zip past, often pulling a trailer; the Ozzies liking nothing more than camping in the Nowhere. From time to time a road train thundered by with a huge outward thrust of air pressure like a mighty wave breaking over you. Many of the road trains were pulling three giant trailers, each the size of a railway container.

Away from the petrol stops, I saw no people. Not one. I saw no houses or buildings. An occasional track led off into the God-knows-where. I saw one, leading into the wilderness, signposted to Cook. That evening in the Nullarbor Roadhouse I saw three old guys in the bar in leather jackets, tattoos everywhere, and the distinctive long wispy grey beard of the Harley-driver.

In the Nullarbor the old enmity between Harley drivers and people on real motorbikes was temporarily suspended.

"Hi guys," I said, "You on Harleys?"

"Well, no, mate, we've owned a few, but we're on the train."

I had looked at the map earlier and noted that the famous trans-Australia Sydney to Perth train, containing the longest bit of straight railway in the world, did indeed run through the Nullarbor but about 100 kilometres north of the road I was on.

"On the train?"

"Yeah, the three of us, we drive the big trains. They do it in stages with relays of drivers. We do the Port Augusta (where I would be in two days' riding) to Cook leg."

"Ah yes," I said, "I saw the sign to Cook about 20 kilometres back."

"That's right, mate. There's a dirt track 100 kilometres long and we live at the end of it by the railway stop."

"Wow, is it a big town?"

"Well, no. Not too big, is it, Brian?" he turned to his fellow greybeard.

"Ah wouldn't say…" began Brian, "what's your name, mate?"

"Miles."

"Yeah, well, Miles, I wouldn't say it's that big. Four houses. And we live in three of them. Nice place though, but not a lot to do between runs on the train so we pop down here for a few cold ones and a bit of company."

'Here' involved a 240 kilometres roundtrip from Cook.

"So where you headin,' Miles?"

"Perth to Brisbane."

"Yeah, that's a good ride. Next time you do it, mate, pop up to Cook and we'll throw something on the barbie for you."

I get easily bored. That may be why I don't fish or play golf. But I never got bored crossing the Nullarbor. Priscilla throbbed away happily underneath me, requiring no effort. I could take my hands off the handlebars and she just went straight on. I had lots of music including some playlists given to me by a music-mad friend in London before leaving, but I didn't listen to music on this trip. I tried using the time to think about people and important things: what did Brexit mean, was Donald Trump imaginary, what would I do when I grew up, but my brain refused to engage with any of those subjects or with anything else but living in the moment, entranced, literally entranced as if by a spell, by the open wilderness flicking past and nothing else.

I had a perpetual smile on my face and happiness in my heart. An experience like no other. Yes, I did get a sore bum after many hours in the saddle, but I could always stand up on the foot-pegs for a few minutes to alleviate that. I made myself stop every hour and half in one of the off-road parking spaces advertised by signs saying, "Drowsy Drivers Die". Lacking a comma after Drivers I took this as an observation, not a command: "Drowsy Drivers, Die!".

When I stopped I would dismount, stroll around, shake my legs to loosen up the knees, take off helmet and jacket, and feel the breeze on my face before going on, refreshed. When I stopped on long bike trips in Europe I often lay down in the grass, rolled my jacket up as a pillow, and had a short nap. I tried this in the Nullarbor on the first day. There was no grass so I lay down on the dust in a patch of speckled shade from a eucalypt. Just as I was nodding off a colony of red ants persuaded me this was a bad idea. I did not repeat the attempt.

Bruce, as I had christened my satnav, possibly first cousin to my previous Ozzie satnav, was a much more relaxed companion than the Satnav Harpy of Japan. He spoke seldom although, as we were on one of the longest straight roads on earth, there wasn't much for him to say. In any case, Bruce was work-shy. He worked for two days and then gave up. He went completely blank. That too was strangely relaxing. Instead of looking at a screen which counted each kilometre and told you how many hours and minutes till you arrived, I had nothing, just the wind and the sun, and the throb of the motor until I reached the next way point.

Three days of straightaway and meditation and then I was able to say we had crossed the Nullarbor. Saying it made it sound like a gigantic deal but to me it had been closer to three days in a zen trance.

The Nullarbor crossed, Priscilla, Queen of the Desert was snoozing in the carpark of the Ceduna Foreshore Hotel Motel, and I was looking out over something immeasurably big and blue and wet. The reward for completing the crossing was a rest day by the seaside. I sat in my room gazing out at the wide blue sea, and watched a gentle surf stir the pebbles on the beach. I had a couple of cocktails, drank some delicious local wines, picked up some shells on the beach, ate some indifferent food, dozed, and read.

Batteries recharged, I was back on the bike for a cross-country trip to Port Augusta. Although we had now left the Nullarbor behind, the terrain was still flat and featureless. Another zen day on the road.

When I had checked into the Crossroads Ecomotel in Port Augusta I told Alan, the owner, that I had biked there from Perth.

"Miles, that's a hell of a trip on a bike. Tell you what I'm going to do. I'm upgrading you to a clean room."

"Gosh, Alan, that's great. I can tell you that after a few nights in Nullarbor roadhouses a clean room will make a nice change."

In my Nullarbor roadhouses the sheets had always been dark brown or dark blue, presumably so as not to show the stains of the things that had died there. I had spread as many towels as I could find on top of the beds and slept on those rather than the sheets. "Being upgraded to a clean room will be great. Much appreciated. Thank you, Alan." Alan looked at me as if I had just lowered my trousers.

"Miles, what are you talking about? Not a clean room, mate, though let me tell you all our rooms are spotless, but a keeng room. One with a keeng bed."

"Ah, of course. Thanks, Alan. A king room would be ace."

My command of Ozzie English was still rudimentary.

Ozzie English is splendid and nowhere more so than in the place names which tell you so much of the short history of this wonderful continent since the white man first arrived. These thoughts about place names came to mind as I biked a day later into Broken Hill. Just before getting there I had passed 'Old Lake Dismal'. How many people had died to give it that name? And shortly after leaving Port Augusta we had biked round Mount Remarkable, which was nothing special, and later, the Daydream Mine, how many fortunes were lost there? Probably by people who ended up on Dustholes Station or scratching a living by Ratcatchers' Lake.

The white man had been too tired to make up names for everywhere, so he kept the aboriginal names for most of them. Those are pure poetry. Try singing out loud some of the places I had passed or would be passing near Broken Hill, "Neckarboo … Wallangarra … Boolcoomata … Mooleulooloo … Mount Wooloolahra … Ramamaroo … Bulgamurra … Booroomagga … and Mullengudgery."

One of these days when I am old and grey, I shall retire, like Yeats to Innisfree, and call my little cottage Mullengudgery.

I checked in to the Red Earth Motel in Broken Hill. Broken Hill has a lot of red earth. Although I had just crossed from the state of South Australia into New South Wales, Broken Hill kept South Australia time as it was so far from anywhere else in New South Wales. It was often referred to as the Capital of the Outback. It is also the place where Priscilla, Queen of the Desert, the original one in the Terence Stamp movie, had come to rest. Every year, for the last thirty years, this extremely macho town has been holding a Priscilla festival featuring drag queens from all over Australia. It's called the Broken Heel Festival.

About 140 years ago a man called Charles Rasp had been herding some mangy sheep round there when some aborigines showed him a rocky outcrop which had a break in the top of it, hence Broken Hill. It seemed to be made up of hard shiny stuff. This was a boomerang-shaped deposit with the middle sticking up in the air and the two ends going unthinkable depths down into the red earth. Mr Rasp's hill turned out to be the biggest silver, lead, and zinc deposit the world had ever seen. Nowadays, most of it has been mined but the people who started Broken Hill Proprietary, the company set up to mine the metal, used their profits wisely. Today, BHP is not only the biggest company in Australia but the biggest mining company in the world. Sadly, the headquarters were now no longer in red earth territory but in downtown Melbourne.

The next day, we were going to head east, which meant more long straight roads, but soon after the air would change, the scenery would change, and Priscilla and I would be throwing ourselves through the bends of the Blue Mountains. Yee-hah.

I had 4,500 kilometres behind me and I'd yet to see a bandicoot. Well, a living one. There's a lot of fur-splodge on the Ozzie highway and identification can be a problem. Roos are easy because you can still see the poor creatures' tails sticking out after a road train's roo-bars have thrown them off to the side of the road, but telling the difference between wombat-splodge and bandicoot-splodge is a challenge.

So far, in ten days on the road, I'd not seen much in the way of live animals. One roo had hopped across my bows, obviously one who had not read Roos' Standing Orders, "No roos allowed on the road between dawn and dusk". Meanwhile I had seen several hundred dead ones. There were times when you'd find ten roo corpses in a half a mile. They were easy to spot because there was always a coven of crows feasting on their remains who flapped and hopped lazily away at the very last minute to return as soon as we were past. Fortunately for me, no eagles with eight-foot wingspans had yet appeared. Some corpses had been there for days. I had learned to hold my breath until I was well past them as the anchovy-sweet stench of rotting roo was not a pleasant one.

We'd passed lots of smaller corpses, wombats, foxes, and, who knows, maybe even a bandicoot or two.

I'd seen a dozen or so emus, all alive and trotting along by the road in a ditzy kind of way. Emus were splendid. Their feathers stuck up off their backs like a Victorian governor-general's cocked hat. They didn't walk, they didn't run, they trotted. This made their feathers bounce up and down. When it came to booty-shaking, Shakira had nothing on an Outback emu. Despite their reputation for stupidity, I had yet to see any emu-splodge on the road.

The most common living wild animal was our old friend the goat. Goats are far too bright to get run over. I assumed the goats were wild. Everyone loves goats although they should probably be made extinct as they have a fair claim to being the most destructive animal on the planet after man. There are many parts of Africa, on the fringes of the desert, where grazing goats eat every tiny seedling as soon as it pops its head up thus ensuring that what might otherwise be pastureland is turned into barren desert. Ask anyone who lives in Somalia.

I thought that not only had I crossed the Nullarbor but I'd also crossed the Outback. An email from an Ozzie friend who was following my progress told me that that would have been an absurd and empty boast.

The Outback. Australia, like Caesar's Gaul, is divided into three parts.

First is the settled part round the coast with cities such as Sydney and Perth, as fine as any in the world. Between them are hundreds of neat communities many of which would look at home in Ohio or Wisconsin. That is settled Australia. The fringe beyond it is the Bush. The Bush is sparsely populated, but it has roads and resources and you are unlikely to get too badly lost in it. Beyond the Bush is the Outback. That's everything else. Most of it has little water, few roads, and a lot of red earth. Somehow, aborigines have learned to adapt, their extreme knowledge of and sensitivity to nature allowing them to survive where no-one else could, cousins in spirit to the pastoralists of the Sahel in West Africa. The Outback is bigger than you can imagine. Think of India, double it, and you have the Outback. Multiply France ten times (please God, no, one France is quite enough) and you have the Outback. What the Amazon is to forest, and Siberia is to frozen waste, the Outback is to wilderness.

While crossing the Nullarbor, I had taken a detour and biked down a dirt path heading south from the road. I knew what I was looking for but not what to expect. A few kilometres later I found it. I had no conception of the impact it would have. One moment I was biking down a nondescript dirt track through scrubby bush and then the road came to an abrupt end in a dirt clearing and the land in front dropped away. I was staring out over the shimmering blue of the Southern Ocean viewed from the top of a three-hundred-foot cliff. I was on the northern margin of the Great Australian Bight.

I put Priscilla on her stand, took off my helmet and gazed out over this infinite expanse of blue. To the south was the Antarctic. Brave men had crossed this angry ocean in small boats searching for lands no one knew existed. This was a place of such grandeur that it humbled you to look at it. After twenty minutes, I put my helmet back on, remounted Priscilla, and continued on with a memory I will never lose.

The road I was taking was the only road connecting the east, Pacific, coast with Sydney and Brisbane, to Perth and the Indian Ocean on the west coast. The only join between those extremes was the Eyre Highway, the road Priscilla and I were biking along.

Edward Eyre, together with his aboriginal companion Wylie, was the first European to traverse this path in 1840–1841, on an almost 3,200-kilometre trip to Albany, Western Australia. Heading into the who-knows-where was an act of extraordinary bravery, almost effrontery, for a man born in Bedfordshire. He had originally led the expedition with John Baxter and three aborigines. Halfway there, two of the aborigines killed Baxter and vanished with most of the supplies. Eyre and Wylie survived only because they bumped into a French whaler, under the command of an Englishman, Thomas Rossiter, after whom Eyre named the location Rossiter Bay. In 1845, Eyre returned to England and later became Governor of Jamaica.

The Eyre Highway did get traffic. Every fifteen minutes or so a 4 x 4 or a road train thundered through. Ozzies being Ozzies, I knew that if I had fallen off my bike in the middle of nowhere, a friendly Ozzie would have scooped me up in no time at all. Surprisingly there was a telephone signal almost all of the way and, every 20 miles or so, you came across a piece of road with extra wide shoulders which was designated as a landing strip for the Royal Flying Doctor Service. Australia has learned to look after people in the wilderness. The frontier spirit was still alive.

I wished I'd had the time to meet and talk to some Outback aborigines. The white Australians seem to be doing their best these days to assuage their guilt about what their predecessors did to them, just as some white Americans are trying to make it up to the few remaining indigenous ones. The irony is that the indigenous Australians and Americans embody so much of what young people today are trying to recapture, the ability to live in peace with nature without harming it, and to learn from it.

Most of my knowledge of indigenous Americans comes from reading *Bury My Heart at Wounded Knee*, the heart-breaking story of how the invading white man in North America broke every treaty he signed with the red man, forced him off his lands, made him change his way of living, got him drunk, and reduced him to living in reservations far from his home lands. I suspected the story in Australia was similar to that in the US. I remembered learning four years earlier when I had been riding a bike round Tasmania, that the last indigenous Tasmanian person had been killed around 1900. I didn't know how true the Tasmanian extermination experience was with that of mainland Australia, but I suspected it was less so because in Tasmania there had been no place to hide. In Australia the aborigines had the Outback.

I had seen quite a few aborigines in the small towns I'd been through, keeping shops, eating in road stops, and doing much the same as their white equivalents but these were people who had adopted European "civilisation". There was a larger world of aborigines who had kept much of their traditional way of life and thinking, despite European Man's attempt to "civilise" them out of it. They lived, many of them, where no-one else did, in the Outback.

Bruce Chatwin, best known for *In Patagonia*, wrote a book, *Songlines* about aborigines in Oz and how their songs connect them with the earth and their ancestors. This introduces us to the concept of the Dreaming which plays such an important part in aboriginal life and thinking. I became fascinated by the Dreaming and found myself thinking about it as I drifted through this vast empty continent. I took to reading up about it online. I may have got it wrong but this is what I found out.

The Dreaming encompasses everything in life, everything that grows and flowers, and they in turn are guides to the animal kingdom where things can be found to hunt or be harvested.

All the wisdom that is passed down, the rituals, the ripenings and the decayings, the art, the songs, the dances, are all parts of the Dreaming. Unlike our bibles and Qurans, none of this is written down, it is everywhere and is an inescapable part of every human. There is no God and there are no priests to act as intermediaries, just the Dreaming. The Dreaming is literally everything.

Westerners sometimes talk about the aboriginal "Dreamtime" but that's wrong. None of the hundreds of aboriginal languages has a word for time. The word Dreaming expresses the timeless concept of moving from dream to reality. Who would not want to have the time to get to know these extraordinary people and to learn from them? When I biked across the Nullarbor, I thought about it as being like meditation. Maybe I was on the fringes of The Dreaming.

An extraordinary thing happened when I left Broken Hill and was eating up the miles to Cobar, my next stop. I saw a hill. Not a very big one but the first hill I had seen in 4,000 kilometres. Broken Hill, despite the name, didn't really have a proper hill, only mounds of waste from which the minerals had been extracted. Since I had left Albany, now as far behind me as London is from Damascus, it had been flat, flat, flat, and the road had run straight, straight, straight. Although the hill was nothing special, seeing it made me feel like a transatlantic sailor encountering his first land bird as he crossed the Atlantic.

Ahead be mountains.

I was so excited by the change that the next day I decided to cut out a scheduled overnight stop in Dubbo and bike a double distance to get to the Blue Mountains. The road to Dubbo initially ran straight and flat, as it had done for so many days, but beyond Dubbo everything changed. The road began going up and down, it had bends in it, real corners, real hills and valleys. I hope you believe me when I say how much I loved the Zen trance of the Nullarbor but, at heart, I am a biker and bends are to a biker what garlic is to a Catalan. Priscilla and I were entering the Blue Mountains. When I had plotted my route I could have headed straight for Brisbane after Broken Hill and cut my journey a couple of days' shorter, but I had planned the southerly detour to the Blue Mountains to add a good wodge of garlic to my Ozzie lunch.

It wasn't just the topography. Everything changed in the landscape. The last 4,000 kilometres had been not just flat but wide and open, no houses with gardens, no trees but gums, no lawns, no fences, no villages. Suddenly I could have been in the Napa Valley. Everything was neat and orderly. Houses had neat paddocks surrounded by white picket fences, and avenues of ornamental trees leading up to grand houses. Here there were eucalypts but also imported trees and plants from Europe and Asia. March is early autumn in Oz and now I saw the first autumn colour as the imported trees turned to gold. Eucalypts are evergreen. Their leaves didn't colour in autumn.

The road snaked along a valley floor and then up over a saddle with hills filled with rows of vines on either side. I stopped for a coffee in Mudgee and saw a map proclaiming that Mudgee had thirty-eight wineries in the surrounding countryside.

And the bends. The intoxication of once more banking into a bend, the bounce – turn – bounce – turn of a skier in a field of fresh powder. How glad I was to have done the trip this way. BikeRoundOz had tried to get me to start in Brisbane and finish in Perth as that would have fitted in better with their schedules but that didn't seem right to me. I wanted to cross the ocean of flatlands before getting into the white water of the hills. The other way round would have been wrong.

At 5.30 pm we puttered into Katoomba, a famous beauty spot in the Blue Mountains known for its spectacular view over the Three Sisters rock formation. It is also known for its wildly over-priced hotels, but when I got to my room in the Echoes Hotel and looked out at the view they could have doubled the price and it would still have been a bargain. I'm not sure I have the words to describe the view over the Blue Mountains. The sun was setting, a great rift opened up in front of me, stretching for 40 miles from the hotel, everything was cloaked in green, and the air was luminescent. How lucky I was to have arrived in the brilliant evening sun because the next morning I threw back the curtains for an early morning view, and all I could see was a white bank of fog. The eaves dripped with drizzle.

I didn't care. I had seen the view the day before and the fog meant that I wouldn't be tempted to go off exploring. I could have a real rest day. An old friend who had returned to live in Sydney biked up to Katoomba on his terrifying Ninja to join me for dinner and spend the night in the hotel. He had proposed that we biked together for the next day. I thought about it and said no. Long solo bike trips are like single-handed sailing trips. They have to be done alone. You cannot take someone on board for a bit of the way, however short. That turns it into something else. My friend understood.

A day later, rest day over, Priscilla and I set off under a clear sky to slalom our way through the Blue Mountains. It was beautiful driving on beautiful roads, a country of waterfalls, big rivers, and fat cattle gently grazing.

What a contrast with the nothingness of the Nullarbor and the Outback. I had learned more about the Outback from an English friend who now lived much of the time in Australia. She had sent me an email about it: "Australia was settled first along the coast (east and south). Then land leases were granted to pastoralists. The Great Dividing Range stretches north to south down eastern Australia, cutting it off from the rest of the continent. Venturing beyond, or out back of the range meant going into the unknown. If you were travelling inland beyond the Range, you told people you were going 'Out Back'. This term then became a noun and everything west of the Range is Outback." Of course, so obvious when you know it. And that's what I was now biking through, the Great Dividing Range, of which the Blue Mountains were a part.

Since I re-entered civilisation, Australia continued to offer surprises. What a pleasure it was to wake up in Spicer's Vineyard Estate my last stop before the ocean, draw back the blinds and look out over fields alive with dancing roos. A hundred yards from my room two big old boys were having a boxing match, reared up on their hind legs like two mutant March hares, while a female roo sat nearby in the long grass, smirking seductively. It is difficult to look at a roo and not smile. There is something so good-natured about them, and how good it was to see them alive after passing so many of their dead cousins on the road in the previous ten days.

Soon after leaving Spicer's and the dancing roos we saw something big and blue with great combing waves thundering onto a beach, empty but for half a dozen stripy birds, a solitary man, and three long-stemmed roses lying on the tideline. Who knew what their story was? Thirteen days ago we had left another empty beach behind us, the Indian Ocean, a continent away as I looked out over the Pacific.

I checked into the hotel Halcyon House on Cabarita Beach, a kind of posh shack of a place, my body buzzing with health and happiness. I changed my clothes and popped down to the bar for a celebratory cocktail. I was sipping it at the bar and began talking to Marika from Bergamo, the cocktail waitress.

"What brings you here, Miles?" she said, "Are you on business?"

"Not exactly. I'm on a journey. But today I finished it."

"Oh, good. Now you can relax. Where was your journey?"

"Across Australia. On a motorbike. Perth to here, 5,800 kilometres, the whole continent."

As I was telling her this I could feel myself choking up. I couldn't go on. I pretended to have a coughing fit. She saw through that, patted the blubbing septuagenarian on the arm.

"Mister Miles, I understand. Enjoy your drink. I come back later. You tell me then."

I should put off celebrating until after I had said goodbye to Priscilla, my companion of the road. That was going to be a sad parting.

A friend who had moved back to Australia from London came up from Byron Bay to join me for the day. She had been admiring Priscilla in the parking lot.

"Hey, Miles, look at the number plate."

I did: MDU 13.

"Yes, MDU is Miles Down Under," she said.

"Wow, so it is. And 13 is the number of days it took me to cross Australia."

As my dear ex-wife, the Jungian psychoanalyst, likes to say, there is no such thing as coincidence.

A day later, I was in a hotel in Brisbane and feeling lonely. I had handed Priscilla over to Joe, BikeRoundOz's man in the outskirts of Brisbane, and said goodbye. When I had emailed him to fix a time to return Priscilla, he signed off his reply not with "Best regards," or "Bonzer, mate," but with "Rubber Down, Bubble Up". I liked that. I may start signing my emails with Rubber Down Bubble Up. The least I can do is to get a coat of arms featuring a biker, head couchant, bum ascendant, on a Beemer rampant.

When I told people I met, which I did as often as possible, that I had just crossed Oz, they did a double-take as, to an Ozzie, I looked like someone who might have difficulty crossing the road.

"Awesome, mate. How was it? How long did it take? Good on yer…"

Even Joe, despite having a garage full of over-powered bikes, had not himself made the crossing.

"Not bad, Miles," said Joe, "Yup, 75, you're definitely the oldest we've had who's done it."

Of course, I put on the modest expression of someone who had just done something fearsomely brave and daring but, in true English style, didn't want to boast about it. I implied that what I had done was up there with Shackleton's return from Antarctica and Thesiger's crossing of the Empty Quarter.

My secret was, and now that the journey was over I could say this without tempting Providence, that the journey had been, as Biggles might have said to Ginger, a piece of cake. Yes, it had been a long way. When I returned Priscilla she had 5,946 kilometres on the clock for our trip against the 5,900 kilometres that Google Maps and I had estimated. The extra 50-odd had been my turning back to refuel in a no-petrol wasteland somewhere north of Esperance.

Crossing Australia was a journey I had to do. Few things made you more grateful to be alive than going into hospital, unable to walk more than 200 yards without stopping for breath, and coming out a few days later, aortic valve repaired, bouncing with energy. A year ago, the idea of planning a motorbike trip had been unthinkable. It seemed then that my biking days were over. Planning a trip to Waitrose had been a challenge. Thanks to the operation, my horizons, which had shrunk to the intervals between bus stops, were once more infinite.

In my house on the Norfolk coast I have a small slate slab which has inscribed on it, "Nothing matters but the longest journey". It sits above the fireplace. When I sent friends emails about this trip I was going to include that line until I looked up the whole poem it came from. It's by D H Lawrence, a poet who, when he is on song, is one of the best, someone whose special talent is how man and nature interact.

When you read the poem, you will understand why I didn't include it

THE HOPELESS BIKER

in emails sent home to friends from a man biking across Australia. Lawrence's "longest journey" was to death.

> *And round the great final bend of unbroken dark*
> *the skirt of the spirit's experience has melted away*
> *the oars have gone from the boat, and the little dishes*
> *gone, gone, and the boat dissolves like pearl*
> *as the soul at last slips perfect into the goal, the core*
> *of sheer oblivion and of utter peace,*
> *the womb of silence in the living night.*
> *Ah peace, ah lovely peace, most lovely lapsing*
> *of this my soul into the plasm of peace.*
> *Oh lovely last, last lapse of death, into pure oblivion*
> *at the end of the longest journey*
> *peace, complete peace!*
> *But can it be that also it is procreation?*
> *Oh build your ship of death*
> *oh build it!*
> *Oh, nothing matters but the longest journey.*

D H Lawrence did make the process of dying sound a lot more cheery than boarding an easyJet flight at Gatwick but I was not ready for that journey and I thought that putting it in something I sent friends would cast the wrong light on the trip and probably worry people reading it.

I reminded myself that Lawrence also wrote, "Life is there to be spent, not to be saved."

But, "the longest journey" is what Oz had been about, just one with a different destination to that in Lawrence's poem. I looked back over the trip with a feeling of infinite joy and gratitude. There wasn't a moment of boredom or regret. It had much in common with a long solo sailing voyage. I've never sailed across the Atlantic but I know many people who have. If you're going to do it, you go south to the Canaries in November when the northeast trade winds have moved up out of the tropics and you push off with a steady wind at your back for twenty-odd days. You live entirely in the voyage, your mind at one with your surroundings, and just that bit of your subconscious ever alert for a tanker commanded by a drunken captain that might run you down at midnight, just as I had that bit of my subconscious on permanent roo-watch.

All the trip had been good. The beauty of the forests of Margaret River, the breathtaking Blue Mountains, but the long straight-ahead kilometres of crossing the Nullarbor had been the best. That I shall never forget, the landscape so primeval, the job to be done so simple. There was the night stops at the lonely roadhouses, forecourts brightly lit red and yellow like a Hopper painting, and, if I peered out from behind the blinds of my motel cell at two or three in the morning, the sight of a giant horizontal rig, a three-trailer road train lit up along its entire length, growling its way round the forecourt and snaking off like a prehistoric beast into the night to gather speed on the straight-ahead to Perth.

I had also been lucky. I am no mechanic, which is why I ride BMW bikes, but even BMWs go wrong sometimes and I don't want to think about what would have happened if Priscilla had had a tyre blow at 120 kph in the middle of the Nullarbor. Living in the moment meant that you didn't think about that, although I did do a double-take when I returned the bike to Joe, saying,

"Great bike, Joe, never gave me a moment's worry."

"Good, mate, lucky you didn't check your back tyre then. That's shot. I'll need to replace that before she goes a mile further."

Joe drove me back into Brisbane. We swapped biker tales.

"Hey, Joe, have any of your bikers ever had roo problems? Mark told me that as long as I avoided dawn and dusk I was OK."

Joe snorted with laughter.

"Yeah, we always tell you that, otherwise you'd never rent a bike, but they can be a problem. We get a few hits."

"Really?"

"Yeah, Miles, a couple of weeks ago, I had three Swiss guys, not quite as old as you, in the Outback and I got a call from headquarters in Sydney saying the Swissies had a man down and could I go and pick him up as I was the nearest."

"Jesus, what had happened?"

"He was a good biker. Was on a 1200 GS just like you. The other two guys were ahead of him. Roo came up under his handlebars from nowhere and hit him in his left armpit. Knocked him over. When I found him, the bike was bent but rideable but he had a broken arm. Funny thing was he'd hit the road on his right side. Luckily his leathers stopped him getting gravel burn. But, get this, it was his left arm that was broken, not the one which had hit the road."

"How come he broke his left arm then?"

"It was the roo. They're solid muscle. If you have 100 kilos of muscle jump up from under your handlebars and hit you, it's going to break a few things. Lucky it wasn't worse."

"How about the roo? Dead?"

"Nah. No sign of him. He hopped off."

"Glad Mark didn't tell me that. Was this at dawn when they're out feeding?"

"No, mate, middle of the day."

Fortune smiles on the foolish. Sometimes the important thing is to do it, not think about doing it.

11

MEXICO: BAA HAA BOY

Mexico did not live up to its billing. I had just spent two weeks biking round the Baja peninsula. Old Mexico hands had promised me that I would be mugged, kidnapped, and gang-raped, probably all three at the same time. A well-connected Mexican friend had emailed me with the names of Israeli-trained security goons for me to use and the phone number of the best kidnap negotiator in the country. A friend in Los Angeles had read that *los bandidos* were in the habit of beheading people they didn't like in the border area and playing bowls with their heads.

What a let-down … I spent two weeks in Baja without once being mugged, kidnapped, or gang-raped, not even a little bit.

I was completely new to Mexico but, slightly to my surprise, I found that I loved the place and loved the Mexicans. Didn't even bother to lock the bike at night. I was originally going to do the Baja trip by myself. I'd always wanted to do it. It's one of the epic bike journeys, a two-thousand-mile round trip from the US border, and it's home to one of the legendary off-road races, the Baja 1000. If you're curious, go to YouTube and enter "Baja 1000". Skip the boring talking-heads bits in the videos and look at the road action. The videos do make it look much more hairy-chested than the trip we took but that's fine with me.

THE HOPELESS BIKER

How come Mr Solitary Solo-Biker ended up with two and then three companions? Well, it's one thing to bike across Oz or round Iceland or New Zealand by yourself. You know that if you fall off your bike or get hit by a passing roo, a nice trucker will scoop you up and speed you off to hospital. And you know that he will speak English and won't nick your passport.

In Mexico? As I later discovered I would have been more than fine by myself in Mexico because the people were so nice, but I didn't know that in advance. All I had heard were horror stories. If I fell off my bike I would be stripped naked and thrown in the gutter, or so I was told.

There was a terrific woman called Karen who had worked for me a few years back. At that time she was in her mid-twenties and had a big Triumph bike. She used go to the Ace Café, the bikers' Mecca on the North Circular, get to talking with the boys in leather on their Ninjas and Fireblades and rocket off to the Black Forest with them.

Karen came from Glasgow, the Gorbals.

You do not mess with a girl from the Gorbals. Karen had left work to go travelling three years ago: Burma, Indonesia, Vietnam, Australia, South America, much of it on a bike. She supported herself en route by doing reiki and hypno-therapy. Thanks to the magic of Instagram I knew exactly where she was, Peru, in an Andean village doing ayahuasca and mushrooms.

I had emailed her.

"Karen, how would you like a trip round Baja? I'm going and I need a bodyguard. I'll pay for your bike hire."

"Miles, I'm there. When do we start?"

Problem solved. I now had close protection, Gorbals style. No-one would touch us. My Spanish is non-existent, and I knew that Karen, after mooching around Latin America, spoke excellent Spanish. It was only when we got across the border into Mexico and I asked her to remind me what the Spanish for 'beer' was that I realised my bodyguard's Spanish was even worse than mine. Ho hum.

Shortly after signing up Karen, I bumped into Haz in London. Haz, aka Richard Harrisson, was in his early thirties, a man so charming that he

could get a job selling snow to Inuits or sand to Saudis. Instead he was selling sunshine to Kenyans. No-one knew exactly what Haz did, least of all Haz, but it seemed to involve plastering unspoilt bits of the Kenyan wilderness with solar panels.

Haz loved to bike. He liked it so much that four years earlier he had taken his 1937 motorbike, yes, that's 1937, and, along with his buddy Tom on another 1937 bike, ridden it from London to Cape Town. The bikes broke down at least twice a day. Haz and Tom, brilliant mechanics both, disassembled them and put them back together, having stuck silver paper, duct tape, and chewing gum on the leaking bits and sailed on through Egypt, Sudan, Ethiopia, Kenya and…

There had been a problem in Ethiopia when some confusion over Haz's papers resulted in him spending a week in Addis Ababa Central Prison in a cell with 53 Ethiopians and one shared hole in the floor, but he managed to get his liberty after eight days and fled on the bike, before they discovered more problems with his papers, for the Kenyan border a thousand kilometres away. Google Maps showed no direct road to the Kenyan border but fugitives from Ethiope justice couldn't be choosers so off he went in the dead of the Addis night. He got most of the way there when he dived into a giant pothole and the front half of his bike became part of the back. Fortunately a passing truck had stopped soon after, Haz had charmed himself and the bike remnants onto its back, and pretty soon they were safe over the Kenyan border.

"Miles, I've always wanted to do Baja. Count me in."

"That's brilliant, Haz."

Now I had quite an expedition. A Glasgow bodyguard who spoke no Spanish, and a sunshine-salesman on the lam from Ethiopian justice.

We Baja Three met up in Los Angeles where we were renting bikes from Eagle-Rider. Eagle-Rider were good people as I remembered from El Paso on Easter Sunday. They had branches in lots of places and rented a huge range of bikes. If you were looking to get a big Beemer or Honda under you, Eagle-Rider were your men.

We stopped off to see our friend Tarik Wildman, newly reunited with

Susie, his wife, who lived in Santa Monica. Tarik had been the leader of the trip I had made through the mountains and deserts of southwest United States. Tarik was a fetishist. His fetish was for old Alfa-Romeos. He had several, all lovingly restored by him. His favourite was a dark blue 1959 Giulietta Spider convertible which he had bought as a wreck when he was in college with money he had made working on an oil-rig in the Gulf of Mexico. If Audrey Hepburn had been a car, she would have been a 1959 Giulietta, pure understated elegance.

Tarik wanted to come with us in the little Alfa but Susie, like me, had heard the horror stories and pleaded with him not to go. "Too dangerous." You didn't argue with Susie so, urging us to keep them updated with frequent pictures on Instagram, Tarik and Susie waved us on our way and he and the Alfa stayed behind.

A day later, we were in Mexico in the elegant seaside town of Ensenada, the start point for the Baja 1000. Haz and I had each picked up at Eagle-Rider a big BMW 1200 GS Adventure, the twin of the bike I had ridden across the Nullarbor. Karen was on a smaller but still chunky Triumph 800. She'd always been a Triumph girl.

People had warned us how tricky getting through the border at Tijuana would be. Allow a couple of hours, they said. Grasping police, *bandidos*, customs checks, bribes, long waits ... We followed the signs for The Border after we left the freeway round San Diego, went through a corrugated iron fence ten feet high, Trumpito's Wall, were slowed by some road bumps and then found ourselves speeding away.

We ... were ... in ... Mexico. No-one had stopped us. No-one had asked for any papers. *Buenos dias*, and have a nice day, señor.

A couple of hours on a beautiful road swooping along the Pacific, so different from the ten-lane suburban boredom of Route 805, the freeway passing San Diego, and we cruised up to the Hotel Coral y Marina in Ensenada. I was not sure what our hotels would be like. Eagle-Rider had booked them for us as part of our rental packages. I had feared they might have saved themselves money by putting us up in cheap motels but, no, everywhere we went we had good hotels, local ones, with local character, one or two of them had maybe a slight surplus of local character, but there wasn't one we didn't like. (OK, there was one but let's leave that till later.) They had showers, flushing loos, loo paper, clean sheets, not a *cucaracha* to be seen, and they always had a bar with refreshing margaritas, just the thing after a long day on the road.

All three of us had ridden long distances on bikes in the past but we'd never done it together. That night we nervously enquired what each other's riding habits were. Did one of us like to get up at dawn, bike all morning, and arrive before lunch? We had about 350 to 420 kilometres most days which usually meant six to seven hours saddle-time with extra time for coffee, fuel, and lunch. Did another like to get up late, leave later, and then rush to reach the destination before the sun set at 6.30 pm? To our relief we found that the three of us had a similar pattern. We aimed for an 8.45 am departure every day, did a bit of dawdling on the way to take photos, admire a view, and have something to eat, and usually arrived in the mid-afternoon in time for check-in and a margarita.

Baja is to bikers what Kathmandu is to hippies. We knew its reputation but none of us had done any reading up in preparation. We shared the belief that being surprised while travelling was better than raising expectations and being disappointed. Where's the fun in discovering a secret village that Lonely Planet had already told you was the best-kept secret in Baja?

I had bought two maps on Amazon, imaginatively named Baja Norte and Baja Sur. The maps showed us that there was only one real road in Baja, Mexico 1, which wound its way down the west, Pacific, coast for a few hundred kilometres, then snaked inland over what looked like mountains, before hitting the Sea of Cortes, the gulf that lay between Baja and the rest of Mexico. From there it headed south along the Gulf before once more going wanderabout in the empty middle of Baja and finally down to the southernmost point and Cabo San Lucas. That would take us a week. After Cabo we would head back north, looping round the southern bit of the peninsula on a different road before rejoining Mexico 1 for the trip home.

Although we would be following the same road we would be stopping in different places on the way back.

I had always been sceptical about Mexican food, knowing little about it and having tended to dismiss it as unidentifiable glop leaking out of a pancake. From the very first day I discovered how wrong I was. An astonishing Mexican breakfast greeted us in the Coral y Marina. What a contrast with the day before's granola and rubber omelettes at the Los Angeles Airport Crowne Plaza, the hotel in which Eagle-Rider had billeted us. The Coral y Marina had everything. The Mexicans love vegetables. And beans. And tacos. And melted cheese. And of course eggs. Few Mexican meals go far without an egg popping up, and none exist without tacos of one sort or another.

The Full Mexican, Coral y Marina style, was a thing of wonder. Half a dozen smiling staff stood ready to cook you literally anything you might want. *Huevos rancheros*? Coming right up, señor ... *Quesadillas* (melted cheese is big in Mexico)? *Si, si* ... Chicken *enchilada*? Of course, with salsa, señor? Or would you rather have *huevos divorciados*, two fried eggs one smothered with fiery red salsa, the other with green? I decided I would eschew eggs and tacos and go for a nice helping of *mole poblano*, shredded chicken gently stewed with chilis, fruit, and, of course, chocolate. And I couldn't resist a bit of beef with chili on the side. Now I was set up for anything the Mexican road could throw at me.

We hadn't been sure how bikers would be greeted at Mexican hotels. Would we be sent round to the tradesmen's entrance? We had of course been warned by the old Mexico hands before we set off, the ones who had promised us a good gang-raping, that our bikes would be stolen as soon as we crossed the border, even if we had them locked, chained, and in a cage. The Coral y Marina set the pattern for the rest of our trip. We biked into the parking area in front of the hotel and looked for a safe place to put the bikes.

A uniformed doorman began waving at us. "Oh God, now where's he going to send us?" I said to Haz. "I think he's beckoning us over," said Haz. In front of the hotel entrance was a drop-off area with a gleaming black Mercedes S parked in it. Lesser cars were waved away.

"Please, señor, park here," the doorman gestured to a spot opposite the Mercedes.

Soon our three bikes were lined up like objects of devotion opposite the hotel entrance. Other hotel people sprung out to help carry our pannier bags into the hotel.

"We have secure underground parking if you prefer, señor, but *vuestros motos grandes se ven bien aquí.*"

He was right. Our bikes did look pretty damn good next to the Mercedes. Stuff the secure underground parking. This set a pattern for the rest of the trip. Most of our hotels had parking lots behind the hotel but nearly everywhere, as soon as we arrived, the doorman would be ushering our bikes as close to the front entrance as possible. We did have locks to put on the wheels. I never used mine. This wasn't London, where you turned your back and you found your bike had emigrated. It had happened to me with my London 1200 GS being spirited out of a "secure" underground parking lot at dead of night in a van, all captured on CCTV. "Well, are you going to get the bastards?" I asked Constable Plod. "Nah, mate, too much bovver. Your bike's in Lagos by now." It never entered my head that anyone would nick our bikes in Baja.

So many things about Mexico, or at least about Baja, were better than what we had been led to believe. It reminded me of other "problematic" countries I had been to in recent years, Eritrea, Iran, Iraq, North Korea, Syria and Libya (those last two visits were both before the Arab Spring), South Sudan, and Somaliland. Before going to these places, people told you scare stories about how dangerous they were, press reports made you believe that you would be mad to leave your hotel without bodyguards, and yet, when you arrived in any of these places to see them for yourself you found that the pre-trip clichés were 100% wrong. The people were charming, welcoming, and usually more honest than in the UK or US, getting about was relatively easy, and you never felt in danger. The one exception had been Iraq, a country irretrievably broken by the US-led invasion but let's not talk about that.

We had been told that Mexican roads were appalling. Potholes everywhere. Yes, we found that there were places where the road surface was bad but most of the time the roads were smooth and well-cambered, nice long bike-friendly curves round the flanks of the hills. Straight roads can get boring on a bike. Sometimes on a straight road we found ourselves slaloming from side to side, often in unison like synchronised swimmers, to break the monotony and to feel the bikes move underneath us.

We left Ensenada and biked though San Quintin, the richest agricultural land in Mexico and now the biggest tomato producer in the world. We made the occasional detour down dirt tracks to get a coffee from a kiosk on a cliff-edge and look down at the Pacific surf pounding an empty beach. It was interesting how, in most of the Baja, the land turned its back on the sea. On both sides of the Baja the sea must teem with fish. I had expected to find scads of picturesque fishing villages but they were few. The people of Baja were farmers and peasants more than sea-farers. In this respect it reminded me of Sicily and Crete, the two big Mediterranean islands where the people tend their sheep and goats, harvest their olives, and kill each other in family feuds over disputes about land ownership, but do their best to avoid getting in a boat, in contrast to the smaller Mediterranean islands which are populated by sea-faring venturers whose arid land is of little value.

We were glad to get away from the busy towns of the farmlands and start our climb into the hills. The traffic evaporated, the repair shops and gas stations disappeared, and we were in wide open country, the earth flecked with yellow, gold and purple wild flowers and the sky noiseless but for the thrum of three bikes carving their way south through empty Mexico.

As we climbed away from the flatlands we found ourselves biking through hill-sides of grape rows and signs to wineries, inviting us to stop for a tasting, a tempting thought but one we resisted. Mexican wine. There was a surprise. Our first night in Ensenada we had had a stunning red Bodega Santo Tomas tempranillo-merlot. To make sure it wasn't a fluke we had followed it up with a bottle of cabernet-syrah from the same producer. Also memorable. There may well have been a third bottle of…

I love drinking the local wine in funny places but it can turn out to

THE HOPELESS BIKER

be a disappointment, Bolivian sauvignon, anyone? No thank you. Mexican wine was serious stuff, the equal of Chile and Argentina. I had had no idea that Mexico turned out wine of this quality. If you thought about it just across the border in California they were growing world-class wines. South of the border Mexico had identical climate and soil ... From then on every night we made a point, after a preliminary margarita throat-clearer or two, usually served in a glass the size of a goldfish bowl, of getting stuck into the Mexican reds. We were never disappointed.

We left the Pacific and climbed into the hills. There were no buildings, no tilled fields, just the odd wandering cow that had scant knowledge of the right of way rules.

Our biking rhythm was to stop every hour and a half or so, stretch our legs, drink some water, and admire the view. If there was a roadside restaurant we popped in there for a coffee or a snack if it was lunchtime. We took it in turns acting as lead bike. On day three we were biking through some dramatic scenery at the foot of an old volcano. I was leading and thought this might be a good spot for a photo opp. I slowed to a crawl and nosed the bike off the road onto some hard gravel.

The hard gravel turned out to be six inches deep and hard as quicksand. I felt the front wheel sliding away and, in slow motion, the bike slipped away from me and fell. As previously mentioned, BMW 1200 GS bikes have the celebrated "boxer" engines. These have two horizontally-opposed cylinder-heads sticking out like ankle-crushers either side of the bike.

As my bike went down, I felt the left-hand cylinder-head come down on my ankle and trap it under the bike. A fully-loaded 1200 GS weighs 560 lbs. Ow. The engine was still going but fuel didn't seem to be coming out of anywhere. Phew. I managed to turn the engine off. Karen sped up and managed to free my trapped leg.

"Och, Miles, are you OK?" She helped me to my feet.

Haz skidded to a halt and ran over. Lifting a big Beemer that has been dropped is not easy. They are heavy beasts. Haz bent down like a weightlifter, grunted, and in one clean movement, the bike was upright. Bravo, Haz. He wheeled the bike out of the soft gravel and put it on its stand somewhere more firm. Haz, like me, was a rowing man. He had rowed in a good Imperial College crew. Thank God I hadn't gone biking with a cricketer.

I gingerly tried moving my foot at the ankle. It hurt but I could move it. A good sign. The trouble was that this was my left foot and on a bike you use your left foot for changing gear. You pushed the gear-pedal down for first gear but then had to put your foot under the pedal and push it up for the other five gears. That was going to be painful but do-able, I hoped.

We had stopped for a photo in front of the volcano. It seemed silly to miss that. If you look carefully at the picture taken you would see the big cylinder-head sticking out from the side of the bike and a man testing his left ankle to see how functional it was. And you would see a second picture of his companions-of-the-road, Señor Macho and Miz Gorbals, having a good laugh at *el viejo* who has just dropped his bike.

We eased our way back onto the road. Changing gear was no fun but we only had another 100 kilometres to go and fortunately the big BMW engines have a lot of torque so I could slip the bike up into sixth as soon as we got over 30 mph and stick there.

We were now in what would have been the Badlands, if there had been anyone around to be Bad. No sign of any people let alone a habitation. The scenery changed from rolling fields to huge cactuses and boulders, which, as we approached Cataviña, a famous stop on the Baja 1000 where people attempted to repair cars and bikes broken by the local tracks, the boulders turned into rocks the size of houses. The lack of roadkill suggested that there were few animals in this austere landscape, but overhead huge birds wheeled. Were they raptors or carrion-eaters, majestic hawks and buzzards, or sinister vultures? I thought of the condors I had seen when biking through Patagonia, and of the eagle I had seen snatching a dove in mid-flight. I wished I knew about birds.

After Cataviña, we were in the wilds. The road surface deteriorated and the landscape, often breathtaking in its austere beauty, was somewhere you would not want to find yourself marooned in at night. Our problem was that we were in danger of that happening. We had failed to buy petrol in Cataviña. True, there was no gas station, but there was a large table by the roadside with a *bandido* selling petrol from jerrycans under a hand-painted sign saying "PEMEX".

Haz and I had bigger tanks than Karen. Scrutinising the map it appeared there was a gas station in Jesus Maria. Jesus was a long way from Cataviña. We calculated we would just make it without buying bandido-gas. Two hours later when our low-petrol warning lights came on, saying 50 kilometres to go, we calculated we were about 60 kilometres short of Jesus and salvation. Luckily it was mainly downhill. We normally cruised at about 80 mph. We cut our speed to 50 mph, we were careful not to accelerate up hills, we didn't waste energy braking for corners. We made it. Karen's dashboard told her she had 3 kilometres left.

That night we stopped in San Ignacio, the first really Spanish colonial place we had been. We went round the ancient church. We had a margarita in a café on one side of the square, sitting under stately trees that must have been planted by Spanish missionaries. Then we had a margarita on the other side of the square. And then we went back to the first café and sat outside eating *camarones a la diabla*, sweetly fresh shrimps in a spicy sauce, drinking excellent Mexican wine, and being serenaded by a tiny choir of local girls in traditional clothing who had come to entertain *los bikers*.

Meanwhile Tarik, stuck in Los Angeles, had been working himself up into a FOMO frenzy. WhatsApp messages buzzed in every thirty minutes, "Where are you?" "What's the weather like?" "Is it safe?" "Are the roads good?" To annoy him we said that conditions were beyond perfect, the driving was the best we had ever had, and what a pity that he was missing the experience of a lifetime.

Next day, we were on our way to Loreto, our first stop on the Sea of Cortes, the east side of the Baja peninsula. We had heard good things about Loreto, the site of one of the first Spanish missions. A couple of hours before getting there we stopped at a deserted beach with a food shack on it to have lunch and stretch our legs. Well, actually, the beach was only deserted in the sense that there were no buildings other than a food shack on it. Between the shack and the sea, drawn up like Xerxes' army on the shores of the Hellespont, was a phalanx of gleaming Recreational Vehicles, RVs, some the size of a bus. This was the case with several of the "empty" beaches we found. They were often over-run by RVs. Their owners were nice enough people, mainly retired Americans who migrated to Mexico in the winter months and lived in their RVs. I remembered that their Australian equivalents were called grey nomads. Finding the local beach shack crowded with grey nomads did detract from their charm.

The sooner Mexico builds a wall to keep these invaders out, the better.

While we were munching our fish tacos in the beach shack we managed to get a wi-fi connection. We posted a couple of make-you-jealous pics on Instagram, carefully taken so you didn't see the RV army on the beach. We noted that Tarik had also posted a pic on WhatsApp of the Alfa-Romeo. Haz clicked on the pic to blow it up.

"Hey, guys, look at this. I don't believe it."

There on WhatsApp was a picture of the Alfa with a signpost in the background saying "Loreto 415km". The photo had been posted a few hours earlier. Meanwhile we were munching tacos on Playa Santispac, some 120 kilometres short of Loreto.

"What on earth," Haz said, "The crazy fool is trying to catch us. He must have driven through the night."

We contacted our deranged friend on WhatsApp and exchanged live location pins showing where each of us was.

"I am 44 miles away," said Tarik, "Order me something for lunch. Let me know exactly how to find you and flag me down if I go past."

Half an hour later, we were downing excellent Dos Equis beer and chatting with grey nomads who thought our bikes and us, particularly Karen, were super-cool. We were telling them about our friend following in the Alfa and we were debating whether to hide our bikes behind the biggest RV so Tarik couldn't find us, when we heard a snarl in the distance. Bumping down the path to the beach was a small blue sports car, roof down, and engine revving to make as much noise as possible. Inside was a large man glowing red with terminal sunburn.

The car skidded up to the shack and did a couple of doughnuts, spraying sand and dirt over us, the RV people, and the bikes. The horn beeped three times, the car braked to a halt in a flurry of dirt, and the large sunburnt man jumped out, clasping his hands above his head in a boxer's salute. We cheered, the nomads cheered, and I said, "Dr Wildman, I presume."

Tarik was not one for hiding his light under a bushel. He liked to make sure everyone knew when he arrived somewhere. We got the impression he had consumed several pints of Red Bull to stay awake as he had had to drive through the night to catch us up. Thanks to the Red Bull he was speaking so fast as to be unintelligible.

He had started two days behind us and had caught us up on the fourth day. Susie, we learned, having read our WhatsApps and seen that Mexico was as safe as Cheltenham had lifted her embargo, perhaps helped, she told us when we got back, in her decision by the fact that Tarik wouldn't talk to her as he was too busy tracking us on Instagram and sighing loudly.

Now we were four. Our pattern remained the same, except that Tarik suffers from ADHD and hates anything steady, including cruising along at 80 mph as we had been doing. He would start behind us in the morning and then, half an hour into the day's trip, come roaring past at 110 mph, the little Alfa's engine a-scream, until he became a disappearing dot between the cacti on the horizon. An hour later we would go round a corner and there was the Alfa parked by the road with Tarik, grin on face, gin and tonic in hand, music blaring, and a bar laid out on the boot. His boot contained little luggage but a fine enough selection of alcohol to stock a night club bar. Whenever we stopped for petrol he would buy ice to put in his insulated container in the boot.

We were now deep into Mexico proper. The US, apart from the occasional appearance of the RV army, was a world away from these open uplands, the tiny villages, the welcoming roadside shacks, the boulders and cacti, and the eternal smiles. We loved it.

I was feeling increasingly embarrassed about my negative preconceptions about Mexico but how wonderful to discover first-hand how it really was. Everyone we spoke to was helpful. No-one badgered us. We came across nothing but honesty and felt that, as someone once said to me in Ethiopia, "Miles, if you drop your wallet on the ground here with $100 in it, it will be returned to you with $105."

The food was a revelation. Everything was fresh and full of taste. Guacamole, normally boring green sludge, was here nothing but taste, texture, and spice. Tomatoes had originated in Mexico, and what tomatoes they were with their fruity, vine-ripened depth of flavour, a different vegetable to the hydroponic Dutch tomato of a London supermarket. Fish and shellfish were sweet with freshness. Stone lava-bowls overflowed with beef and vegetables, everything with tacos. The delicious wine. And did you want your margarita made with tequila or mezcal? Karen explained the difference and I still didn't understand but I preferred the tequila.

Every night I went to bed with a smile on my face.

We had a rest day in Los Barriles, a windswept, kite-surfy, beachy place, a day's biking from Cabo San Lucas, the southernmost tip of Baja. Haz rented a windsurfer and skimmed up and down the beach hoping we were videoing him. Karen appeared and disappeared. I suspected her of doing secret reiki in her room. She had explained reiki to me; it sounded unconvincing. What could she be doing?

Tarik rearranged the gin, rum, and vodka bottles in the boot of the Alfa and bought some limes. I had hoped to go for a walk along the endless yellow-sand beach but my ankle, the one on which I'd dropped the bike, had swollen to twice its normal size, so that getting a shoe on was a problem, let alone walking. Instead, I stationed myself at the beach bar, drank Cinzano spritzers (an excellent, not very alcoholic, hot-weather drink, best with a slice of orange and lots of ice), and attempted to get enough bandwidth to download *The Times*. Internal bleeding had made my swollen foot a spectacular sunset blue-red-purple colour. I proudly showed my companions a photograph of it with my sock off at lunch. They blenched.

That night, we decided to go out for dinner. We found a lovely place in town. Tarik took pity on my hopalong status and gave me a lift in the Alfa. There is a photo of the two of us, *dos viejos*, out on the pull in the Alfa. What good-looking boys…

The one place everyone knows in Baja is "Cabo". People we had talked to in Los Angeles said, "Yeah, Baja. You'll have a great time. Cabo is awesome." Cabo, the Spanish for Cape, actually describes a strip along the southern coast of Baja, with two towns 20 miles apart, Cabo San Lucas in the West and San Jose del Cabo in the East, a golf course-infested strip of coast in between. Anything but awesome.

My advice would be to go to Baja and keep as far away from "Cabo" as possible. Cabo San Lucas is the one everyone knows. It was a wannabee Ibiza. Cabo's beach had a Blue Marlin, a Mango Deck, a Zipper's, and used to have a Nikki Beach but that seemed to have sunk. On the East Coast US the college kids went to Fort Lauderdale and got drunk for spring break, on the West Coast they went to Cabo, and got even drunker.

Every beach bar and restaurant was filled with drunk semi-naked spring breakers. The streets had some of them, vomiting.

But, hey, when in Rome … we did somehow discover an excellent club which was I can't-remember-how-many-miles out of town. We ended up dancing on a rooftop there at 2 am. I don't recall how we got there and I don't recall how we got back. Haz was wafting around charming Cabo-ista babes, Karen was throwing impressive Glasgow shapes on the floor, and I was instructing Iliana, a charming Polish girl, in the finer points of my celebrated aeroplane dance. Tarik was talking to Jack Daniels.

We were not sorry to say goodbye to Cabo and head back to the real Mexico. An hour north of Cabo was Todos Santos, the anti-Cabo, a place of soul. Todos Santos was the Baja Kathmandu, a hippy heaven. There were no clubs in Todos Santos, not a golf course to be seen, no sports cars, and no bare-bummed spring-break girls checking into hotels. Just chill. Lazy bars, good places to buy local art works, shady shacks to eat *chile rellenos mariscos*, dip a nacho into spicy guacamole, and get photographed, as we did, with the bikes and the Alfa in front of Hotel California. Some say that Todos Santos is not the original Hotel California. I, and the hotel, think otherwise. While the Eagles' famous song may suggest you can never leave, we did succeed in making a getaway.

We were homeward bound, heading north, the sun behind us. We were looking forward to a rest day in Loreto, our favourite town, the one we had spent a night in on the way down. Loreto was perched on the edge of the Gulf of Cortes. It had a Spanish colonial centre with cobbled streets and a dignified church. Nearby were deserted beaches not yet discovered by the RV Army or the spring-breakers.

I had two things I wanted to do in Loreto. Buy a Mexican sweater because the nights would be cold when we got back in the mountains. And I wanted to go off on the rest day morning and find a beach shack where I could sit in the sun, drink a Dos Equis, pound away on my iPad catching up on some writing and nibble a nacho. I succeeded in both.

I found a shack on the edge of the mirror-calm Gulf of Cortes where I spent a happy few hours writing, interspersed with fish tacos and good Mexican beer. And I found a wonderful thick woollen poncho. Unlike most ponchos, this one had a hood, my first hoodie.

The other thing to do in Loreto was to sit in the balcony bar of the Mission Hotel, where we were staying, and watch the pelicans. Loreto was the pelican capital of Baja. There must have been fifty of these birds, so ungainly on the land, so graceful and menacing in the air, wheeling and turning over the patch of sea in front of the hotel. One would plunge like a rapier into the sea, leaving just a plop of water behind it, to reappear seconds later with a fish in its beak.

We loved Loreto and we checked out reluctantly with two long days' biking ahead of us. As we moved north it was getting colder than it had been on the trip down, particularly in the high places, and the road was bad in parts. I put on my new Mexican sweater under my biking jacket. Good move. The first day we had to cross from the Sea of Cortes to spend the night in Guerrero Negro on the Pacific.

We had stopped there briefly for lunch on the way down. We hadn't liked it. It was unlike anywhere else in Baja. Guerrero Negro was founded in 1957 by the secretive American shipping billionaire, Daniel Ludwig. Its lagoons and flats made it the perfect place for producing salt and soon Mr Ludwig had the biggest evaporative salt mine in the world. Salt flats are not attractive things. Sinister slicks of purple and yellow chemical water lay by the roadside.

Guerrero Negro was known for two other things, its Mexican army base, and for being the embarkation spot for watching grey whales birthing. In February, when we were there, the grey whales had popped down from the Arctic, checked into nearby Scammon's Lagoon and were giving birth to calves bigger than hippos. We probably should have got in a boat and gone out to see this happen. We didn't. Bikers on a journey are not sightseers.

Thanks to the army base, Guerrero had the essential facilities that soldiers needed, strip clubs, tattoo shops, and massage parlours. It also had the only dodgy hotel we stayed in, the Halfway Inn, halfway between Cabo and the US border. It was a creepy place painted sherbet yellow and purple. And the margaritas were diluted.

We were happy to check out of the Halfway Inn the next morning and head north. We would be going through Cataviña where we had stopped on the way down, this time not stopping for the night there but heading all the way to San Quintin, a long 440 kilometres.

"Looks bad," said Tarik, looking at the clouds. Tarik is an amateur glider-pilot and knows his weather.

"Wouldn't want to be on a bike on a day like this," he said cheerily as he checked that the convertible top on the Alfa was all snug and rainproof. I had to agree with him. The clouds were low, thick, and threatening. A north-westerly gale was blowing. As we started up the bikes we noticed that the road surface was slick and shiny with water.

"Let's hope that's blown through," said Tarik.

It hadn't. As we moved off it began to spit with rain and soon we were biking into a horizontal sheet of wetness. Memories of Japan. Another

Lady Macbeth day. We had over 400 kilometres of this ahead of us. It was like being sprayed by a water-cannon. The road surface was pocked with potholes, many with jagged edges that could shred a tyre if you hit them too fast, as one of us would soon discover.

As previously mentioned, helmet visors do not have wipers on them. If you are going fast enough most of the rain will be blown off by the slipstream. We weren't going fast enough. We were feeling our way through the storm at 50 mph, often slower. My visor was a blur of water. I was driving all but blind. I was tracking Haz, the most adept biker of the three of us, but that was difficult. Today of all days was the day that the big trucks had come out to play. Every few minutes a giant Freightliner or flat-faced Peterbilt would thunder past throwing out a wave of spray and, even worse, a wash of wind that knocked you sideways before it sucked you back the other way.

Overtaking a truck was worse. You had to wait for a straight bit of road, of which there were few, throw yourself out from behind the truck into the opposite lane, praying you would have enough visibility to see an oncoming Freightliner, and then accelerate through a wave of spray and wind, the bike being buffeted from side to side like a canoe in the rapids, all the while keeping an eye on the road for a pothole that might throw you under the truck's wheels. Meanwhile the rain was penetrating every crevice of your "waterproof" rain gear. You could feel icy water soaking down your neck and your back and somehow even into your crutch.

We stopped after an hour and a half to fill up with gas.

"Karen, how are you doing?" I asked.

"Och, Miles, I'm fine. No worries."

She flashed me her big smile. What a woman.

Despite my Mexican sweater, I was cold, very cold. We were hardly making 50 miles an hour. At this rate we still had five or six hours' biking ahead of us, possibly more. At least we could stop for lunch in Cataviña. We would be able to warm up there. By 1.00 pm we were approaching Cataviña when we passed a man on his knees by the side of the road. He appeared to be praying to a sports car. It was Tarik. He had hit a pothole which had wrenched the rear left-hand tyre off the wheel-rim, bad enough in a car but I did not want to think what that would have been like if it had happened to the front tyre of a bike.

Tarik was soaked. His smart gliding jacket, a present from Susie, was as waterproof as blotting paper. Haz took one look at Karen and me. I was now blue and shaking so badly with cold that I could hardly speak.

"Miles, Karen, you go on to Cataviña. There's nothing you can do here. I'll stay behind to give Tarik a hand."

Haz the hero. This was an instruction we readily obeyed.

Thank God Cataviña was only 5 kilometres down the road. We parked the bikes, stripped off our wetter outer layers in the lobby of the Mission Hotel where we had stopped for lunch on the way down, and went to the dining room in search of warmth. I couldn't remember ever being so cold. I wasn't shivering, my whole body was shaking. The waiter took one look at us, dashed off into the kitchen and reappeared with two mugs of hot black liquid.

"Drink this. Mexican coffee. Coffee and tequila." I slurped mine down. I felt a tiny shaft of warmth inside me although I was shaking so hard, I had to hold the mug in both hands to stop it spilling.

Fifteen minutes later, Tarik and Haz splashed in, Tarik looking like a spaniel which had been hauled out of the water. We ordered bowls of hot soup. More Mexican coffees. I was still shaking. Haz got out his iPhone and checked Google Maps.

"Another 186 kilometres to go."

We looked at each other glumly.

"Miles," said Haz, "You need to get some dry clothes on before we get back on the road."

I nodded. My fingers were still blue.

"Wait," I said. "I've got an idea."

I stumbled off to the lobby. Two minutes later I was back.

"Guys, I've made a decision. I spoke to the guy on the desk. They have four available rooms. I've booked them. We're staying here. We can't go on."

Never had three faces brightened more quickly.

"Miles, best decision you ever made," said Tarik, thumping his palm on the table and bellowing with laughter. We all laughed. We were happy. We hugged each other.

The world had become a better place. Tomorrow we would drive through San Quintin, we didn't want to stay there in any case, and get to Ensenada, leaving us within easy striking distance of the border. Tomorrow the sun would shine.

Lunch over, I went off to my nice warm room, took off my clothes, and stood under a steaming hot shower for fifteen minutes. That felt so good. I had almost stopped shaking. Then I dried, put on layers of dry clothing, thank God the sturdy BMW panniers had once again proved to be watertight, slipped under the duvet, pulled it up to my nose and drifted off to a warm sleep.

Four hours later, I woke up. Even my feet were warm. Warmth had never felt so good. I knocked on Tarik's door. Haz and Karen were already there. The Alfa had a tiny boot, but Tarik knew what to fill it with. Eight bottles were on display plus limes and ice which Tarik had sourced from the hotel.

Next day, the gale had dropped to a gentle breeze, the sun shone, fluffy white clouds flecked a blue sky, and the forecast was good. I set off with a song in my heart. The day we had just undergone had been as bad as it could get for a biker.

We cruised into Ensenada at tea-time with smiles as wide as Wisconsin after a great day's biking. Tomorrow was going to be "*Adios, Mexico*". We had lost our hearts to it.

We were not looking forward to tomorrow because we had been told that you could get into Mexico from the US easily enough, but the border was a "one-way valve". Getting back into the US from Mexico was a nightmare. Queues at the border post could go on for four or five hours as part of Trumpito's immigration policy.

Trying to go through at Tijuana, the most direct route, was madness.

Tijuana was the world's busiest international border crossing and the US immigration officers, we had heard, had instructions to keep the bastards out at all costs. Instead we would head up into the hills and try to cross the border at Tecate, about 60 kilometres inland.

Next day when we set off from Ensenada, destination Los Angeles, that proved to be an inspired decision. The route to Tecate turned out to be the Ruta de Vinos. We snaked our way higher and higher round long sinuous biker-friendly bends through hillsides tidy with vine-rows. We could have been in Chianti. Once more the sun shone.

A couple of hours after leaving Ensenada we were in Tecate. And there was The Wall, an ugly twelve-foot-high corrugated iron barrier. The Mexicans had treated it as a joke and painted it with lurid graffiti, many of which had personal remarks about *el Donaldo*. You had to love the Mexicans.

We puttered along and joined a queue of cars. In fifteen minutes we found ourselves crossing out of warm, friendly, you-are-welcome, Mexico and into "SIR, step-out-of-the-vehicle-SIR-with-your-hands-over-your-head," USA. It would be nice if I had a horror story to fit the script but, no. I paused the bike by the immigration booth and handed my passport over. The bike papers and insurance were in my tank-bag ready for inspection. The immigration guy gave the passport a perfunctory glance through his Ray-Bans, said, "Hey, nice bike", and gestured with a flick of his head for me to enter MAGA-land. Fifteen minutes after joining the queue we were through and back in the USA.

Three hours later we were saying goodbye to our bikes at Eagle-Rider. It was over.

My biking boots, companions on so many journeys, across Australia, round Japan, Iceland, New Zealand, Tasmania, across the Andes, the Alps and Pyrenees, so many places, were now leaking and held together by duct tape. I gave them a decent burial in a bin of the Crowne Plaza Hotel in Los Angeles.

I tried not to think about it, but I knew as I dropped my tattered boots into the bin that Baja would be my last rodeo. I have loved biking, and it has been a big part of my life. Writing this book has brought back the memories with such force. Many of them are of times when I was close to going over the edge but didn't. If my trips had been all sunshine and smooth roads, they would never have entered my soul the way the way they have. I am in Norfolk, gazing out as the sun sets over the marshes, and the trips flash by as if they had been yesterday.

When I handed the keys over at Eagle-Rider, I was a few months short of my 77th birthday. I had ridden the equivalent of twice round the world and apart from the odd bruise I had never fallen off the bike and never had an accident. How lucky I had been. I often thought back to the *Das Boot* memory that had stopped us taking the extra day's trip up the coast of Goa with Zander.

You may remember how the U-Boat, having accomplished its mission with great bravery, was sailing in triumph back into home port with the sailors standing on deck waving deliriously to the cheering crowds, when Providence in the shape of the RAF loomed up out of a clear sky and bombed them into oblivion.

I didn't know when my *Das Boot* moment might come, but those moments come too often for bikers. They come, like the RAF, out of a clear sky when you least expect it. They come when a dog runs into your path, or when you are banking into a blind mountain bend and an oncoming bus decapitates you, or when, like Tarik in the Alfa, you shred a tyre and get blown into a tree because you are on two wheels not four, but come they do. I didn't know how many beans I had left in the jar after Baja, but I did know that if I fell off my bike at 77 I wouldn't bounce.

Stopping while I was ahead was a good idea. I knew that my daughter and other people who cared about me would be happy they no longer had to worry about *el viejo* disappearing for a final trip down Ruta Cuarenta.

AFTERWORD

This is a book about the joy of biking and the thrill and terror that can go with it. Riding a bike is about leaving behind the dreary, spirit-dampening things that beset our everyday lives. Heading off to somewhere you have never been is about finding out first-hand what lies on the dark side of the mountain.

I'm often asked, "You've biked all over the world. What was your favourite place?" That always gives me pause. Argentina, Che, and the Andes? Surviving a typhoon in Japan? The craziness of India? The zen of the Nullarbor? The shock and awe of Death Valley? The geysered wildness of Iceland? Chilling in Baja? Then I realised that the reason I loved going to those places so much was that each one involved discovery, learning new things at first hand. That gave me my answer –

"My favourite place is somewhere I have never been."

I hope that bikers read *The Hopeless Biker* and recognise what binds us bikers together and sends us off down the unknown road. I hope that non-bikers also get it, understand the X factor, and find themselves wishing that they too were heading over the mountain, as they lean into an S-curve on a high Andes pass with a 1000cc of motorbike howling underneath them.

"Nothing matters but the longest journey."

I have been lucky to have made the journey and survived.

ACKNOWLEDGEMENTS

I love writing. I would do it even if no-one ever read what I had written. Sometimes, I have to write things out to find out what I feel about them. For me, writing is a solitary occupation so I only have myself to blame for this book. I would however like to say a big thank you to the Bealies, Sarah and Kate Beal of Muswell Press, who took this book on despite it being a travel book by an old white man. I would also like to say a big thank you to Jean McNeil and Fiona Leney, both professional editors, writers, and book people. I sent them the book in draft form and asked for their comments in the hope that the book might appeal to women and to non-bikers. They both replied, independently, with excellent comments, and said that although they were generally hostile to biking that they loved the book, even the scary parts, and it left them wanting to throw a leg over a big bike and follow me round the bend. And a big thank you to Emma Charleston who worked her usual magic with the maps.

TWO GOODBYES

I would like to say farewell to two people who were with me on my last rodeo, the bike trip round Baja: Haz, Richard Harrisson, my biking hero, the free-est of free spirits, who was killed two weeks after Baja in a paragliding accident; and Tarik Wildman, my honorary younger brother, a man who personified that living well is the best revenge and who died in his sleep while this book was going to press. Go well, guys, I'm so grateful to have shared so much with both of you. I loved you.